"Greg Dobbs is a brilliant storyteller. Someone I always counted on to file the smartest, most interesting reports. He delivers once again with *Life in the Wrong Lane*."

– Rick Kaplan, executive producer, CBS Evening News. Former executive producer, ABC World News Tonight, former president, CNN

"Greg Dobbs lifts the curtain hiding the magic and mayhem behind a television correspondent's reports on war and confrontation. He bursts the pomposity of network news by confessing that he once surrendered to a cow. Then he switches to a terrifying tale of escape from slashing machetes and tank fire, after being dumb enough to try to do a stand-up in the middle of a firefight during the Iranian Revolution. This book shares the stories behind the stories, the ones foreign correspondents save for each other on late nights in smoky hotel bars when the story's been filed ..."

– Ann Imse, Associated Press Moscow correspondent during the fall of the USSR

"This volume is written in the brilliant and impressive style that we have come to expect from Greg Dobbs. The adventures that he describes are both hair-raising and hilarious, and give us back-door access to the kinds of problems that journalists meet. You will enjoy it, guaranteed!"

– Tom Sutherland, longtime hostage of terrorists in Beirut

"Dobbs captures the adrenaline, the fear, the fury, and the funny parts of being eyewitness to history. These 'stories' behind the stories reveal what it's really like to dive for a deadline or put your life on the line for a story. Greg Dobbs is a newsman's newsman; relentless in his pursuit of a story, brutally honest in his reporting, and hilarious in his tales of the hunt."

– Tom Foreman, correspondent, CNN

"Greg Dobbs's *memoir de guerre* of his salad years spent reporting for network television is, as only a journalist could find it, a delightful gambol through the battlefields. With a keen eye for detail, Dobbs manages to capture the humor and absurdity of situations that just about any normal human being would find terrifying, insane, or life-threatening. And like a number of us who were privileged to live through the era when the big broadcast networks felt it their obligation to at least attempt to cover news stories from the outside world, Dobbs recalls those marvelous times when coverage expenses were secondary and a correspondent faced possible reproach for one reason only: missing the story.

–Jim Bittermann, CNN senior correspondent, Paris

Engaging. Illuminating. A recipe book for how the sausage is made—and what it tastes like."

–Frank Sesno, GW University and former CNN correspondent

LIFE IN THE
WRONG LANE

Another book by Greg Dobbs:
Better Broadcast Writing, Better Broadcast News

LIFE IN THE WRONG LANE

*Why Journalists Go In When
Everyone Else Wants Out*

GREG DOBBS

iUniverse, Inc.
New York   Bloomington

Life in the Wrong Lane

ISBN: 978-1-4401-5276-4 (sc)
ISBN: 978-1-4401-5274-0 (dj)
ISBN: 978-1-4401-5275-7 (e-book)

iUniverse books may be ordered through booksellers or by contacting:

iUniverse
1663 Liberty Drive
Bloomington, IN 47403
www.iuniverse.com
1-800-Authors (1-800-288-4677)

Printed in the United States of America

iUniverse rev. date: 8/18/2009

For Carol, who patiently put up with my perilous trips and long absences with love that exceeded the vows we made when we married.

And for Jason and Alex, great guys who grew up with their father sometimes missing weighty events from first steps to first dates.

Without my family's forbearance and support, I would instead have had to enroll in law school to make a good living, which at different times in my career has sounded like something I should have done. But it never would have provided the voyages and adventures that allowed me to produce this book. Or to live life in the lane where I've lived it.

CONTENTS

PREFACE

I CALL THIS BOOK *Life in the Wrong Lane* because that's where journalists live: in the one lane heading toward a catastrophe. Everyone who's normal is in the other lane, any other lane, going the other way. They're getting out.

Although my travels, first for ABC News and nowadays for HDNet Television, have taken me to many troubled corners of the country and the world, *Life in the Wrong Lane* isn't a travel guide about exotic places, or a contemporary history of the events I've covered. There are better people to write about both. No, it's about all the funny, funky, scary, stupid, dangerous, distasteful, unwise, and unbelievable things journalists experience just getting to the point of reporting a story, experiences that possibly are even more interesting than the stories being covered, but which never become part of the stories we finally report to our audiences.

Public interest about what journalists have to do to cover difficult and sometimes dangerous stories grew during the hunt for the Taliban in Afghanistan in 2001, and again with the American invasion of Iraq in 2003. What I write about is of that genre. It doesn't matter whether it happened in 1979 or 2009, because while the events inevitably change, what it takes to cover them doesn't. These stories are about adventures normal people swerve to avoid, but journalists seek.

Think of life as a highway. A divided interstate highway. And somehow, you've missed those omnipresent, red "Wrong Way" signs, and have gotten going down the exit ramp into the oncoming traffic lanes. Is that ever the right lane? No. Not for anyone but us. In fact, we go looking for the signs saying "Wrong Way." Those are the ones that guide us. Oncoming traffic is our livelihood.

This is obvious in some places, less obvious in others. It was the wrong lane for instance—the fast one, but the wrong one—that got me to war-torn capitals like Beirut and Kampala and Tehran, places where I've had to run for my life, while colleagues who ran with me weren't so lucky. Other times, every lane was the slow lane—and to my way of thinking, the wrong lane—when I had to sit around unpleasant places just waiting for news to break, such as the first shot in the long-awaited war in the Gulf, or the two-thousandth death from religious violence during the troubles in Northern Ireland. (Our motto is, "When the news breaks, we fix it.")

Maybe the best example is the Gulf War, when it was shaping up in 1990 and due to explode at any moment in the deserts and oil fields of Kuwait. Our bosses didn't have to "assign" anybody to the lane leading to Saudi Arabia. Nearly everyone already had his or her passport in the pocket and hand in the air. Did we go for the cozy climate? Nope. For the scenic beauty? Uh-uh. The food? Certainly not! We went, at risk of life, limb, and stomach lining, because the Gulf was the biggest story of the year, promising perhaps the biggest adrenaline rush of the then new decade. In the news business at that particular time, the lane to the Persian Gulf was the only lane worth taking.

I first spent two and a half months there during Operation Desert Shield. Although it was furiously hot and far from home, I complained only once: on my birthday, because when you blow out the candles on your cake, you get lots of sand blowing back in your face. But when Desert Storm broke and the fighting started, I was forced to change lanes; ABC reassigned me to report from the civilized chambers of the United Nations in New York, where the anti-Iraqi coalition had been created. Normal folks might think the U.N. is a much more appealing place from which to report the war than the desert. Long lunches, clean shirts. Normal folks would be wrong! The fast lane at that point led through the Arabian Desert. The United Nations, after having played a major role in the action against Saddam Hussein, once again had become the slow lane. Spell that slooooooooooow.

Naturally, by the standards of normal, family-oriented, forward-looking human beings, the slow lane usually is the best lane, certainly the safest. However, anyone watching us work would figure out pretty easily, we're not normal, we don't place safety high on the list, we don't get our kicks the usual way, we don't always put family first, and we're incapable of looking too far forward. I wouldn't call these the *qualities* of a dedicated journalist, merely the qualifications.

What this means is, we thrive on chaos. The more distant, the more unpredictable, the more adventurous, the better. Media critics who think we always want something bad to happen somewhere in the world are wrong. Sort of. We don't wish for chaos. We just wish to be there when it strikes. This is true, by the way, of everyone on the coverage team.

In many businesses—advertising, public relations, publishing, commercial art—there are creative people and technical people and logistics people and business people. In network news, all those qualities must be wrapped up in every member of the team. The correspondent is primarily responsible for conducting interviews, gathering information, and writing and narrating the final product. The producer, in addition to sharing the task of assembling all the elements into a comprehensible story, has to be the correspondent's eyes and ears when the correspondent is wearing blinders and earmuffs. The cameraperson and the sound technician, between their technical skills, endurance, and artistry, have to provide compelling components that hold the viewers' interest and make television different from the radio and print media. The editor is the one who works with the rest of us to take all the words and sounds and pictures we've collected and put them together to make some sense. Each is a journalist. Each is hooked on the chase.

It's not that we have a monopoly on that kind of passion. Some Americans, after all, get their thrills watching twenty-two men pound their way toward opposite goalposts in pursuit of pigskin bloated in a funny shape. The difference with journalists is, we get our thrills watching different kinds of contests.

Sometimes, they're contests against time. In twenty-three years with ABC News, one of my greatest thrills was standing by the rubble of the collapsed freeway in Oakland, California, four days after the 1989 earthquake, and watching a fellow named Buck Helm get pulled out alive.

Sometimes, they're contests against authority, contests to overthrow the misguided leaders of despotic governments. Nothing gave me more satisfaction than reporting from Poland about the courageous members of the Solidarity Trade Union who stood up and said to their communist overseers, "We shall overcome," (and eventually they did).

And sometimes, they're contests against extinction, the classic battles for turf that inevitably mean more men (and nowadays, women) go away to war than come home. War is destructive, but whether you work for the United States military, a company like Blackwater, or a national news organization, if you live to tell the story, war is also exciting.

This book is not an atlas of troubled places. Nor is it an encyclopedia of major events. Rather, this is simply a collection of my "war stories," "bar stories," call them what you will. I like to think of them as letters home from the field. They tell the tales that never ended up in my reports on the air. They're probably a lot more interesting. But a bit less accurate. Time has passed, dialogue faded. Excuse me if I get a few names, a few words, a few places wrong. Then again, just like a news story, how will you ever know the difference?

I begin every chapter with a short explanation of what attracted me to each place. There are tales to tell from the Soviet Union and Saudi Arabia, Budapest and Beirut, Afghanistan and Uganda, South Dakota and Salt Lake City. Also from Poland, Northern Ireland, Cairo, Khartoum, Iran, Libya, Yemen! The events I got to cover are part of history, but the experiences are evergreen. And I got to every one of them by living life in the wrong lane.

ACKNOWLEDGMENTS

FROM THE MOMENT iUNIVERSE'S Vice President of Editorial and Production, Robin Lasek, told me in our first telephone conversation that when she got my manuscript, she couldn't put it down and read it well into the night, I knew I liked her. And my affection never waned. Despite the thousands of manuscripts that come through her computer, she gave me disproportionate attention and personal encouragement from the beginning of the publishing process to the end. And she put her best people on the case.

Like Editorial Evaluations Coordinator Lynn Holm. She laid out the rules that make the difference between a letter to family and friends, and a published work. Did you know that "Muslim" is capitalized whether it's an adjective or a noun, but "atheist" isn't? Neither did I, until Lynn became my grammatical guide.

And Line Editor Elizabeth Day. Simply put, she's the best. How could I not like a woman who accompanies the manuscript she has edited with a note saying, "I have to tell you, I didn't want this editing project to end!" But beyond a huge stroke to my ego, her greatest contribution was her superlative editor's eye. I've been a writer for a long time, but still, I made some rookie mistakes. She caught them. When something seemed wordy, she suggested ways to simplify. When something seemed confusing, she suggested ways to clarify.

I wouldn't have met any of these talented people in publishing, though, if not for my good friend and fellow author David Henderson. Through our partnership in a Web site called *BoomerCafé.com*, he knew that I had written all these stories, but more as a journal than a book. He saw the possibilities and put me together with Kevin Weiss, the CEO of iUniverse. This book grew from that. It pays to have generous friends.

Two men famous for their success in broadcast journalism and, to the industry's sorrow, now gone, deserve my deep thanks. Paul Harvey, for whom I worked as an editor when I was a young man, taught me to write more sharply than I otherwise would. Not by sitting down with me and going word-for-word through a script, but by trusting me—green and fresh from graduate school—to produce a few scripts for him, in his incomparable voice. Peter Jennings taught me to be a relentless journalist, and he taught by example. Peter was best known as an anchorman but he lived by the reporter's axiom, "If your mother tells you something ... check it out." I don't do justice to the example set by either man, but without them as unintentional tutors early in my career, I probably wouldn't have lasted long enough in the big leagues of broadcast news to cover the stories that fill this book.

Finally, my biggest debt of thanks goes to all the people behind the scenes whose names whiz by in the on-screen credits faster than a viewer can absorb them: the cameramen who made me look better than I look, the audio techs who made me sound better than I sound, the editors who made sense of the visual ingredients I brought home on film and videotape, and the producers who made sense of the thoughts I brought home in my head. The guy with his face on the air usually gets the kudos when a story is good. If life were fair, the face would be a composite.

This book is the product of teamwork. Every story I tell inside is too.

Greg Dobbs, 2009

first thing in the morning to screen and produce the piece you've just shot, retrieve your luggage, and head for the hills. Or in the case of universally flat Chicago, the lakefront.

The assignment desk had different plans. "Why did you fly home?" was how the conversation started.

Why did we fly home? "Because we did the story, we couldn't stand another winter day in South Dakota, and we didn't figure you'd let us fly to Honolulu instead." Why did we fly home, indeed!

"What do you mean you 'did the story'? The story happened while you were in the air."

"What are you talking about?"

"A couple of hours ago, they occupied Wounded Knee. Now the feds are moving in to surround the place. Isn't that where you were?"

Yep. And it's where we were headed again. Like I said, we probably should have seen it coming.

This time, too late for a commercial connection, we chartered. It would be far more expensive, but by the time our Chicago bureau chief made it to the airport to join us, we couldn't even have caught the last commercial flight back to Denver, let alone to Rapid City. Anyway, even if we could have made it to Rapid City, the Pine Ridge Reservation was a several-hour drive. From Chadron, Nebraska, to which our chartered plane would fly, Pine Ridge was just across the border.

As we approached Chadron, the airstrip was dark. We figured it was because no one knew we were coming. Chadron isn't real high on the list of twenty-four-hour airports. When our pilot finally reached someone by radio on the ground, he was told, "Circle for a few minutes; I'll head out there and light it up."

And that he did. With his automobile headlights. Chadron's airstrip was dark because it didn't have any lights of its own. Not a whole lot of people ever try to land at night in Chadron, I guess.

Luckily, ABC in New York came through with its part of the logistics. Three Avis rent-a-car employees from Rapid City had driven all the way down in three separate vehicles to meet us when we landed. They explained that their trip would cost extra, and that if we didn't drive the cars back to Rapid City ourselves, they'd also have to add a drop charge to the bill when we were ready to give them their cars back. We took two four-door Plymouths off their hands; they drove home together in the third.

The first news reports of the Indian occupation of Wounded Knee had said only that several hundred militants had taken over the trading post. The second reports had added a new factor: U.S. marshals and police from the BIA, the Bureau of Indian Affairs, were rushing to cordon off the area so that no more militants could get in. It was about 2 AM. By the time we loaded the cars and headed north into South Dakota, that's all we knew.

Just inside the reservation, we learned more. Each road into Wounded Knee was blocked. It was one of the first moves the BIA police had made. Non-Indian journalists were no more welcome than Indian militants.

So we went to a ranch house four or five miles away. It was the same house where earlier that day, or I guess by now it had become the day before, we had interviewed a white rancher whose house and cattle were on reservation land he leased through the U.S. government. That was one of the very issues AIM was protesting.

He hadn't been wild about having a network news team knock on his door to do the interview, so we figured he'd be even less wild about having the same team knock again in the middle of the night. But we had to start somewhere.

Thankfully, the rancher was sympathetic. Not to the Indians. He was hoping they'd all get thrown in jail for a good long time. But he was sympathetic to us. After all, at least he'd gotten a few hours' sleep. We'd had none, and wouldn't get any for a while.

He gave us doughnuts. He gave us use of his bathroom. And he gave us a map that he himself drew, guiding us over hill and dale to reach the occupied trading post on foot.

The rancher had just two requests. First, don't tell anybody he helped us. Second, get our cars off his property. Park them by the road, hide them in the woods, ditch them in the creek, but don't leave them here.

I think he had a better idea of how long we'd be stuck in Wounded Knee than we did. And that's when it struck me: "We're not going to give up until we've gotten rid of Uncle Sam," Dennis Banks had warned us. That could be a long time!

Of course, if we were destined to spend a few days or longer with hundreds of militant Indians in Wounded Knee, there wasn't much at this point that I could do about it. Except head back to the rancher's bathroom and start winding as much toilet paper around my fist as I could fit in my hip pockets. Which I did. You never know.

We came up with a plan. Since it looked like we wouldn't be able to freely move in and out of Wounded Knee, our bureau chief, Bill, would keep one of the cars and stay on the outside to coordinate our coverage if need be. Just how we would *provide* that coverage under those circumstances, we didn't know. And for that matter, we didn't know whether there'd be any way to coordinate it either.

But aside from Bill, the rest of us, after stowing the other car, would hike in and try. That meant the camera crew, which in those days had three men (John, Jack, and another Bill), the correspondent, which on this trip was Ron, and the producer, which in those early days of my career with ABC News, was me.

By the time we had our act together, it was almost dawn, which meant we might be seen by someone who wanted to stop us. But we figured federal authorities would have needed at least as much time as we did to get *their* act together. In short, maybe they had already shut down the roads into Wounded Knee, but they probably hadn't yet sealed it off from anyone going in on foot.

At least we hoped not.

It turned out we were right. Within a couple of days, they did put hundreds of U.S. marshals, BIA police, and FBI agents around the perimeter of Wounded Knee. But for the moment, not twelve hours into the occupation, this rugged South Dakota rangeland was still wide open.

The only thing in our way was barbed wire. Most of the rolling grassland in this part of the country was subdivided into quarter sections, and each quarter section was defined by a barbed wire fence. If the Indians could have made a penny for every foot of barbed wire strung across their reservations, they wouldn't need any financial help from the government.

It only took a couple of hours to get in, because the rancher's map was right on the money. Every fence, every hill, every hollow showed up right where he said it would. At first, I was grateful that he got us where we wanted to go. By a few days into the occupation, I thought of it more as his revenge on us.

Thank goodness for the rancher's doughnuts, though. Just half a day into the seventy-one-day occupation, all the fresh and packaged food in the white-owned trading post was already gone. Three hundred to four hundred Indians, and a handful of journalists, can go through one small store pretty fast.

All that was left was flour. Shortly before the occupation, the trading post had gotten in a huge shipment of big bags of flour. Indian women, part of the occupation force, were now baking it into biscuits.

At first, they were sweet and tasty. Within a few days, they became just adequate. By the time we finally pulled out of Wounded Knee, I'd have preferred corned beef and cabbage, *and I hate corned beef and cabbage.* But biscuits were all we ever had to eat. For the duration of our unexpectedly long stay, with only one exception, biscuits were the sum total of our meals inside Wounded Knee.

But it was one hell of an exceptional exception!

One of the Indians' protests, as I said before, was that white ranchers could go to Washington and lease the best of a bad lot of land to graze their cattle. What that meant was, there were some fine, fat cattle grazing not too far away. But the Indians couldn't just walk out and grab one. Remember the security cordon of federal officials? It was getting tighter and tighter.

Well, about two weeks into the occupation, Indians and journalists alike were fed up with biscuits. Some were even getting sick. Pity, with those tasty, fat cattle so close.

Then one night in early March, we were buried by a cold and blinding blizzard. Actually, I wasn't nearly as cold as everyone else. The Indian leaders, who had taken over one of the two trailers that belonged to the white owners of the trading post, had assigned the twenty or so journalists who were covering them to the other trailer. Early on, I had secured the top of Wounded Knee's one working TV as my sleeping place in that second trailer. It was one of those big old console models, and if I curled up tight in a fetal position, none of my limbs hung over the side.

More important though, it was up against a wall of the trailer, and it was the wall that was heated, which meant I didn't get really cold until almost everyone else already was—especially most of the Indian occupiers, who were sleeping in the poorly heated trading post, or on the floor of the church.

Anyway, about two weeks into the occupation, at two or three in the morning, someone started ringing a bell. A great big bell to summon all within earshot to the road outside the trading post.

I kind of hated to leave my tiny, hard perch. You can get used to anything. But I left, along with everybody else.

The snow was thick. And blowing almost horizontally. No place gets blizzards like South Dakota's.

Standing in the middle of the road was a bull. Or a steer. To tell the difference, you've got to get down and look. But I didn't. I wasn't curious. Just hungry.

The animal had a rope leash around its neck and was covered in snow. But it sure looked tasty.

Three Indian braves had snuck out of Wounded Knee in the blizzard and rustled this animal. They led it back and proposed to slaughter and cook it right there on the spot. There was only one problem: no one knew how.

The whole point of this increasingly difficult occupation was to enable the inhabitants of Indian reservations to return to Indian ways. But out of several hundred Indians gathered in a circle around this potentially delicious meal, no one knew how to kill it and cook it.

Except Aaron. Aaron was there for NBC. He was NBC's soundman. Aaron was a black man, not an Indian. But in an earlier life, he had been a chef at a Chicago restaurant. In training for that job, he had learned how to do what we needed done that cold night in Wounded Knee. He stepped into the middle of the shivering circle. "Let me show you."

Under flashlight illumination, Aaron opened his pocketknife and slit the animal's throat. Then with the help of the braves who had stolen it, he hung the animal from a rafter in the trading post's overhanging roof to bleed. Aaron told everyone we should let it age. At least a few days anyway.

But no one really wanted to. Everyone was savoring the idea of meat, *now*.

So Aaron struck a deal. "Tell you what," he told Russell Means and Dennis Banks, who had assumed control of the animal now that leadership really counted, "I'll butcher it so there are enough small portions of meat for every Indian, and we'll just take the liver." "We," in this case, meant the journalists.

Well, "we" were none too happy with Aaron's deal. We were just as hungry for a good piece of steak as the Indians were. On the other hand, they were the warriors. We were just the journalists. Moreover, it was too late to renegotiate.

But Aaron knew what he was doing. He explained to us over the campfire he built that we had the better half of the bargain. The meat of a four-legged animal that had been walking around just an hour earlier is way too tough to chew. Fresh liver, on the other hand, can be cut with a spoon. Of course most of us didn't have a spoon, or anything else. But the slice of fresh liver that I held in my bare hands, roasted over a campfire on a freezing field during a blizzard in South Dakota, was about the best food I had ever eaten.

Several Indians, on the other hand, chipped their teeth.

Actually, while the blizzard made it possible for the Indian braves to sneak out, and then back in again with the bull/steer on a leash, you could sometimes get in and out of Wounded Knee at night without the cover of a blizzard, as long as you didn't need to drag a big four-legged animal along. I had to do it three times. That was my lot when I drew the short straw.

What happened was, there were maybe ten or twelve news organizations inside Wounded Knee. The three broadcast networks (nobody had invented cable yet), a few national newspapers, a couple of national news magazines, and a regional reporter or two. In those days, that was major coverage.

There was one telephone there (don't forget, nobody had heard of cell phones either). It was outside the trading post. One telephone for several hundred Indians and a dozen journalists, all of whom seemed to need it at once.

So every print reporter with a story to file could do it by reading his copy over the phone if he was willing to wait an hour, sometimes two or three hours, for the chance. And even then, the line was tapped. We could hear the clicks. It may seem kind of silly for a reporter to care whether someone's listening in when he files a story that will be printed for all the world to see on his newspaper's front page the next day, but it's the principle of the thing.

Anyway, it wasn't really an issue for us because film couldn't be transmitted on the phone. Nor could newspaper and magazine photographs. So, with help from our people outside the security cordon, we had to create what we called "the transportation pool."

Every afternoon, we held a drawing. Several long sticks, one short one. The loser would leave the moment it turned dark and smuggle everyone's material out to a waiting courier and then try to make it back in again before dawn. As a courtesy, news organizations with only one person there, or the loser from the day before, didn't have to participate. We would sink or swim together.

The second night we were there was my first loss in the lottery!

Waving a stick the whole way so I'd find the barbed wire before it found me, I got out of Wounded Knee without incident. Several times, I came over ridge tops to see the hand-warming fires or hear the stay-awake conversations of the feds, but out of sheer luck, I detected them before they detected me, and went around. It took about three hours to reach the highway.

At this point, we hadn't perfected our links with the couriers who would meet us on the outside, so I had to hitchhike ten miles or so into the town of Pine Ridge to find Bill, our bureau chief, who would take all the material off my hands and get it into the right ones.

Had a federal agent, or perhaps an antagonistic rancher picked me up along the road, the written and recorded material I carried on everyone's behalf might never have seen the light of day. But no matter; my good Samaritan was an Indian. He was happy to get me where I was going.

After handing off my cargo, and gulping down two or three candy bars, which I had sorely missed, I didn't relish the idea of going back in alone.

Sure, I got out without incident, but hiking through a line of armed agents at night in the snowy hills of South Dakota, waving a long stick ahead of me most of the time to catch barbed wire before it caught me, was kind of scary. And not much fun. Certainly not fun enough to do it twice between sunset and sunrise.

Luckily, I met up with another journalist who had just gotten into town and wanted to get into Wounded Knee. His name was Art, and he was a cameraman for a company that syndicated news film to TV stations that weren't network affiliates.

"I'll make you a deal," I said. "I'll take you in, but if we get caught, you be the decoy and let me get away." These are not the kinds of things they teach you in journalism school.

So at a bit before midnight, we ditched Art's rented car along the highway somewhere near where we had left our own cars a couple of nights before, and set out for Wounded Knee.

The first time I'd gone in a few nights before, five of us shared the burden of carrying camera and batteries and microphones and film and tripod and other equipment. This night, it was just the two of us.

Among other things, I took the tripod. With everything else in the load, there was too much to carry to leave a free hand to wave a stick out in front of me as I had done for hours while coming out, but by pointing the tripod out front, feeling for barbed wire, it almost served the same purpose.

There was snow on the ground, but a starry sky and a bit of moonlight. In case you think that's good news, think again. It wasn't bright enough to actually help us see the barbed wire. It was just bright enough to make Art and me stand out against the white snow. That meant we had to stay just below the ridgelines if we could, even though that's where the drifts of snow were deepest. But if we didn't, we were sitting ducks. Or hiking ducks, if anyone was watching.

The trouble with crossing through barbed wire at night, with or without snow on the ground, is that you never know whether you've merely climbed to the other side, or crawled *into* something. This fact didn't occur to me until we did precisely that.

We had crossed through three or four barbed wire fences uneventfully. It wasn't easy because at each one I'd have to put my equipment down in the snow, crawl through while Art held the strands apart, take each piece of gear Art handed me over the top, hold the strands apart for him to crawl through, and then pick everything up and start out again.

This time though, we never got that far. I put everything down and with Art's help, crawled through. But before I could grab hold of the first piece of gear, something grabbed hold of me. A dog. He had my cuff in his mouth. In an instant, several more were barking wildly and racing to join the fun. I could hardly see them, but I didn't need a good look to have a fair idea where I was. It was some kind of dog pen, and the dogs were all over me, growling and barking and snapping at my pants.

I'll tell you this: you can get through a barbed wire fence mighty fast when you want to. Just grab the top strand with your gloved hands, pull it down, and pull yourself over. You will lose a little skin. But that's better than losing a leg. And you don't even need Art's help.

After that, we were scared. Not just that we might stumble into another dog pen, but that there surely must be some feds hotfooting it toward the noise of the dogs. So we decided to get as far from the pen as possible, as fast as we could.

What that meant was, we couldn't carry on along the hidden ridgelines. We'd have to cut straight across the reflective fields and take our chances. That's when we got caught.

The first sign was maybe a hundred yards ahead of us, at the top of a hill, silhouetted in the dark night. A lone figure, erect, like a statue at the top of a treeless slope, the barrel of his rifle standing out against the night sky. He seemed to be peering right down at us. If he was a fed, he was just waiting to clamp on the cuffs.

We stopped short and whispered to each other. Fed, or Indian, or angry rancher? No way to know. But it didn't really matter. Whoever he was, he wasn't acting real friendly.

We could cut fast to the left or right and hope to outrun him. We were weighted down with tens of thousands of dollars in camera equipment, but who knows? Maybe in this deep snow, we could move just as fast as he could.

And maybe we couldn't. Furthermore, outrunning him might not be our biggest challenge. What if he shoots at us? Could we outrun the bullet?

So we decided to surrender. After all, if he was an Indian, he'd probably help lead us back to Wounded Knee. If he was a rancher, he'd probably read us the riot act and tell us to get the hell off his land. And if he was a fed, well, we were just journalists. Sure, we were trespassing, and sure, we had illegally crossed a government barrier, but if this was an agent, what would the government do to us except slap our hands and send us home?

"We're journalists and we're not armed." I tried to keep my voice calm as we took maybe a dozen steps in his direction. But he was calmer than I was; he hardly moved. And he didn't say a single word back to us. So now, Art spoke.

"I'm Art Levy. I'm a cameraman for TVN. My partner is Greg Dobbs. He's a producer for ABC." And with that, we took another dozen steps toward our captor.

But he didn't respond. Or move. We could still make out the shape of the rifle's barrel.

"We'll put our hands in the air, just to show you we mean no harm." Art seemed to have the right idea now. Just as we could only see this guy in silhouette, maybe that's how he saw us. And all our protruding equipment, which just as easily could have looked to him like weapons as TV gear. Picture me, walking along with this long tripod sticking out front. In the darkness of the night, it looks like a long gun. "Just give us a few seconds to put all our equipment down."

We set everything down in the snow. That should reassure him. And we put our arms in the air. That should too. And we took a few more steps. He didn't take even one. This was beginning to worry us. It's bad enough to get arrested. Worse still to be captured by some nut with other things in mind. But that was how it seemed to be shaping up.

"Look." My turn again. "We're going to keep coming toward you, slowly, unless you tell us to stop. And we'll keep our arms in the air. But we want you to see us, and we want to show you our press credentials, and show you that we don't have any weapons."

He didn't say not to, so we began stepping through the deep snow. One tall step after another, closer and closer to the mysteriously still and silent figure. Remember, it's a dark night. We'd have to be nearly nose-to-nose to make out more than just his shape.

Which is what it took. It wasn't until Art and I were just a couple of yards from this stoic figure that we could see that he wasn't an Indian. Or a rancher. Or a federal agent.

This guy had four legs. We were surrendering to a Black Angus bull. With a long horn that stood out above his head like a rifle.

We were so shaken, we apologized. To the bull. He still didn't respond.

We backed away, all the way back to our gear, and resumed our hike. Another barbed wire fence or two, and we came to a river. This was no surprise. The crew and correspondent and I had crossed one on our hike to get into Wounded Knee the first time a few nights before, and I had crossed the same one a few hours earlier this night on my way out.

The trouble was, Art and I crossed five on our way back in. *Five.* Seemed like an awful lot of rivers for the South Dakota plains.

Now, you should understand what each river crossing required.

First of all, the closer we got to each river, the thicker the brush. By the time we reached the water, we were having to pull the brush apart to step through.

Second, since it was February, each river was covered with ice, but not always thick enough to walk on. Sometimes it was, sometimes it wasn't. What this meant was, each and every step was a tender test. You'd kind of put your weight on one spot, and if it didn't give way, you'd take the next step. If it did give way though, you'd fall through. We fell many times. Clear up to our hips.

Third, because of the camera gear, we had to cross each river two or three times to get everything across, always holding our cargo high above our heads to keep it dry. It wasn't long before we were soaked to the waist. But we'd done our job; we were soaked, but the equipment wasn't.

Fourth, we had to cut through the same thick brush on the route away from the riverbank. It was a great adventure the first and maybe second times. After that, it was just cold and wet.

Eventually, each time we came to a new river to cross, it was depressing. Not that we could shiver any harder than we already were. But it meant we were still some ways from the campfire we were counting on to dry us out.

Finally around dawn, we crossed our last river and, with a sense of amazement I never admitted to Art, we found Wounded Knee. We came dripping in at about the time most occupiers were rising from that night's hard, fitful sleep.

"Why are you so wet?" We thought it was a pretty stupid question, considering that we had discovered so many rivers in the region. But in one form or another, it's what everybody asked, until one Indian occupier, who knew the reservation because he lived there, heard our explanation and roared. I mean, he almost couldn't stop laughing. And when he did, he pulled a map from his satchel.

"You crossed the same river five times."

He opened the map and sure enough, there was one river, just one. It curved back and forth like a never-ending S. Left, and then right, and then left, and then right again. For some two miles, we had gone straight down its spine. A hundred yards to either side and we'd have crossed it just once. By now, we might already be dry.

We covered the occupation for only the first three and a half weeks, and then, when it was obvious that peace talks to end the stalemate were going nowhere, we pulled out. The negotiations were being held every few days in a colorful ceremonial teepee about two hundred yards from the trading post. The militants had given the government a guarantee of safe passage for its negotiators, who included South Dakota senator and, only the year before, Democratic presidential candidate George McGovern.

Each session began with the negotiators sitting around smoking a peace pipe. Once they started, the television soundmen would quietly crawl up to the rim of the tent to stick so-called "shotgun" microphones under the seam. It was forbidden, but sometimes they got away with it for a few minutes and recorded some interesting insights into the negotiations.

The trouble was, everyone—Indians and government officials—was growing impatient. The standoff was cold, dangerous, and so far for both sides, fruitless.

There was gunfire many nights. Two Indians and a federal agent died during the course of the occupation. But on one particular night of gunfire, a medic was hit. He was a sympathetic white medical student from New York who had driven to South Dakota, snuck into Wounded Knee, and offered his skilled support to the militants.

He wasn't killed or even seriously injured. His thigh was just grazed by a bullet. He was treated with a tourniquet before losing much blood, and he never lost consciousness. But this innocent humanitarian was a casualty of the war, and AIM's leadership meant to make the most of it.

So at about two in the morning, the leaders rang the bell. Every time Means or Banks wanted to summon all the occupiers and observers (that was us) to a rally, or to applaud our meat on the hoof just a few nights earlier, they rang this huge bell. Frankly, I'm not sure I ever asked where they got it. Maybe it was sitting around when they took over Wounded Knee. Maybe they learned to bring one in with them when they took Occupations 101.

Anyway, they rang, and everyone answered, gathering in the trading post.

A rostrum had been set up for speeches. It was elevated on some packing crates that had been found out back. Russell Means held a typed copy of the government's latest peace proposal over his head and began his tirade.

"The federal government is a pack of hypocrites. Its negotiators talk out of both sides of their mouths. They say they want to make peace, but then they restart the war." And at that, the injured medic was carried in on a stretcher. His bearers held it high so that everyone could see who'd been hit. Then they gently set it down on the floor, at the foot of the rostrum, and Means continued.

"The government cannot be trusted. The government makes promises it has no intent to keep. We cannot deal anymore with the government. We will cut off the talks." And to prove his point, Means produced a cigarette lighter and then a flame, and set the printed proposal on fire.

Sensational. A strong protest. A meaningful message. Not to mention good television.

Except for one small mistake. Russell Means let the paper burn to the point where his hand might get scorched, and then he let it drop to the front of the rostrum. Right onto the chest of the injured medic lying at the foot of the rostrum, whose shirt caught fire. He wasn't in danger for long. Several Indians rushed to quash the flame, and then rushed his stretcher out of the hall and out of harm's way. Who'd have thought he'd be safer in the snow?

Ever since then, I've always thought this small event proved one point: the "handlers" who stage-manage politicians serve an important purpose. At the very least, they keep the politicians from setting their supporters on fire.

It was only a week or so later that we pulled out of Wounded Knee. The story was beginning to repeat itself, not to mention break the bank at ABC News. In those days, you see, ABC, which stands for American Broadcasting Company, was still recovering from its long-held reputation as the poorest network, symbolized by the fact that many people thought the letters stood for "Always Be Cheap." In its early years, in fact, the whole network might have folded if not for the profits of a single hit show, such as *Maverick*. There really hadn't been any money to waste, not in news, sports, entertainment, or any other division of the network. Eventually, when ABC broke into the big leagues in every division, thrift was a habit hard to break.

Believe me though, we broke it with a vengeance. For example, a few years after Wounded Knee was the premiere of a successful new broadcast in the news division. It was *Nightline*. Its first year was both a ratings and a critical blockbuster. Some editions of the broadcast were costly to produce, and some were cheap. Or at least, they could have been. But the broadcast's boss knew how to play the game, so he put people in charters when they could have flown commercially, and ordered up hours and hours of satellite time he didn't need.

Why? So that when he went to his bosses to ask for next year's budget, he could justify a high level of expenditure, and given the show's success, they couldn't turn him down. At that point, the waste was locked in. An old trick, tried and true.

But back to Wounded Knee. In 1973, there wasn't any waste to lock in, because there wasn't any extra money to spend. That's why, when we hired the charter from Chicago to Chadron that first night of the occupation, we turned down a jet in favor of a turbo-prop. CBS and NBC were racing up in jets, and that meant they'd beat us there, but they'd spend another thousand or two to do it, which we couldn't.

Then, once we landed and got the lay of the land, we realized we couldn't let the plane go. In those days, you couldn't just set up a portable satellite dish in a pasture and transmit to a transponder 22,000 miles up. These days you can, but back then, you could only feed from a television station with the right links to the outside. The closest one for us like that was in Denver.

What that meant was, early each afternoon, one of our people on the outside would take the film we'd smuggled out the night before, get on our turbo-prop, and fly down to Denver, and then go to our affiliate, cut the story, and feed it via a complicated network of land lines to New York. Our competition was doing the same, although faster.

It seems kind of silly, looking back. Those of us inside Wounded Knee may have been in competition with one another, but we were able to form a pool of convenience and cooperate to get our material the first ten miles. No one complained. Yet our colleagues on the outside each then flew the next few hundred miles to the same city in separate aircrafts, each occupying a single seat and each costing his network a couple of thousand dollars a day.

The others could afford it. We couldn't. First, because there was that daily roundtrip to Denver. Second, because the three-man camera crew and I all were union employees who were on the clock *on overtime* twenty-four hours a day. That was because for those three and a half weeks, we never saw a pillow. Sorry, but that's the contract.

So with the story no longer changing, ABC decided one day to pull us out. Me first, that night. I would smuggle my last load, and then carry ABC's material myself on the turbo-prop to Denver. Correspondent and crew would follow the next morning.

I got to the town of Pine Ridge before sunrise and found a bed. We wouldn't leave for Denver until just past noon.

In the meantime, another set of peace talks had started. Russell Means's antics notwithstanding, both sides were eager to claim victory and go home.

This time, there was quick progress. On the same morning I had gotten out, McGovern and his colleagues had carried in a concession, and the

Indians had offered one of their own. The two sides met for less than an hour, with McGovern promising to dash back to Washington that very day and plead in person for approval.

But when he and another team member from the Justice Department got to the Pine Ridge airstrip, which everyone was now using because it was even closer than Chadron, their government plane wasn't there. However, I was. I offered them a ride. Next time, I think they'll wait for a better offer.

We took off into the clouds, and then into the unstable air blowing east from the Rocky Mountains. Remember, other than that delicious snack of barbecued liver a week or so earlier, I'd been living on biscuits. My stomach was fragile. Too fragile for the flight.

What's worse, it was a small aircraft. An uncomfortable bench in back, and four regulation airplane seats further forward, facing each other in pairs. I, in the same clothes I'd worn for weeks, was across from the guy from Justice, who was wearing a suit and probably had showered that same morning. We gave McGovern, also suited and suitably tied, his own pair of seats next to ours.

He was the lucky one.

Before we even leveled off, I got sick. Instant nausea. There wasn't a whole lot of food in my stomach, but what there was came out. Without warning. All over my traveling partner from Washington. McGovern wasn't physically hit, but like everyone else aboard, including the cockpit crew, he was hit by the stench. After someone's been airsick, you don't want to be confined with them for another hour or so in a sealed tube. Trust me on that.

We landed in Denver, they thanked me most *in*sincerely for the ride, and probably headed for the nearest men's store to buy new suits.

I couldn't. There was a story to put on the air. And after doing so, there was a commercial flight home.

I could have bought new clothes, had a good meal, taken a hotel room *and a warm shower,* and caught the first flight in the morning. But you have to understand: the longer you're away from your own bed, the better it sounds to get back to it. Especially after nearly a month with no bed at all. So after getting our story on the air, I caught a cab and rushed straight from the TV station to the airport. I was determined to sleep in my own bed that very night. I bought my ticket and went to the gate.

Until then, I'd been so much on the move that I hadn't thought about how I looked or *how I smelled.* But at the gate, I got a clue. When I sat down to wait to board, people on both sides moved away. When I took my seat on the plane, the guy in the seat next to mine asked for another. Actually, sitting next to me wasn't as bad as sitting across from me. I knew a man from the Justice Department in Washington who would swear to it.

The next day, I slept late and stayed home.

The crew had just gotten home too. Jack, the soundman, called me.

"When we got out," which they had done by hitching a ride with the government negotiators, "we went to get the cars. We were kind of surprised, but they were still there."

"Good," I said. We had all half thought they would be stolen after all that time.

"No. Not good." Jack was a guy who had to be asked the right question. "Why not?"

"Because they were shot full of holes. The tires, the bodies, the windows, everything. The cars are totaled."

To this day of course, none of us knows who did it. Or how many did it. Indians, white ranchers, law men? Don't know, doesn't matter. But the cars were rented in my name. That mattered! "What did you do with them?"

"Greg, you don't understand. We didn't do anything with them because we couldn't do anything with them. The cars are destroyed. They can't be driven. Ever. I'll send you the keys."

So I did the only thing I could do. I called Avis in Rapid City.

"Remember the two cars your people drove down to Chadron, Nebraska several weeks ago for ABC News?"

"Yes."

"Great. First, let me tell you where they are. They're parked off the highway running east out of Pine Ridge, probably four or five miles from town. But second, let me tell you how they are. Apparently someone's used them for target practice and they're totaled. I don't even know if you're gonna want to pick them up. We took the insurance, so I suppose the insurance company will buy you new ones. Meanwhile, please send me the bill. I'll pay the drop charge."

It was years before any of us had the guts to rent a car again in Rapid City. Especially from Avis.

THE LIGHT AND BRIGHT SIDE OF AN EXECUTION

Utah, and Eagle Pass, Texas

GARY GILMORE WAS A *double murderer.*

One night in 1976, just three months out of prison for a previous felony, he went to rob a gas station in Orem, Utah. He took the clerk into the bathroom, had him lie down on his stomach, and shot him twice in the head. Gilmore had his girlfriend's little sister waiting outside in a pickup truck. The next night, Gilmore went to rob a motel. He had the clerk get down behind the registration desk, and shot him in the head too.

Altogether, for two nights' work, Gilmore got a few hundred dollars. In no time at all, he was caught.

Tragically and coincidentally, both of his victims left behind young pregnant widows. And one baby apiece.

Gilmore's murder spree came at just about the time the United States Supreme Court was reconsidering the constitutionality of the death penalty after a moratorium of nearly a decade. Was the death penalty cruel and unusual punishment? Was it inequitably applied, depending on a murderer's race? Were convicted killers deprived of fair and reasonable trials, and equally fair opportunities for appeal?

The Court decided the answer to each of these questions was no. Executions for capital crimes could start again in America.

Gary Gilmore's death date was set. But he wasn't the only man in the country with a schedule to die. In several states, where elected officials had been eagerly waiting for the Court's decision, murderers were given death dates, and setting their appeals in motion.

What made Gilmore stand apart from the rest was that he didn't appeal.

In fact, he told the civil rights organizations who wanted to keep him alive to "get off my back." Gary Gilmore was thirty-six, a habitual criminal who had spent half his life in jail. He didn't want to spend any more time there. He wanted to die.

On January 17, 1977, he did. He died at the hands of a firing squad inside an old cannery at Utah State Prison. It was the start of a new era of executions.

•   •   •   •   •

Norman Mailer got it slightly wrong.

In his thick book on Gary Gilmore, *The Executioner's Song*, Mailer wrote that after reading that a condemned man in Utah actually wanted to be executed, "ABC correspondent Greg Dobbs rang in (to Utah's attorney general) from Chicago and said, 'I'll be out this weekend, can I interview you? Can I come to your home?'"

Slightly wrong, because it wasn't that simple.

It was a Friday, and I had just gotten back to Chicago from a trip. I sure wasn't trying to come up with another story idea to take me away over the weekend again, so I was in the bureau, keeping a low profile, going through my pile of out-of-town papers, looking for story ideas to pursue the following week.

This little bitty item on Page 3 of the paper right on top, the *Salt Lake City Tribune*, caught my eye: "CONVICTED KILLER FIGHTS APPEALS." At first I thought it was a misprint. It was probably meant to read, "CONVICTED KILLER FIGHTS TO APPEAL."

But no. In a little sidebar box, not an inch and a half long, the piece said that a convicted double murderer in Utah had told the NAACP and the American Civil Liberties Union that he did not want their help in appealing his death sentence, set for ten days hence. The short article didn't even carry his name.

It wasn't the prospect that this fellow might become the first man to be legally executed in the United States after a decade-long moratorium that got my interest. It was the prospect of a man going to his death because he wanted to.

So yes, although it was a more detailed conversation than Mailer related in the book, I called the state's attorney general. And the convicted killer's lawyer. And the civil rights groups that wanted to appeal Gilmore's death sentence. And the warden at Utah State Prison, who would be charged with carrying out the execution.

The long and the short of it was, Gary Gilmore was demanding that the liberal anti-death penalty groups back off, and they were refusing.

The timing of it was, he would appear the next Tuesday before the Utah Supreme Court, which, at the behest of these groups, had given Gilmore a stay of execution. He would ask the justices to overturn the stay and let him die six days later.

The beauty of it was, so far as I could tell, no one else in the national news media knew a thing about it. So on Sunday, we flew out. There went the weekend. And the next two and a half months.

Two days after we got there, in the Utah Supreme Court, Gilmore told the panel of very conservative justices, "I believe I was given a fair trial and I think the sentence is proper and I am willing to accept it like a man." By a vote of four to one, they granted him his wish. At eight o'clock the next Monday morning, he would die.

We had asked to be in court with our camera to hear his historic plea, but were turned down. "No pictures." So we did the next best thing. Since just about every employee of the court was curious to see Gilmore in the flesh, they all abandoned their offices to sit in the ornate courtroom, which was in a corner of the state capitol. And that gave us an opening to sneak into the office just adjacent to the courtroom, lock the doors to keep anyone else out (like, say, CBS News), and shoot the whole hearing through a small window in the door.

Then at the end, as guards fortuitously began to lead the prisoner right toward our hiding place, we unlocked the doors just in time and filmed Gilmore as he walked past, getting him to say a few words to boot. But that, of course, was the end of our scoop. After our piece played on the *ABC Evening News* (the predecessor to *World News Tonight*), showing a prisoner with his hands cuffed and his legs shackled begging to be shot, all flights into Salt Lake City the next day carried journalists. And most stayed, because the story kept growing.

To begin with, Gilmore's protectors, whom he saw as his opponents, found another way to save his life. They got the governor to order the State Board of Pardons to review Gilmore's conviction and decide whether his sentence was justified. Ultimately, they would conclude that it was, but the catch was this: the next meeting of the board would be Wednesday, November 17, two days *after* the scheduled execution. Gilmore's date with death would have to be postponed.

And that's pretty much how the story evolved. The Board of Pardons, the state supreme court, the United States Supreme Court—everyone got into the act. Gilmore's execution was on-again, off-again several times.

Sometimes it was Gilmore's own fault, because he tried to speed up the process himself. Twice he managed to get hold of some sleeping pills and overdosed. Each time, his appointment with the executioner passed as he lay in the hospital recovering. And once again, at least on his first attempt, we were the first to find out. Quite by accident.

Part of the fascination with Gary Gilmore had been his girlfriend, a thrice-divorced young mother of two, named Nicole Barrett. Nicole had stuck with Gary. He had beaten her, he had lied to her, he had committed two murders while dating her, but still, she loved him, and now regularly visited him on death row.

I wanted to talk to her. Gilmore had become the subject of national curiosity, and she was one of the keys to his thoughts. So, early in the morning on November 15, the day Gilmore originally was supposed to have died, I drove alone down to the prison, halfway between Salt Lake City and Provo, arriving just as visiting hours began. Someone had told me that Nicole always visited Gary first thing in the morning so that she could make it to her job on time. I would try to meet her on her way out.

I waited in the car for more than an hour. Seemed strange, because I also had been told that Nicole never stayed that long. Just as I concluded that she hadn't come that day and prepared to give up, a thin, attractive young woman came out of the main entrance and began to walk toward Interstate 15, which ran right by the prison.

She did not fit the description someone had given me. On the other hand, maybe the description was wrong, and if this woman was getting picked up on the interstate, I didn't have much time to find out. I jumped out of my car and ran after her.

In a situation like this, you don't go rushing up and blurt out, "Hey, aren't you Nicole Barrett?" First of all, you feel stupid if you're wrong. Secondly, even if you're right, you'll turn her off before you get the chance to spit anything else out.

So I decided to take the soft, familiar approach. "Hi, Nicole, my name's Greg Dobbs, I'm with ABC News. I'm awfully sorry to bother you right now, really. I know how tough all this must be for you, but blah blah blah blah blah ..." Actually, at a time like this, there's no way you can avoid sounding like you've got something to hawk, but you do the best you can.

The trouble was, the prison sat below the interstate, so my short sprint up the freeway on-ramp to catch her left me out of breath. Instead of my intended calm, thoughtful approach, it came out like, "Nicole (huff puff huff puff), I'm a reporter (huff puff huff puff), can I talk to you (huff puff huff puff)?"

"No." She didn't even stop walking. Something wasn't working.

"Look (huff puff huff puff), I really don't want to be bugging you right now (huff puff huff puff), but if it's not me, it's going to be someone else (huff puff huff puff)." One problem was, I hadn't had a moment to catch my breath.

"I don't want to talk to no reporters." This time though, at least she stopped when she said it—not that she stopped for me; we had reached the shoulder of the interstate, and she was hitchhiking. She stuck out her arm and stuck up her thumb.

"Tell you what," I said, finding my opening, "I have a car. Let me take you to work. I'll tell you why I think it might help you to talk with me, and if you still say no, I promise you, I won't bother you again."

Nicole took a moment to think about it. So far, no one had stopped to pick her up.

"Okay. I'll go with you." She told me it always took a long time to get a ride because *not many drivers want to pick up a hitchhiker in front of the state prison.* So we walked back to the parking lot and got in the car.

"Where do you work?" I had to know which way to go on the interstate.

"I ain't working today. You can drive me home."

"Where do you live?" Hadn't done my homework.

"Orem. I'll show you."

Off we went. Funny thing was, I didn't ask her a thing about Gilmore. The only purpose of this ride was to win her over to do a lengthy on-camera interview about Gilmore, although I had to restrain myself from asking all the questions in my mind right there on the interstate.

The fact is, we drove most of the time in silence. I had very little in common with this inarticulate young woman whose greatest love was a convict condemned for killing two innocent young men. And she had very little in common with me. It wasn't until we pulled into her neighborhood in Orem that I undertook my mission.

"Nicole, I told you that I'm a reporter. My name is Greg Dobbs, and I work for ABC News. I also told you that I think an interview on a national TV network can help you. That may sound self-serving, but let me tell you why. You know that every reporter in Utah right now wants to talk to you. And every last one of them is going to try, and keep trying, and you're not going to have a moment's peace. Sit down with me and my camera crew, and we'll go over everything there is to talk about. You've got to understand, I don't want to pry into your personal life, or even your life with Gary. He's the one we all really want to talk to. It's just that none of us can, and so you're the closest link. Talking with you will be like talking with him. Then, if you go ahead and do it, you can tell every other reporter who requests an interview that you've already done one, you've said everything there is to say, and you're not doing any more."

Hardly a unique argument, but I hoped she hadn't heard it before. It's not hard to remember all these years later, because I've used it so many times since. We were pulling up to her apartment house just as I finished.

"Okay, pick me up tomorrow."

Simple as that! Much easier than I expected. I thought at least she'd want more details. But don't look a gift horse in the mouth.

"Are you visiting Gary?"

I remember her long pause. "Yeah."

"What time do you leave your apartment?"

"No, don't get me here. Get me at the prison."

I noticed that her eyes never met mine. Not once.

"I'll be happy to pick you up here and give you a ride, then bring you back to do the interview."

"No, pick me up there." Then she got out. Since Nicole didn't have a car, I wondered why she didn't take me up on my offer to give her a ride.

The next morning, I found out.

The crew and I showed up in the prison parking lot before visiting hours even started. Leave nothing to chance.

But Nicole never came. We kept our eyes on the off-ramp, and she never showed up. But after being there only fifteen or twenty minutes, two ambulances did. They rushed through a gate in the electrified fence and pulled around the side of the prison. I got this funny feeling in the pit of my stomach. Nicole yesterday, the ambulances today. I got out of the car and ran into Warden Sam Smith's office. He was at his desk.

"I just saw two ambulances race into the prison. Does this have anything to do with Gilmore?"

"Looks like someone slipped him some pills and he overdosed."

"Is he dead?"

"Not yet."

Not yet. That meant they'd rush him to a hospital to try to keep him alive. So that they could shoot him later on.

I ran back outside. Just as I reached the car, one ambulance sped out of the gate. It turned north, to Salt Lake City. We gave chase. Luckily, the cameraman had his camera on his lap. Sometimes they'll stow it in its case in the trunk. Getting it out would have cost us a minute. We couldn't afford it. We had another scoop.

Gilmore had OD'd. The state wouldn't kill him quickly enough, so he would kill himself. And while pretty soon word would spread, it was a scoop for the moment, and we had probably the only opportunity to get dramatic pictures to back it up. The ambulance, you see, had clear glass windows. Had it been a windowless ambulance as most are today, or had the glass been translucent rather than transparent, our shot of it speeding up the freeway would have been worth about three seconds on the news that night.

But it had big, clear windows, and we could see two paramedics in the back, adjusting the oxygen mask on Gilmore's face, pressing on his chest, taking every heroic measure they could to keep him going until he reached the hospital.

This was good stuff! The fact that we could see them working on the patient was fine. The fact that it was through the window of a speeding ambulance was even better. We'd all keep our jobs at least another day.

The cameraman had climbed over the back of the front passenger seat to get to the rear left window seat. I was driving, and concentrating on keeping our speed steady and our position in the right lane absolutely parallel with the ambulance in the left lane. At 80 mph, that's a bit of an art. But as it became second nature, my mind went to work to put some pieces together.

It seemed pretty clear that Nicole was the one who slipped Gilmore the pills, probably right before she met me, which meant she knew he would be dead by now, or should be, which meant she had no plan to visit him. And yet she had been adamant: don't pick me up at home. I remembered her reluctance to look me in the eye. And her pause before saying, "Yeah," she'd be seeing Gary today.

Ohmigod, I had it! When Nicole and I had been together yesterday, she fully believed that today, she would be together again with Gary. *In death.* She must have taken an overdose too.

All this struck me just as we came up to one of those "Emergency Vehicles Only" turnaround points on the interstate. We were halfway to Salt Lake City and probably had all the good videotape of Gilmore being worked on in the ambulance that we needed.

We were speeding north; Nicole lived south. Or at least, that's where her apartment was. She might not "live" anymore at all.

I jammed on the brakes, swerved right behind the ambulance into the left lane and straight for the short break in the center median. The crew went flying. Sorry, guys, no time to explain.

We got to her apartment house and found it crawling with uniforms. Police, fire, medical. She had just been taken away, comatose but alive.

They found the empty bottles in her bedroom. Seconal and Dalmane. Enough to kill two. And they found a letter. The heart of it said, "I love him, I made my own choice, I'll not regret it."

It turns out that the day before, Nicole had stuffed Gilmore's pills into a pair of balloons, and then stuck them up her vagina, and went to visit him. She was strip-searched, but not that far. Then, while necking in the visiting room, Gilmore had pulled out the balloons and stuck them up his own rectum. Some people have to go to more trouble than others to kill themselves.

Incidentally, all this evidently was done right before I picked Nicole up. To think *I* was the one out of breath when we met!

We got directions and raced from Nicole's apartment to Utah Valley Hospital in Provo. The crew and I ran in through the front door and asked for help to find intensive care. Instead, we were shown the way out: "No reporters."

But there's more than one way to skin a CAT scan.

We went back outside. I took off my tie, rumpled my hair, even took some dirt from some landscaped bushes and spread it on my shirt and face. I wanted to look like I'd been in an accident. Then, right back through the lobby. No one even looked.

I found a staircase, and then a set of arrows directing me to intensive care, and before I knew it, I was looking through the glass at Nicole, or at least what I could see of her through the pumps and tubes that were keeping her alive. She was the only patient there. I made a mental note of what I saw, and then turned away and found myself facing a sign saying "INTENSIVE CARE WAITING ROOM." Inside, several women. Most were sobbing.

Beautiful!

I shuffled in, head bowed, eyes to the floor, and took a seat. I'd just sit silently, mournfully, let my presence sink in, and then slowly win their confidence before letting on why I was there. But my butt hadn't hit the vinyl when one of the women snapped through her tears, "What are you, *a reporter?*"

These are the times that try reporters' souls. Do you say yes, and get yourself kicked out instantly? Or do you say no, and get yourself kicked out a little later? I always prided myself on telling the truth, or at least the half-truth to get a story, rather than flat-out lies. So in my most innocent voice: "Well yes, but—"

"No reporters here! Get out!" She wasn't leaving a whole lot of room for argument.

"But I don't want to intrude, I just—"

"Get out right now or we'll get you out!"

Now, a good reporter is a little like a good prizefighter. Know when you've been beaten. Don't go back for more. So, tail between my legs, I left. Retreating down the hall, I still could hear their sobs.

Within just a couple of days, Gilmore was sufficiently revived to be taken back to prison. Nicole Barrett was still in a coma, but Gilmore was the real subject of the story, and he was okay.

On Friday, I asked ABC to have the weekend off so I could fly home to Chicago and spend it with my wife. The company was compassionate: catch the final flight tonight; go back on the last flight Sunday night. Fair enough. Just enough time to make it. I raced to the hotel, threw my suitcase together, and then with briefcase and portable typewriter in hand in that pre-computer age, caught a cab to the airport. I ran to the ticket counter, made my purchase, got stuck with a middle seat, and ran to the gate. Everyone else had already boarded. The flight was full. I was assigned to the bulkhead row in coach, seat B.

I had checked my suitcase, but carried the briefcase and typewriter with me. The typewriter was a nifty little Olivetti, the kind most traveling journalists used back then because, of all the portables made, it was the most compact. It came in a soft, powder-blue case. As I nudged my way past the passenger in the aisle seat, I saw a typewriter just like mine under her feet. An Olivetti. In a soft, powder-blue case.

Her face was familiar, but for just a moment I couldn't place it. Then, it struck me: "What are you, a reporter?" This was the woman who had hit me at the hospital a few days earlier with that broadside. "No reporters here! Get out!" None, that is, except her. It turns out she was *Newsweek's* reporter on the story, Elaine Sciolino, who went on in her career to dominate the world of diplomacy for the *New York Times*.

Diplomacy! She had used none with me.

As we laughed about it over drinks on the flight to Chicago, Elaine explained that she had been in Provo that day to talk to Nicole Barrett, found out about the attempted suicide, and got to the hospital before anyone else. She had used her powers of diplomacy with Nicole's mother. Elaine convinced the mother that if she cooperated with Elaine, Elaine would keep all other reporters off the mother's back. Sound familiar? Elaine kept her promise to the mother. I've always admired her technique.

Ultimately though, we tried hard and came close to interviewing Gilmore himself. Mind you, we were not alone. Everyone wanted such an interview, but we had a special connection. A Hollywood film producer named Larry Schiller had worked through Gilmore's attorneys and opened the wedge with Gilmore by promising to pay his estate a portion of the profit from a made-for-TV movie about his life. Among other things, that enabled Schiller to visit Gilmore in person from time to time.

But Schiller had taken advantage of some prison rules. According to the warden, he had represented himself as a producer for "ABC Television" whereas the truth was, ABC was just one of the organizations to which he *hoped* to sell his movie. So the prison shut him out, and he came to me to forge a marriage of convenience. He would get Gilmore to write a letter requesting a visit with me and a camera crew from ABC News. In exchange, after using the material on ABC, we would permit Schiller to use it in his movie.

ABC News in New York loved the idea. We would do our interview "live" for *Issues and Answers*, which was our Sunday interview show until it was replaced by what became *This Week*. But Sam Smith, the warden, said no. He cited a rule against television cameras coming into maximum security.

We challenged him. We cited the First Amendment, not to mention the arbitrary nature of the prison's rule. First we went to state court. The judge went along, but the State of Utah appealed. That put us in the Utah Supreme Court, which went along with the state. Then we went to federal court. The judge went along, but the State of Utah appealed. That put us in federal appellate court, which went along with the state. Do you ever get the feeling you're just not going to win something? We considered carrying our case to the United States Supreme Court, but ABC decided not to throw bad money after good, and gave up.

Too bad. We already had spent thousands to fly in the cables and cameras and technicians that a live interview from the prison would require. Now, they would be kept in Utah but left idle for a few weeks to cover the execution itself.

Back when he was first sentenced to death, before the compassionate advent of lethal injection, Gary Gilmore had been given a choice: die in front of a firing squad, or at the end of a rope. Utah, a predominantly Mormon state, gave murderers the choice because of one old, unofficial canon in Mormon law: having shed the blood of others, a good member of the Church of Jesus Christ of Latter-day Saints cannot redeem himself by shedding his own. A contrite Mormon wouldn't choose the firing squad for redemption. Gilmore, however, had been raised in an on-again-off-again Mormon household and wasn't particularly observant. He chose the firing squad simply because he preferred a bullet to a noose.

Made sense to me.

The firing squad itself was to be composed of five riflemen. The state had solicited volunteers and received many responses. Every member would be a professional lawman. Only four of the rifles would hold bullets. The fifth would hold a blank. That way, if in the future one of the volunteers regretted his participation in an execution, he could rationalize that maybe he had been the one with the blank. That's standard operating procedure just about wherever firing squads are found.

In an abandoned cannery that has since been demolished on the grounds of the prison, an old, wooden executive's chair with a dark green, leather padded seat and back was placed against a wall of sandbags, which were piled against the stone wall. This was designed to absorb the steel-jacketed bullets that would either miss Gilmore, or go through him.

The warden, long frustrated with the news media that had been hounding him rather constantly for more than two months now, had his revenge. He ruled that since the execution was scheduled for Monday sunrise, but the prison grounds wouldn't open until nine in the morning, journalists who wanted to cover it would have to come in the night before. Into the building? Perish the thought. Into the frozen parking lot, in the middle of January. It became a bonanza for RV rental companies.

ABC ended up with four "on camera" people there. I was there to do the big story: the execution. Tom Schell was there to find a serious sidebar. Stephen Geer, a very funny man, was assigned, believe it or not, to do a story about how the press corps spent the night outside the prison—what he cynically called "the light and bright side of the execution"—and Geraldo Rivera was there for the entertainment segment of *Good Morning America*.

Let's get something straight. Nobody saw the execution as entertainment. It's just that in those days, the entertainment division of ABC produced *Good Morning America* (which subsequently was taken over by the news division). If Gilmore was to be shot during a news segment of the show, I would anchor, but if it were to happen during "entertainment's" watch, it would be Geraldo.

The timing of the execution was fuzzy. It was set for "sunrise," which technically meant 7:49 AM. However, while a stay of execution had been issued by the federal district court in Salt Lake City at one in the morning, the state attorney general's people had flown overnight to fight the stay at the federal appeals court in Denver. Simultaneously, anti-death penalty forces were trying to get relief from the Supreme Court in Washington. Anything could happen.

At about 7:30, the warden set the execution in motion. With our eyes and lenses focused on the prison, from a distance we all saw Gilmore, in black T-shirt and white jeans, shackled top and bottom, led into a van, and then driven to the cannery on the other side of the complex. What we didn't know was, the warden would take things to the point of no return, and then stop if need be.

Meanwhile, finally, reporters and cameras were let into the administration building of the prison. We would be squeezed into a conference room to await word that Gilmore was dead, if he was to be shot at all. At least it was heated!

ABC had two "live" cameras in place. One was in the conference room, and the other was out front, with the prison in the background. From an editorial point of view, the position outside was too far removed from the instant information we needed. But from a visual point of view, with the security fence and the prison cellblocks and the pink sky at sunrise, it was a much better backdrop. So that's where they told me to stay. I would get my information by walkie-talkie from one of our people inside.

At about ten minutes to eight, "news" took over from "entertainment." Signs were that the execution was imminent. We wanted to be broadcasting from the scene when it happened. I went on the air, describing the run-up to this day, describing the night full of eleventh hour legal appeals, describing the scene right then. Then we went to a commercial. It was during the commercial that we heard that the Supreme Court had refused to act, and the appeals court had overturned the stay. Gilmore really would be shot. Any minute now.

Suddenly, all the great plans in the great minds in New York fell apart. "Get Dobbs inside," they were shouting through a phone at Steve, the producer at my side. "Get Dobbs inside so he can tell us the moment Gilmore's dead."

"Okay, he's on his way." Steve was frantically signaling for me to unwire my earpiece, unhook my microphone, and hotfoot it into the administration building fifty yards away. Meanwhile, the voice in New York was ordering up a correspondent to replace me there, at the outside position, as a backup. "Get Geer in gear." I've always liked that play on words.

But Steve, the producer, didn't have time to laugh. "I don't see him." The parking lot was pandemonium right about then.

"Then get Schell into harness."

"He's not here either." Geer and Schell were out doing what they were supposed to be doing—reporting the story.

"Well, who've you got?"

"Geraldo."

Steve later told me there was an audible moan over the phone. Geraldo did not work for the news division. He was known in those days as a loose cannon. Some things never change.

"Okay, get him wired up. We're coming out of the commercial in a minute. Let me know as soon as Dobbs is in place inside."

But Dobbs didn't get into place until the whole thing was over, because I ran into the worst traffic jam Utah has ever seen. It was on the stairway to the second-floor conference room. Prison guards had created a logjam clear down to the first floor by searching everyone going in. And everyone else was just as eager to get in as I was. A loud demand like, "Hey, network news, let me pass," just wouldn't carry much weight.

I got into the room just as the phone rang. It was placed on a long table at the front, and a deputy to the warden, given the dubious assignment of answering the call, did his duty. Suddenly, you could have heard a pin drop. The deputy listened for just a few seconds, hung up, and then said to the hundred or so reporters watching him, "The order of the court has been carried out. Gary Mark Gilmore is dead." It was 8:07 A.M.

I pushed my way to the ABC camera clear in the back of the jam-packed room, and saw that instead of peering through the eyepiece, the cameraman was frantically fiddling with the cables. Something was wrong—*very* wrong. The camera had gone down just before the announcement. That left us just the one "live" camera outside.

And Geraldo was using it to the max. "I think I can hear the shots. Oh my God, I can hear the shots. I can't believe they're doing this. My God, I hear the shots."

I may have included one "My God" too many, but that's basically how Geraldo told the story. Not exactly how a newsman would have done it. What's more, there were hundreds of yards and a few thick walls between Geraldo and the cannery. But who knows? Maybe his hearing was just better than anyone else's.

The rest of our coverage was anticlimactic.

Witnesses to the execution came to the conference room and gave the news media details about what happened. When the warden asked Gilmore if he had any last words to utter, Gilmore had just said, "Let's do it."

Then we were led to the execution site itself. We pawed over the chair, we peered through the executioners' rifle slots cut into a long black drape, we fingered the bullet holes in the leather padding. Every last one of us did.

In the meantime, Gilmore's corpse was already on its way to Salt Lake

City. His eyes would be donated to someone who needed them, his body cremated, and—as he requested—his family would spread his ashes over Utah from an airplane. It turns out that disposing of Gilmore's ashes that way was illegal. It figures.

Incidentally, Stephen Geer's "light and bright side" of the execution never got on the air. To his credit, he killed it.

But the piece I was doing, the big lead, almost didn't get on either.

We were feeding our story from the ABC affiliate in Salt Lake City. Everything had gone well up until the last minute. Not for Gilmore, but for us. We had strong video and a strong story. Steve, the producer, was in the control room on the phone with New York. Our "color bars," the technical standard that tells the videotape operator in New York that our machines' video levels are compatible, were showing on the screen, which the master control room at ABC in New York was seeing.

But they weren't hearing us. We first fed some high-pitched tone, which is an audio standard comparable to the color bars, and then we rolled our tape and fed my recorded narration. But New York wasn't hearing a thing. There were only about ten minutes until the broadcast went on the air, and this was a big story. It had to lead the show. So the fact that New York couldn't hear our audio was a big deal.

One complication was, our picture and our sound were scheduled to travel on different paths. It wasn't preferable, but it was the only routing available. You see, in those days, there were precious few telecommunications satellites in space. That means there were precious few channels available to carry a TV signal. On the day of Gilmore's execution, the three broadcast networks—ABC, NBC, and CBS—were all feeding from Salt Lake City. That means there was an inordinate demand on the satellite. And that means there weren't enough communication channels for everybody. What we ended up with was our picture traveling via satellite, and our sound traveling via ground wire and ground-based microwave. They would meet in Manhattan. That meant the problem, New York's inability to hear us, was either in the ground or on it, somewhere between the cities of Salt Lake and New York.

But piece o' cake; it's not like we all hadn't faced this kind of problem before. The procedure for isolating the problem always worked the same way. People at ABC and people at the corporation providing the means of transmission, such as the telephone company, hit the phones. If they could identify the link where the audio signal comes in but doesn't go back out, they would have isolated the problem and could probably fix it. They began in this case with the technician at the microwave dish closest to New York.

"Uh-uh," he said, "there's no signal reaching me here."

Then the next one to the west. With the same response. The minutes were ticking by, and one by one as the phone calls reached west across the country, the men and women who monitor communications links were telling us that nothing from us was reaching them.

By about two minutes before air time, we had heard from the last technician. He was at the local telephone company office in Salt Lake City. About three miles away. He wasn't hearing our signal either. We reported that to the station's technicians. Actually, we *shouted* it at them. There was no time to lose.

That's when one of them figured out where the last link had to be. He didn't know whether it was the source of the problem, but just that it was the last plausible place to look. If he looked and found nothing wrong, it meant that one of a million wires inside the station itself might be severed, and we would never correct the problem in time. We would not get our story on the air.

He ran out of the control room, into a fire well, and up some stairs. He got out on the roof. The guy was a savior because, sure enough, that's where the link was broken. The cable to the microwave dish on the station's roof was unplugged. Simple as that! I never did find out why. But it meant that our sound had never left the building. The technician plugged it back in and ran back down. About the time our main anchorman, the late Harry Reasoner, was saying "Good evening," New York was finally hearing our audio.

But it was far too late to feed the piece into a videotape machine for playback. My story was close to four minutes long; Harry's introduction would only take thirty seconds, and then it would be show time for Utah. So, on cue from the director in New York, the affiliate's technical director rolled our tape just as Reasoner said, "Here's ABC's Greg Dobbs in Salt Lake City." And our story led the show. Viewers never knew the difference. Unless they saw us at dinner that night. I felt like those ten minutes had aged us ten years.

But everything's relative. By then, after all, Gary Gilmore looked a lot worse. And at least, by a hair, we did "make air." About a dozen years later, on a story of less consequence to the American audience but tougher to cover, we didn't. This time, New York couldn't hear us *or* see us. It was a horrible mining disaster in northern Mexico, about a hundred miles from Eagle Pass, Texas. Late afternoon. Hundreds of miners trapped. *Good Morning America* wanted a piece the next morning.

The plan was, the crew and I would charter down from Denver to Eagle Pass, hire a car and driver, cross the border, cover the story, and race back to Eagle Pass, where a satellite transmission truck from our Houston affiliate, after driving all night, would meet us in the parking lot of a local motel, a La Quinta Inn. What could possibly go wrong?

Plenty, but to that point, nothing did. Our border crossing went smoothly, and then, on the way to the mine, we passed through an otherwise dark and silent town called Nueva Rosita where a small crowd was pouring out of a rustic funeral parlor. It was past midnight. This had to have something to do with the disaster. We stopped. The first two recovered victims were in open coffins inside. Like it or not, that's what sometimes makes TV news unique. We had the first element of our story. Then, on to the mine, where the crew, Ralph and Jan, quickly captured the general fervor of the all-night rescue operation, while I tried to collect a few facts. In Spanish. Finally, high school pays off!

Then, although up to the moment I abandoned them they protested that *neither of them had taken Spanish* in high school, I left Ralph and Jan at the scene to collect videotape for *World News Tonight*, and headed back up to Eagle Pass to rendezvous with the satellite truck (and a producer and editor who had flown in from Atlanta) in La Quinta Inn's parking lot. Plenty could have gone wrong, but nothing had. Until now.

Although the editor barely had time to set up his gear, we pounded out a minute-and-a-half story in about twenty minutes and ran it out to the truck. *Good Morning America* was already on the air and waiting for our piece.

The truck's driver, who was also its technician, had gotten the coordinates of the satellite we would use and already had aimed his satellite dish right at that point in the sky. Just as he was supposed to do. We put the edited cassette in the truck's feed machine and got New York's tape room on the phone to establish the link. But they didn't see or hear a thing.

The truck's technician re-examined everything he had done and assured us that everything ought to be working. But they didn't see or hear a thing. We checked and double-checked the satellite's coordinates with the satellite desk at ABC (which by now knew its stuff). But they still didn't see or hear a thing.

This went on for the whole half hour that we were paying for the satellite. We would have extended the time, but the satellite channels we had booked were no longer available. So *Good Morning America* didn't get the piece. It wasn't sixty seconds after the satellite time was over that it suddenly occurred to the technician from Houston what was wrong. His compass was broken.

Actually, that isn't what was really wrong. He knew that the compass was broken. But he also knew that the highway he had taken to Eagle Pass on the last stretch from San Antonio ran due west. True west. He had used that as his compass. The front of the satellite truck on his way into Eagle Pass was headed due west. He kept telling himself that for the last hour of his long trip. All he had forgotten was, he turned right to enter into the parking lot. The whole time we thought we ought to be hitting the satellite, we were ninety degrees off. The poor guy had driven all night, and then in his fatigue had made one simple mistake. He parked facing due north. Who could really blame him?

Incidentally, since *Good Morning America's* audience never saw our story from the Mexican mine, *World News Tonight* was that much more eager to have a story of its own. So I raced back down.

In America, you cannot bury someone until public officials have authorized it. In Mexico, you have to bury the dead within twenty-four hours unless public officials tell you not to. So by the time the producer from Atlanta and I linked up with the crew, the weeping families of the first dozen or more corpses to be pulled out of the mine already were digging their graves and burying them. I'll always remember one particular angle, where we could see a single line of five or six families, each digging a hole in the ground to bury a loved one. Combined with what Ralph and Jan had shot while I was gone, it added up to some very powerful TV.

Then, back to Eagle Pass. Back to the edit machines. Back to the truck. This time, we knew which way to look for the satellite. We opened our link, and New York heard and saw us just fine. But they never took the feed.

That's because it was the day after an infamous interview between then-CBS anchorman Dan Rather and presidential candidate George Herbert Walker Bush, eventually the first President Bush. On the air, Rather had all but accused then-vice president Bush of lying about the Iran-Contra affair. Bush had all but accused Rather of irresponsibility in his job. Frankly, it was better TV.

ABC's White House correspondent Brit Hume—these were his pre-Fox News days—was doing our piece on the aftermath of this high-profile argument. And he, like us, was up against a deadline. Brit's piece made it on the air barely on time. And ran a minute long. Which meant something else in that night's lineup would have to go. The broadcast's producer in New York had told me to squeeze my story into just one minute's time. I had. Which made it the best candidate to cut when the show ran over.

So at the end of the whole process, we had chartered an expensive jet, rented a costly satellite truck, missed a precious night's sleep, done two dramatic stories on the mine disaster, and *nothing* got on the air. Sometimes I wonder how anything ever does.

I'll close this chapter by jumping back to our coverage of Gary Gilmore with a postscript.

On the Friday night after his execution, ABC did an hour-long special on the resumption of capital punishment in America. Our other anchorman back then, the late Frank Reynolds, would moderate a four-man panel in discussion.

Its members were Tom Wicker, *New York Times* columnist, who had written extensively about the massacre of prisoners at the state prison in Attica, New York, and was strongly against capital punishment; Norman Redlich, dean of the NYU law school, who had written several pieces in legal and academic journals against capital punishment; and Truman Capote, novelist and New York bon vivant, whose epic, *In Cold Blood*, about a couple of killers in Kansas put him firmly in the camp of campaigners against capital punishment.

And me.

The so-called "green room," where we waited to start the show, was kind of funny.

Since I had been away from home for so long, covering the Gilmore story, my wife Carol came with me to New York, and to the studio for the show. Once it was off the air, we would have the weekend together there.

NYU's Dean Redlich brought along his wife and teenage daughters; you don't go on network television every day. Tom Wicker's wife was there, although not in the green room. She happened to be Pam Hill, the executive producer of ABC's documentary unit and producer of this broadcast. And Truman Capote, who was openly homosexual, brought two young, blond boys. They sat on either side of him on a couch, rubbing him, whispering to him, calming him, generally fawning over him.

But why me? No, I'm not asking why Capote's boys weren't fawning over me. I'm asking, why was I included in this distinguished company? All my reports for two and a half months on ABC proved that I knew a thing or two about capital punishment, but they did not foretell my personal bias in favor of it. That was partly because I didn't have firm feelings about capital punishment one way or the other when I started, but the more time I spent on the Gilmore story, the more emphatically I began to favor it.

Since I am otherwise politically left of center, it was assumed at ABC that I would line up against it too. In other words, the deck was stacked. Overtly stacked, but stacked nonetheless.

That's what made it fun. Me against the experts. The beauty of it was that they didn't have any magic up their sleeves. There are only so many ways you can argue an issue. They used theirs. I used mine. It was a draw.

More important for me though, it was a thrill. At that point, I had only been an ABC News correspondent for a little more than three years. Still, in that time, I had never before been able to campaign on television for positions I believed in that had been reinforced by my own firsthand journalistic experience.

After that, I never had the chance again, because most every contract for a correspondent says you cannot publicly express opinions about anything. I mean, I couldn't publicly have supported anyone for dogcatcher.

That's why I had a lot of fun for several years after leaving ABC. I became a talk radio host, and got to tell people precisely what I thought five days a week. Can't have more fun than that!

EXCUSE ME, DO YOU SPEAK ENGLISH?

Budapest, Hungary, and Moscow, USSR

FOR SEVENTY YEARS, RUSSIA *was known as the Union of Soviet Socialist Republics. That was because its rulers controlled not just Russia, but ultimately fourteen other geographically related republics as well. The national motto was, "Proletarii Vsekh Stran, Soyedinyaites!" which we all know means, "Workers of All Countries, Unite!" Eventually, in English it was modified to, "Workers of the World, Unite."*

The trouble was, they took their motto too seriously. After the end of World War II, Soviet leaders had absorbed many otherwise independent and sometimes geographically unrelated countries into their control, if not into their union. Albania, Bulgaria, Czechoslovakia, Hungary, Poland, Romania, and the eastern part of a newly divided Germany all became, to varying degrees, subservient satellite states. To say nothing of nations on other continents, like Angola and Cuba. Thanks to the iron curtain, workers of many countries had to unite, whether they liked it or not.

In one of those nations, Hungary, they never liked it and tried to overcome it. In this fairly small Communist country surrounded on most sides by other Communist states, there was a rebellion in 1956. Fighting in the streets led to an invasion by Soviet soldiers, who quickly crushed the revolt. From that time on, to try to prevent further uprisings, the Hungarian government adopted reforms that were relatively progressive in the Communist bloc. But it was still an undemocratic government, with many policies that mirrored the ways of the Soviets. Only in 1989, with the resignation of its old line of leaders, Hungary finally officially renounced Communism and officially left the Communist bloc.

Eventually, other Communist governments fell too, but the last major country behind the iron curtain to turn its back on Communism was the Soviet Union itself. Its last leader, Mikhail Gorbachev, was a reformer of sorts; he created the conditions that made it possible for other countries like Hungary to break out of the Soviet bloc. But while Gorbachev ultimately opened the door for freedom in his own country (deliberately or inadvertently, we've never truly known), the early days of his era resembled in some ways the autocratic eras of his predecessors, who employed censorship and political imprisonment to hold on to their power. In 1991, Gorbachev was put out of power, not so much overthrown as simply left stranded with no country to govern. The Soviet empire was gone. Its fifteen republics (including Russia itself) and its long-loyal satellites were on their own.

•　　•　　•　　•　　•

One thing you learn working in a dictatorship: you constantly want to wave the United States Constitution under the noses of authorities and say, "You can't do that to me!" You want to, but of course you can't.

It's their candy store, and if they don't care to respect our Constitution, they don't have to.

Too bad. The more I saw of the other side, the more I respected our side and what it stands for, and the more I saw our Constitution as not just a protector of American rights, but as a model for human rights throughout the world. That's why I still want to wave the Constitution at autocratic authorities in foreign lands when they impose censorship. And restrict movement. And ignore human rights.

I was never the serious victim of such abuse, not in the long term. That's only because I didn't have to stay. But I did see the human rights of many citizens violated by their own governments, because their leadership believed in the power of might, not the power of people.

And I did suffer in minor ways from the dictates of the dictators. But while they made the job a little more difficult, they also made it a little more challenging. Which sometimes meant a little more fun.

Actually, my first story is only fun to tell. It was frustrating to experience.

Budapest, Hungary. One of the loveliest cities, rivaled only by Prague, in what we used to call Eastern Europe. It is built like Paris on the Seine, using its river, the Danube, as its social spine. The only difference is that buildings in Budapest are still pockmarked with bullet holes, souvenirs of the unsuccessful '56 rebellion.

Actually, Budapest is two ancient cities: Buda and Pest (pronounced

Pesht). They are connected by half a dozen decorative bridges, some built of mighty iron, some of sculpted stone. On both banks of the river sit the forts and castles and palaces of the nation's capital. Monumental structures erected by monarchs in centuries past. The best way to see them is to stare at the Danube on a windless day. You'll see a reflection of the city's history.

When the Nazis ran in retreat at the end of World War II, they tried to blow up Budapest's buildings and bridges. Thankfully, with the Allies tight on their tails, they didn't get to finish the job. What they did destroy, the people rebuilt.

Except for freedom. After the war, Communists gained control of the government, and Hungary was ceded to the Soviets. It had a constitution patterned after the Soviet Constitution. It had an army trained and armed by the Soviet Army.

And it had lost Saint Stephen's Crown.

Saint Stephen himself almost surely never set foot in Budapest. He lived in Jerusalem. Historians say he made people there angry because he purported to speak on behalf of God. Sometime after Christ's crucifixion, he was stoned to death. But he became an icon in Hungary, because he was a symbol of supremacy, of autonomy, and of independence. Thus, Hungary's national insignia of sovereignty before World War II was a crown named after Saint Stephen. Just as Britain's monarchy is the manifestation of their constitution, Saint Stephen's Crown had become that same thing for Hungary.

American soldiers seized and kept the crown as they chased the Nazis through Budapest. They kept it for safekeeping. And kept it for democracy. But for years, the U.S. government didn't own up to what it held in trust. When finally it did, it said that Saint Stephen's Crown would only be returned to Hungary when Hungary returned to the ideals of the crown, the ideals of pre-war sovereignty.

By 1977, when Hungary had proved itself the most progressive country behind the iron curtain, the United States decided to send the crown home. That's why I got to go.

President Carter's secretary of state, Cyrus Vance, was the courier. He would carry the crown to Budapest, present it to the Communist authorities, and hope for a further loosening of laws that still stood in the way of human rights. Maybe, in a best-case scenario, the Hungarians would even ask the Soviets to remove their four army divisions from Hungarian soil.

We had two stories on our agenda. The big one of course: the pomp and ceremony of the return of Saint Stephen's Crown. And the day before, to put a piece on the air about the importance of the crown to the people, and why its return was such a meaningful national event.

But how do you do that? How do you characterize the feelings of a population of more than 10 million? A population that speaks a language whose only known roots connect to *Estonian* and *Finnish*!

Easy. Do what you do in every foreign country where people don't speak English. Put yourself and your camera crew on a corner across the street from the English Language Institute. Preferably, the corner that students from the institute must cross to get to the bus, or the subway, or in the case of Budapest, the streetcar.

"Excuse me, do you speak English?" I don't know how many times I have asked that question in how many countries. If they don't speak English, you feel silly asking. Why? Well, imagine you're walking down the street in an American city, and some guy says something to you that's perfectly unintelligible unless you speak Hungarian, something like *"Cxpsopkjc, wfcijvqudci?"*

That's how it must seem to many foreigners when we stand on some street in their city and start asking, "Do you speak English?" That's why we love to go to that one street corner in any country on earth where they might actually answer, "Yes."

But in Hungary, in 1977, you couldn't just set up your camera on a convenient corner and start asking questions. Oh nooooooooooooooooo. We needed permission. From two different ministries of government. From the information ministry, we needed permission to shoot any videotape on the streets. From the foreign ministry, we needed permission to actually ask questions.

No sweat. A piece of cake. We were there to report good news. Good news for both nations: Hungary and the United States of America were shaking hands. Saint Stephen's Crown was coming home. Everyone was a winner.

The information ministry said it was okay to shoot our pictures, as long as we did it in the next two hours and kept the camera focused on the faces of the people who stopped, and nowhere else. What were these guys scared of? Were the streetcars pulling missiles we weren't supposed to see?

The foreign ministry said it was okay to ask questions, as long as we kept it to one per customer. In other words, each time someone stopped, we could ask them one question and only one. Okay, I could handle that. These weren't going to be exhaustive political interviews. I just wanted to ask people how they felt about the return of Saint Stephen's Crown.

The ministries actually coordinated our effort. They got together and, between them, provided an "escort." How very nice!

Now, this requires a bit of explanation. In some places, an escort means a guide. Occasionally a fixer. Sometimes a translator too. But in Budapest, 1977, an escort was what we called a "minder." A watchdog. Watching us. For the government.

We chose our corner. Streetcars would stop right in front of us. Foot traffic from across the street wasn't heavy, but it was adequate. Some of them must be from the English Language Institute.

"Excuse me, do you speak English?" I was on my way.

So were they. The first five pedestrians passed me by as if I were yesterday's paper blowing past.

"Excuse me, do you speak English?"

"Excuse me, do you speak English?"

"Excuse me, do you speak English?"

"Excuse me, do you speak English?"

"Excuse me, do you speak English?"

"Yes I do," said the sixth.

Bingo. Let's wrap up this shoot and head for the bar.

"We're from American television," I continued excitedly, "ABC News it's called, and we're doing a story for our broadcast about Saint Stephen's Crown. How do you feel about getting it back?"

Actually, I'm not sure I really got to utter those last three or four words because our "escort" stopped me cold. "Uh-uh," he said, "you are only allowed one question."

"Right," I replied, "I was asking this man how he felt about the return of the crown."

"But you had already asked him a question."

Maybe it was naiveté, maybe jet lag. I just couldn't remember asking anything before I asked about Saint Stephen's Crown.

"You asked him if he speaks English."

There it was, staring me in the face. The whole problem with Communism. Central planning. A bureaucrat higher up in the system had told me, and obviously demanded of my escort, that only one question could be asked. Flexibility? Buy some in duty free on the way out.

"Obviously, when we were told to ask just one question," I argued, "your superior meant one question about the crown."

"No," he came back with all the authority of a man with a badge, "you were told you can ask one question, and you cannot ask more."

The slow stream of pedestrians was growing. The English Language

Institute was disgorging its student body. If ever there was a time when I might find a second willing English speaker, this was it. It had better be. The first guy, sensing the sudden icing from the cold war, had gone.

"Okay, okay, it doesn't make any sense, but I shall ask just one question and see if it works." I didn't even have a copy of the Constitution to wave.

"Excuse me," I started anew to whoever walked my way, "how do you feel about the return of Saint Stephen's Crown?" But of course, I was now exactly like that old copy of yesterday's paper blowing in the wind. I was a guy muttering gobbledygook at no one in particular.

"Excuse me, will you tell me how you feel about the return of Saint Stephen's Crown?"

Nothing.

"Hello, are you glad to get Saint Stephen's Crown back?"

"Hi, how do you feel about Saint Stephen's Crown?

"So, what about the crown?"

Nothing. No one even stopped, let alone spoke. The system had defeated me.

"Okay, you win," I told the escort. "Let's go call the man at the foreign ministry and ask him if I can ask *two* questions."

"I don't know the number." This guy was responsible for the protection and preservation of Communism, but he couldn't reach his superior on the telephone.

"What can we do?" I asked, watching the briefly steady stream of articulate English speakers begin to dwindle.

"We must drive back to the ministry and ask him personally."

That was the death knell. Foot traffic was slowing down, the sun was setting, and the foreign ministry was a good half hour away. That's a full hour's roundtrip. Not to mention the time it would take to get our outrageous request approved. In fact, two requests. Because our allotted two hours would be up, we would now have to go back to the information ministry too and beg for a new window of opportunity.

This meant that at best, with all our approvals in place, we would return to the corner in the dark (which the camera doesn't like) and hope, just hope, to catch someone who was studying late at the institute. Of course if they're studying late, it probably means they're not keeping up in class because their English isn't all that hot. Oh well. The alternative was to turn in a story without a single non-government-Hungarian-citizen-sound bite.

Needless to say, the big man at the foreign ministry didn't get big by being stupid. With a hearty laugh (his; it sure wasn't mine), he told our escort, "Of course they can ask two questions if one of them is 'Do you speak English'!" I think that's when the escort realized he would always be an escort.

Then to the information ministry, where they acted like we were asking to inherit the city, rather than simply shoot pictures in it. But in the end, they gave us another two hours to work. Eventually, and only with persistence, we got our English-language answers. And soon after that, Hungary got its long-lost crown. And all of us got a lesson in the ways of the Communist world. Everything there takes longer.

We never got to the bar.

In 1985, I got an even more personal lesson about Communism, up close and personal. The incident in Budapest had been frustrating. But this one, in Moscow, was exhilarating. Yes, there were victims, but they weren't us.

It was already the Gorbachev era, but early Gorbachev. He had only recently been elected general secretary of the Communist Party. In Soviet-speak, that meant he ruled the country.

As time passes, it is harder and harder to remember that for a while, the United States didn't trust him. He talked a good game, and he banned the sale of vodka, proposed the reduction of missiles, and pressed the flesh with the best of them. But we didn't trust him. The "evil empire," the label President Reagan eventually gave the Soviet bloc under which hundreds of millions had suffered, lived on. Countless political dissidents were still in internal exile or in jail, and it didn't take much to join the club. Vocal Soviet Jews were still agitating to emigrate, with precious little success. And everyone—dissidents and loyalists, citizens and foreigners— everyone was still being watched.

There used to be a misconception outside the Soviet Union about what "being watched" really meant. It's not that everyone had what spies call "a tail." No, usually it was a lot simpler than that. Take license plates, for example. Soviet citizens had white plates with black lettering. Diplomats had red plates with white lettering. Foreign journalists and businessmen had yellow plates with black lettering.

Then, each plate had seven characters: a capital letter followed by two clusters of three digits each. The capital letter identified you by occupation. Journalists were designated by a "K," which is the first letter in the Russian alphabet for the word "correspondent." What that meant was, everyone on the street knew it when a foreign journalist drove by, because the "K" told the story.

But not the whole story. The license plate also identified the country from which the journalist came. It was obvious from the first three digits following the capital letter. The United States was number "004." Canada was "003," West Germany "002," and Great Britain "001." In fact, the ten lowest numbers, from "001" to "010," were reserved for the ten countries most antagonistic in those cold war days to the Soviet Union.

Word had it that the system was designed this way for the cops on the street, because connecting ten numbers to ten countries stretched their mental abilities to the limit. Friendly countries like Bulgaria had high numbers like "139," but so what? Bulgaria was no threat. "004" was.

Finally, the last three digits specifically identified *you*. Naturally, it would take a long list for anyone to instantly recognize you by name from your license plate, but if a car bearing a plate with "K 004" came along where it wasn't supposed to be, it was enough of a red flag to get Big Brother's attention: "American journalist."

What this meant was, every time you drove around Moscow, you could be visually tracked by the cop on the corner, and have that information passed by walkie-talkie to the cop on the next corner. In those days, there were very few corners without cops. And that is what "being watched" really meant.

Maria Casby told the best story about Big Brother watching. She was our producer in the Moscow bureau, an American woman with Russian roots and a terrific linguistic command of Russian. For people like me who made a working visit from time to time, but couldn't say much more than *"da"* and *"nyet"* (yes and no), she was invaluable.

The bureau had purchased a new car, a Volvo, in Helsinki, Finland. Sure, we could have had it delivered, but when there was a trip to take outside the iron curtain, everyone's hand went up in the air. Maria's reached highest. She flew to Helsinki, picked up the car, and began her long drive back. It was wintertime, which meant the days were short and the roads were slick. It meant she probably wouldn't make the five-hundred-mile-plus drive in a day. It meant she ought to reserve a room along the way.

She did. In a small city called Vyshniy-Volochek. Go ahead and say it five times fast. Vyshniy-Volochek Vyshniy-Volochek Vyshniy-Volochek Vyshniy-Volochek Vyshniy-Volochek.

But Maria got an earlier start than she expected. And the roads were dryer than she expected. And she made better time than she expected. Which meant she could skip Vyshniy-Volochek and make it to Moscow not long after dark.

So when she came to the exit for Vyshniy-Volochek, she just kept going. But not for long. Just seconds after passing her off-ramp, Maria had a police car in hot pursuit. Siren, lights, the works. Yet she hadn't been speeding. In fact, as with most drivers on interstate highways in the United States, she was especially prudent when passing through an urban area.

She stopped. The policeman stopped behind her and walked up to the window.

"Miss Casby," he began (in Russian), "you have missed your exit."

Here was Maria, in a town she'd never seen before, still almost two hundred miles from home, and the cop knew exactly what to call her and precisely where she was supposed to sleep. How? Because of her license plate. He had been sitting somewhere out of sight, noting every plate passing by. The hotel was expecting a "Miss Casby" from "K 004." The rest, as they say, is history.

That sort of thing was still quite common in the days of Gorbachev. The Soviet Union was still very much a police state. Big Brother was still very much a presence. For Soviet citizens, the massive popular protests and demonstrations of the late eighties and nineties were just a pipe dream.

But one small group of citizens dreamed anyway.

It was December 12, the date designated every year by the United Nations as International Human Rights Day. A small band of Muscovites let out word with the Western media that they were going to observe Human Rights Day. How? By placing several bouquets of flowers at the base of a statue.

That's what you called a protest those days in the Soviet Union. Laying flowers next to a public statue. It was against the law. After all, the government had exclusive responsibility for municipal landscaping. Therefore, anyone who put down their own floral decor inside the chain encircling the base of the statue was usurping the government and risking imprisonment. That was the level of human rights in the Soviet Union.

The statue, incidentally, was of Maxim Gorky, a legendary Russian novelist who chronicled the misery of the peasant class. It was situated in Gorky Square, which was right on Gorky Street, not half a mile from the Kremlin.

We got there about three o'clock in the afternoon. The beginning of rush hour. It was snowing like crazy. Cold, wet, heavy snow. People were flowing from the buildings. There were lots of government offices in the area, and Moscow's best stores. For the most part, until a bus actually pulled to a stop, commuters huddled under awnings and archways while they waited for it. Why wait in the blowing snow?

In other words, no one just stood getting wet around Gorky Square if they didn't have to.

That's how we first recognized the agents from the KGB, the Soviet Union's brutal secret police (where Vladimir Putin worked before he became a public official and eventually Russia's president!). They were the only ones standing there with two inches of snow on their shoulders. They also were the only ones with exactly the same overcoats. And shoes. Government-issued.

They had heard about the human rights observance too. And didn't plan to permit it. So now there were two groups looking at each other, both looking stupid in the snow. The KGB and the Western journalists. Neither side knew what was going to happen. Or when. We all just stood there exchanging scowls, knowing that when and if the protesters showed up, we'd be on different sides.

Then, from the crowd boarding a bus on Gorky Street emerged a woman. Just one woman in a veiled hat, thick leather boots, a scarf around her neck, and an overcoat. With a bouquet of flowers in her hand. She walked up to the statue of Gorky almost without notice. She raised her left boot above the level of the chain, which was about a foot and a half above the ground, and stepped onto the soil on the other side.

Into forbidden territory. Punishable by imprisonment.

Before the woman could gently lay her flowers on the ground, she was brusquely grabbed from behind. A KGB man for each arm, a third to grab her legs and carry her struggling form to the paddy wagon. The flowers fell pretty much where she probably wanted them, but they didn't get there the way she planned.

Then came another. This time, a man. He clearly had seen what happened to his compatriot, but wasn't deterred. While we were all watching the woman being dragged away, he stepped across the line and suffered the same fate she had. It seemed the KGB *really* disliked flowers.

Then another, and another after her. It was happening awfully fast. Frankly, it was only by the time of the third or fourth protester that we journalistic geniuses figured out what was going on. Then we went to work. Cameras went on, microphones went up, pencils came out. We had ourselves a story.

The KGB saw things differently. These protesters were lawbreakers, hooligans, unworthy of attention. Furthermore, they were despoiling a perfectly nice patch of unplanted soil.

There were more KGB agents than we imagined. Three for every dissident, with enough left over to deal with us. They grabbed at one reporter's pad. They grabbed at my jacket. But none of that was going to affect our coverage. When they started grabbing at the cameras though, it was. Gary, the cameraman with me, had KGB men on either side, each of them struggling to pull his camera away, Gary struggling to keep hold of it. He managed to.

CBS's cameraman didn't. The bad guys managed to pull his camera out of his grip, and it fell to the ground—in an instant that seemed survivable, because the kind of camera the networks used back then was built strong enough to be run over by a tank. But when a KGB agent gave it a swift kick and put the tip of his government-issued shoe right through the lens, the party was over. The dissidents had run out of flowers, and the story had run its course. With adrenaline rushing through our bodies like a New York subway car at rush hour, we retreated to lick our wounds.

Almost everyone was mad. We were mad, because our colleagues had lost a camera. The KGB guys were mad, because they weren't allowed to carry out their work in private. The dissidents, on the other hand, must have been thrilled. They set out to show the state of human rights in the Soviet Union, and got what they bargained for.

We got something too. When we returned to the bureau and began to screen our videotape, we found that we had a good clear view of the whole incident with the CBS News camera. The struggle, the fall, the kick.

We called our colleagues at CBS. Did they want to see it? "Sure!"

We went to their bureau and showed them what we had. Then they put on their own video show. While the lens had been destroyed, the tape had not. Although shaky, it showed a bird's eye view of the whole affair, ending only when the KGB shoe broke through the glass.

It would make a powerful sequence in a story. A slice of life of human rights campaigners in Moscow. We all recognized the possibilities. But we didn't know how we'd get it out. Just as you can wrap rotting fish in yesterday's newspapers, you can lose TV viewers with yesterday's news. We'd have to get this on the air today if we wanted to get it on at all. The trouble was, it was too late in the day to ship it out to the Western world with a courier on a foreign airline. We would have to transmit it via satellite from Soviet TV.

Of course, that was ridiculous. Whenever we fed stories from there and whatever we fed, the censor always had his or her hand on the plug. If the censor saw or heard something disagreeable, whoosh! The plug was pulled, the transmission was over.

All that meant was, we'd have to make sure the censor wouldn't see what we had.

Our plan began with a lucky break, even before we recognized it for the great break it was. Earlier that same day, the United States secretary of commerce, visiting Moscow, had met with Secretary Gorbachev. There was a photo op, and the ABC camera crew and I had been assigned by the "pool" of American networks to cover the event.

It was the first time I got to see Gorbachev in the flesh. Nice man. He smiled a lot. Extended his hand. Even kidded around with us a bit. Although maybe I ought to state that more clearly: he did the kidding, we did the laughing. After all, he was still warden of the gulag!

News-wise though, it was a non-starter. The photo op was just Gorby in his office, shaking the American's hand. No statements. No news. In fact, earlier that day, we already had dismissed the probability of a feed of the material to New York, and when we spoke with New York later in the day, just before heading out to Gorky Square, the powers there agreed.

Now things were different.

We could use the USSR-U.S. meeting as a pretext for a transmission. We would tell officials at Soviet TV that we had an important story about the Gorbachev meeting. Meanwhile, we would tell both networks at home, ABC and CBS, that we actually had something much better and they'd better have their tape machines rolling when the satellite came up because the transmission might prematurely be cut. We would tell them, of course, in the kind of code we occasionally used to overcome the taps on our telexes (precursors to e-mail) and telephones.

Then we actually edited a story about the Soviet and American secretaries, thirty seconds or so worth of a story anyway, and when we felt it had run long enough for the censor to think everything looked legit, we slipped in the scuffle at the statue.

We drove to Soviet TV. The only word that adequately describes the place is "humongous." Truth be known, that word must have been engraved on the entryway to every architecture classroom in the Soviet Union. Every government building there is humongous. Each communicates its power. If the goal is to intimidate everyone who sets eyes on it, it works. "International Control," the room reserved for foreign transmissions at Soviet TV, is buried somewhere in the bowels. No surprise.

The procedure to feed a story was simple. You'd walk in, get New York on the phone, tell them to roll their machines, and you'd roll yours. And all the time, the censor would be watching. But this time, we got her to watch the wrong thing.

It had been our editor's idea. He was an American who once had trained in the U.S. Army as an explosives expert. So, once inside International Control, he disappeared between two tall walls of plugs, "patch boards" they're called because they have hundreds of holes with dozens of wires running from one to another. If you know which ones matter for your transmission to New York and which ones don't, you can wreak havoc. Which is what the editor did, and it was fitting in a country where one of the founding fathers has a powerful cocktail named after him: the Molotov cocktail. In Russian, Molotov means "of the hammer."

While I made small talk with the censor, whose eyes already were on her monitor, the editor who had slipped away planted a small charge in a small hole. Just powerful enough to ignite a small explosion and set a small fire. Just enough to get the censor, and everyone else in the room, to jump from their seats and run for their lives.

In two minutes, the fire was out and the censor was back. But a minute had been enough.

Of course, Soviet diplomats based in Washington watched TV too, and they saw what we showed, and they knew it shouldn't have gotten out, and they sent word back to Moscow, and we had a visit from the authorities.

For a week, no more transmissions for ABC News. That's like telling a child, "For a week, no more cookies." Big deal. We enjoyed the taste of the first cookie so much, we could live on the memory for at least a week. Easy.

TONIGHT THE SPHINX SAID, "SHUT UP"

Cairo, Egypt, and the Libyan border

THERE IS NO PLACE else like Egypt.

And within Egypt, there's no place like Cairo. It is the greatest and the worst of the world's cities.

Cairo was built to comfortably hold 2 to 3 million people. The official estimate of Cairo's population today is more than 6 million. Some guesses put it unofficially above 10 million, with roughly 15 million people in the whole metropolitan area.

The spillovers live on the streets. They live, and eat, and work, and sleep, and die on the streets. Or they live in Cairo's great graveyard, popularly known as "The City of the Dead." In reality, it is a city of the dead and the living. Tens of thousands of Cairenes live in the graveyard, some in the open spaces between the mausoleums, some in the mausoleums themselves. They die there too.

It is Cairo's worst qualities that also are its best. The hot streets of this North African capital never shut down. There is a vibrancy they would envy in New York. Weaving amongst modern cars are wooden carts drawn by donkeys. Working amongst gold merchants in the bazaars are amputees begging for a penny.

The antiquities also represent the best and the worst of Egypt. The best, because even today we don't understand how the pharaohs figured out how to engineer the gigantic pyramids, or how the morticians figured out how to mummify a corpse. The worst, because every Egyptian is shamefully aware that in the four or five thousand years since Egypt was a cradle of civilization, their nation has been unable to come even close to its once unparalleled economic, artistic, and intellectual greatness.

Until the middle 1970s, Egypt's main claim to modern fame was its participation in Arab wars against Israel. Egypt was and still is, with something like 60 million people today, the most populous Arab country. As such, it was always Israel's most powerful opponent, even trapping an Israeli army or two in the desert, although never experiencing final victory.

Then came Anwar Sadat. He wasn't Egypt's favorite leader; he was the West's. Egypt's favorite had been Gamal Abdel Nasser, who in 1952 helped overthrow the last monarch, King Farouk, and led a popular pro-Arab revolution. But Nasser was not a friend of the West, because in his revolution, Egypt would seize everything the West and Western landlords thought they should continue to own, including the crucial and profitable Suez Canal. When Nasser died in 1970, his vice president, Sadat, succeeded him.

Sadat started out as a clone of Nasser, but he won favor with the West when he tossed out the Soviets, even though they had long provided Egypt with money and arms. Then he became the unequaled darling of the West when he accepted an invitation in 1977 to visit Jerusalem, the capital of the Arabs' mortal enemy, Israel. The result of that visit was a handshake, a peace treaty, a Nobel Prize, and the enmity of all the rest of the Arab world. It took nearly a decade, and Sadat's assassination by Muslim fundamentalists, for Egypt to be forgiven.

●   ●   ●   ●   ●

It was supposed to be ABC's Africa bureau. It very quickly became our Sadat bureau instead.

In the past, we'd had a bureau in Nairobi. It was meant to cover the African continent, with the exception of the Republic of South Africa where ABC had a separate bureau because the battle against white minority rule there always threatened to become a civil war, and because, when you were trying to travel from rebellious black Africa to recalcitrant white Africa, or vice versa, "you can't get there from here." In fact, in those days, just about the only way to get from a place like Johannesburg to a place like Nairobi was to change planes in Europe. Hardly the shortest distance between two points!

But the Nairobi bureau never worked out. Not that it wasn't a nice place for the ABC News staff to live. That was the problem. It was too nice.

Use a little logic here: you live in Nairobi, with swimming pools and tennis courts and juicy steaks and shady clubs and cheap domestic help. And an altitude sufficiently high to make the sunny climate fairly dry, contrary to most of the continent. Why would you ever want to leave?

That was the trouble: no one did. Our Nairobi-based staff never pressed to cover stories in the rest of black Africa—rude and rundown places like Dakar and N'Djamena, Lagos and Lusaka—which were absolutely god-awful by comfort comparison.

So, in early 1977, ABC moved the bureau, lock-stock-and-camera, to Cairo. It was a brilliant stroke ... *not*! In Cairo, it could be faster to drive to a government ministry to ask for information than to get through on the usually-not-working phone. And with the bulging volume of cars, not to mention the traffic-jamming donkey carts, it could be even faster to walk there than to drive.

And every step you took could be depressing. First of all, literally: the streets and sidewalks were so full of potholes that you could twist your ankle in a depression if you didn't watch out. Secondly, emotionally: there was some poor soul begging for "*baksheesh*," the Arabic word for charity, from almost every doorway. *Baksheesh* takes many forms. Because Cairo was so poor, you were encouraged to litter, since someone would be able to make use of whatever you threw away.

So the theory behind moving our bureau from Kenya to Egypt was this: Cairo is such a hard place to work that the ABC News producer and correspondent based there will beg to get out. But they never got the chance. Just a few months after ABC set into this ancient, bulging, hot city on the Nile, President Sadat flew to Jerusalem. The Middle East changed forever. And the story began to seem like it would last forever too.

There was the Israeli-Egyptian handshake, and there was the virulent reaction of almost all the other Arabs. They didn't just criticize Sadat for trying to make peace, they isolated him. Diplomatic relations were cut; the Arab League moved its headquarters out of Cairo. Suddenly, no matter how hard the correspondent and staff based in Cairo begged to get out, they were turned down. Their job, and mine when flying in to replace our resident reporter, was to cover Sadat like a blanket. We made the presidential death watch in Washington look sloppy.

Generally, I am a staunch defender of the news media, with all its flaws. But I'll admit that those flaws do exist. The flaw when we attach ourselves to a particular story is that we tend to make mountains out of molehills. Every movement, every word, every sneeze from a guy like Sadat got publicized and analyzed. He'd go to make a local speech; we'd follow. He'd go to pray at a local mosque; we'd follow. He'd travel to other parts of

Egypt to escape the pace of Cairo; we'd follow. About the only place to which we never followed him was the bathroom. We know our limits.

My longest stay in Cairo lasted two and a half months. Our correspondent based there was taking a couple of weeks of vacation, and then going to Washington to cover the peace talks between Sadat and Israel's Prime Minister Begin, hosted by President Carter at Camp David, and then traveling through the United States with Sadat, and then taking some more vacation.

Two and a half months. Long enough for my wife to come, because if one thing was for sure, I wasn't about to leave. Most of the places I went to cover stories, she didn't want to go. Nor did I want her to go. Rhodesia during its independence war, Iran during its revolutionary war, Northern Ireland during its civil war.

But Egypt. Exotic Egypt.

Of course, I had come back from previous trips and told Carol I hated the place. It was hot, it was noisy, it was depressing. And the food? I like good food, and there is certainly good food to be found in Cairo. But what do you think is the specialty at the city's better restaurants? Pigeon. Grey meat.

Cairo was the only place in the world where a suitcase of mine was permanently lost. If that's not an omen to stay away from a place, I don't know what is. I was there for only a few days on that particular trip, and an aide in our bureau took me to a store to buy a couple of shirts, some socks, and some underwear. Everything else was fine, but the only socks they had were glittery, like a woman's made-up face at Mardi Gras. It was bad enough walking around Cairo with glittery socks. But flying all the way home to Chicago *without crossing my legs* so the socks wouldn't show, that was the last straw!

Anyway, I already had seen everything I wanted to see in the city: the Giza pyramids, the great Sphinx, the Antiquities Museum, and the unparalleled bazaar at Khan-Khalili.

And a camel. I had ridden a camel. Some things in life don't need to be repeated.

After that, Cairo was just a place to which I had to go and couldn't wait to leave.

But Carol couldn't wait to come. She knew that Egypt was a nation of wonders, ancient and modern, and that if you weren't wearing blinders like mine, you could have a remarkable experience. Although her first one was unwelcome, and it was my fault.

It was summertime, and it was hot. I had been in Cairo for two weeks or so when she was scheduled to come. On the phone from our flat in drizzly London, she asked about the weather and what to wear. "Sundresses." My answer was that short. It was too hot for anything else. So she even wore one on the plane. Not a promiscuous sundress, just one where her shoulders showed.

Of course, getting off the plane, it was covered by her raincoat. Remember, she came from London. We got out of the airport and into the cool chauffeured car that was one of the perks for people working in Cairo. The raincoat stayed on.

Then, once in the center of the city, rather than eat up time checking Carol into my hotel (in a place like that, you don't just take a new woman up to your room without checking her in), we went straight to the bureau, which was on the East Bank of the Nile. I wanted Carol to get a feel for Cairo right away.

We put her things in the office, left her coat on my desk, and went out for her first walk. Carol got a feel for Cairo all right. A feel from every Cairene she passed. People were pinching her left and right. It was a punishment. Her sundress, modest by Western standards, was outrageous in Egypt.

We went right around the block and back to the bureau. She closed the door to my office, changed her clothes, and never again took a sundress out of her suitcase until she got back home to London. Where she almost never needed one.

My favorite story from my wife's time in Egypt happened when I wasn't with her. But it's a good story about Americans adapting to Arab ways. Sort of.

With Cindy, the American wife of our Cairo-based videotape editor, Carol went down to Upper Egypt. That's how you describe the country's geography: "down to Upper Egypt." The Nile river flows from south to north before emptying into the Mediterranean, so the top of the river down at Egypt's southern border is "Upper Egypt," and you move up toward "Lower Egypt" the further north you go.

I already had told Carol about the art of negotiation in the bazaar, the marketplace. I had passed on what I had been told myself: never, never, *never* pay the asking price. "The story," I told Carol, "is this: when the merchant begins the negotiation with a starting price, you come back with a counter offer. A low one. Come in at 20 percent of what he asks, and he'll bring his price down in response."

I guess I forgot to finish the story. She was in a rug shop in Luxor, part of the ancient Valley of the Kings. There were two little woven rugs that she had her eyes on; both were hand woven by rural Egyptian villagers, both depicting rural Egyptian scenes. Perfect souvenirs.

Carol asked the merchant, "How much for this one?"

He said, "One hundred pounds." Egypt's currency is a legacy from England's days as colonialists.

Carol said, "I'll give you twenty." She had learned at the hands of a master.

The merchant came back with, "Eighty pounds."

Carol snapped back, "Twenty."

Uh-oh, evidently I never did finish explaining to her how the system works. This time the merchant's voice began to waver. "Seventy."

"Twenty." I had said 20 percent; she was sticking to her guns.

Trying to salvage a bad deal, the merchant came down to fifty pounds, then thirty, and then, when Carol just wouldn't budge, sold her the rug for twenty pounds. Then when she said she'd buy the other one for twenty pounds too, he succumbed. But not without a lecture.

"Madam," the merchant said to my wife, "somebody must teach you how to bargain. If I start at 'a hundred' and you offer 'twenty' and I come down to 'eighty,' you must offer something like 'forty.' I go down, you come up, and we do this until we meet somewhere in the middle." Of course what he failed to say was, the rugs weren't worth any more than twenty pounds apiece. Otherwise, he never would have struck the deal.

So Carol learned to negotiate the easy way. Her lesson about resisting beggars came a little harder.

We were having coffee outdoors at Khan-Khalili, which is Cairo's splendid semi-covered bazaar, one of the best in the Middle East (the others being Fez, Morocco, and Istanbul, Turkey). Jewelry and carpets and copper and brass by the bundle.

We were with Aida, one of the Egyptian women who worked at the bureau. She was telling us horror stories about beggars. She said that when one beggar, well known because of his prominent perch, was found dead, investigators went to where he slept and found the equivalent of more than $80,000 stashed away. Aida told us there were syndicates that bought babies from peasants, amputated one or more of their limbs, and then put these pathetic little urchins out on the streets to beg. The people who ran this particularly unpleasant business were known as "the cripple-makers."

And as Aida talked, adult beggars constantly came to our table, among others, asking for *baksheesh*. Carol and I were a soft touch. A penny here, a penny there, but we spread lots of pennies around.

Then came a little boy. A thin, sad eyed, hungry looking little boy. Maybe five or six years old. Dressed in a filthy, white gown, which they call a *"galabaya."*

"Baksheesh?"

Carol went into her purse. A penny or two wasn't enough. She gave him a pound, which was about the same thing as a dollar. He looked like he had never before seen that much money at one time. Surely not in a single bill. His sad eyes turned bright, and he kind of wandered around near our table, staring at this one-pound note that he held almost unbelievingly in front of his face.

Then a man walked up to the boy, said something nasty to him, and snapped the pound note right out of his fingers. The people who ultimately get the *baksheesh* are the ones who don't need it.

The lesson almost applied a few days later, too. It was *Ramadan*, the year's most religious holiday for Muslims. It is a thirty-day period of daytime fasting. From dawn to dusk, not a morsel of food or fluid (or, hardest of all for some, tobacco) is supposed to pass their lips. It is also a special time for special portions of *baksheesh*. What that means is, if you see someone in need, don't even wait to be asked.

This was a Sunday, a regular business day in Cairo where Friday is the day of the Sabbath, but a day when ABC's demands would be few. Carol and I had gone by the otherwise empty bureau only to let me check the news wires and send a couple of telexes to ABC in New York. It was faster than the phone.

I was typing on the telex keyboard when the doorbell to the bureau rang. Carol offered to answer it. She opened the door, and there was this guy, about six feet tall, with a dark complexion and a bushy black beard, wearing a *galabaya* at least as filthy as the little beggar's at Khan-Khalili, but with even more holes.

Carol didn't even wait for him to beg. She mumbled the Arabic phrase she had learned for "wait a moment," left the door ajar, walked past me to her purse, and then returned to the man and began to pull some Egyptian money out.

He stopped her. In English. Almost perfect American English. I say "almost" perfect, because he had a New York accent. "I'm just here to see Greg."

It was Mark, otherwise known as Abdullah, the local NBC bureau chief, a good Jewish boy from New York who had transferred to Cairo and promptly converted to Islam. His parents must have been thrilled.

Carol, however, was embarrassed. I was simply amused. But Abdullah was probably pleased. In the interest of authenticity, he had been working hard to cultivate the "feel" of a full-fledged Muslim peasant. He had pulled it off.

Incidentally, with the exception of the NBC correspondent and producer assigned to their bureau by headquarters in New York, Abdullah pared down NBC's staff there to only Muslims. It was rumored that from time to time he flogged them for ineptitude. And that they accepted it. And critics say the news media is too liberal? It's a big world out there.

Actually, the picture a lot of Westerners have in their minds' eyes of Cairo and its people is inaccurate. Not flat-out wrong, just not altogether right. True, you could hardly take two steps without tripping over some pathetic beggar. But not everybody was poor, and not everybody was wrapped in rags.

I probably saw Cairo's crème de la crème at a Grateful Dead concert. Yes, you read it right, a Grateful Dead concert! It was while President Sadat and his wife were at Camp David, hammering out a peace treaty with Israel.

Just like American first ladies, Mrs. Sadat had pet projects to improve the lot of her nation. One was birth control. Egypt had and still has one of the world's fastest-growing populations, and one of the world's lowest capacities to feed and house them. Through Mrs. Sadat's efforts, millions of dollars had been donated to distribute oral birth control pills. But peasant women who understood barely a fraction of what they were taught about birth control stuffed them in the wrong opening. The others, who understood nothing at all, fed them to their cows.

Mrs. Sadat's other pet project was the Museum of Egyptian Antiquities. It is the world's repository of information and artifacts for one of the birthplaces of modern civilization. The great Egyptian exhibits that have toured the United States, such as the renowned King Tut exhibit, came from there.

The trouble is, there isn't enough money for the preservation or the exhibition of most of the wonders of that ancient world. To this day, they are still stacked up, broken and collecting dust, in the basement. That's not good for tourism. Mrs. Sadat tried to raise money to change it. The Grateful Dead concert, in the shadow of the Giza pyramids at the edge of Cairo, was a benefit for that cause.

Maybe Jerry Garcia and his band really wanted to help Egypt's first lady raise some money. Maybe they just wanted to be the first American band ever to play at the foot of the pyramids. It doesn't really matter. What does matter is that they almost didn't play.

The officials responsible for the regular sound and light show at the pyramids, and at the great carved statue of a lion with a man's head that is known as the Sphinx, just to the east of the pyramids, decided that night to make some money. No, not for the museum. For themselves. They told the band that they wouldn't turn on the lights without a great big gift of *baksheesh*. Several thousand dollars. The band, already envisioning an album cover showing them playing on the Egyptian desert with the floodlit pyramids and Sphinx as a backdrop, said, "No lights, no music."

Not being a Deadhead, I had never thought of their sound as music anyway, even when the lights were on. But that's not the point.

The band thought it could pressure these officials into doing what Mrs. Sadat wanted them to do. But the Sadats, as I said before, were out of town. It took two or three thousand screaming young Egyptians, well educated and well dressed, to convince these highway robbers, who were supposed to turn on the lights for nothing, to do so. Their alternative, it appeared, was to be ripped apart, limb from limb.

Then came the concert. There were a few people in the audience who apparently had heard the Grateful Dead before, but for most, it was the first time. And it showed. Unlike an American concert where fifty thousand fans may stay on their feet and sway lovingly and dance on their seats and reach out from the front rows to touch their musical idols, everybody in Cairo simply seemed stunned.

I mean, it was loud. And discordant. And compared to the gentle rock and roll to which Egyptians until then had been exposed, it was confusing. Barry Manilow, they might have understood. The Grateful Dead, they didn't. Some trickled out before the intermission, although most stayed. They looked catatonic.

We stayed too. Cairo's producer John and cameraman/editor Bob and I had come with the camera gear to see whether there was a story to be done: "Western Music Reverberates for First Time Across Sahara Sands." We hadn't checked it out first with ABC in New York; we just thought, if it's any good, we'll offer a show closer for tomorrow.

We shot the first half or so of the concert, but then gave up. Visually, the scene made a pretty postcard, but no story. The state of the Egyptian nation would be no different tomorrow than it had been today. Except its hearing.

We had gone out to the pyramids with Moustafa. He was a former Egyptian Army colonel who got sent to England for training and made the minor error while he was there of marrying an English woman, even though he still had a perfectly good wife back in Cairo, and that got him drummed out of the army. So now he worked for ABC. He was one of our bureau drivers. And he spoke good English.

When we got back to his car, Moustafa was almost in shock. Not because we got back to his car, but because we stayed so long.

"How could you stand that sound? It is not music. It is noise. Bad noise." Clearly, a Barry Manilow fan.

"Moustafa," Bob said to him, "that's the future. That's what young people listen to today."

"If young people listen to that terrible noise today, they will hear nothing tomorrow."

Moustafa had a good point. After three hours with the Grateful Dead, I could hear almost nothing already.

But Bob was still trying, in jest. "Moustafa, this was a great concert. The cream of Egypt learned how to be just like Westerners."

"If this is what Westerners have," said Moustafa, "please keep it to yourselves."

"But Moustafa, even the Sphinx smiled for the first time."

"No," Moustafa said, "the Sphinx has been silent for four thousand years, but tonight, for the first time, he spoke."

"What did he say?"

"He said, 'Shut up!'"

Incidentally, we got back to the heart of the city so late that we never did get around to telling New York that the story was a bust. Then again, why would we? We had never told them we were going.

But when we checked into the bureau the next morning, a telex awaited us from ABC New York. "Why missed Grateful Dead concert at pyramids?" They had heard about it despite us. A stringer for the wire service United Press International had written a colorful piece about the introduction of Western music to the Middle East, including some terribly inventive phrases like, "Egyptians were dancing in the aisles."

I didn't actually say this stringer went to the concert. All I said was, he *wrote* about it. Dancing in the aisles? I could have done pushups in the aisles, and nobody would have stepped on me. Egyptians at the concert were stunned, nothing else. They were more silent than the Sphinx. But ABC wanted to know why we hadn't covered the concert. And when we told them we had, they wanted to know why we hadn't offered a piece.

"Because there was no story," was my telexed reply.

"Why not?" was theirs.

"Because nobody was dancing in the aisles. Nobody was dancing at all. It was a non-starter."

"But UPI says it was a revolutionary event."

"UPI got it wrong."

"Then can you do a piece and knock it down?"

Do you understand what the jerk at the other end in New York was saying? If this UPI report is wrong, do a piece that discredits it. As if the first report mattered!

It reminded me of the fiasco years earlier when ABC prematurely reported the death of Spain's dying dictator, Francisco Franco. The first report from ABC News said, "Spanish dictator Francisco Franco is dead." The second report said, "Whoops, no he's not." Which led *Saturday Night Live* to report for weeks on Franco's condition, immortalizing ABC's report with, "Franco is still seriously dead."

Two more stories I want to tell you about covering the news in Egypt. Both underscore the paranoia of developing countries.

When Sadat flew off to Camp David, we went out to an Egyptian air base in the Sinai Desert to watch him go. To me, it promised to be fascinating. It is said that from the air, the enemy can't see if there's an air base down there in the desert. Every hangar, every bunker, every building is painted the color of the desert sand.

It was also the first time the government had ever permitted foreign journalists to enter such a base. You have to remember, until just a few years earlier, the Soviets had taught the Egyptians everything they knew about paranoia. Even alongside minor bridges crossing minor ditches in Cairo, there were still signs printed in Arabic and English, "No photographs."

Security at the gate of the air base was pretty tight. The president was flying off to sign a peace treaty with Israel. A lot of people would rather see him dead. So though security was tight, it essentially followed the same rules as security these days at most every airport in the world. No, in those days, they didn't take away your tube of toothpaste, or make you take off your shoes, but they did open every compartment, every pocket of what we were carrying. They had the cameraman turn on his camera to prove that it worked. They had the soundman turn on his video recorder. They had me play my audio tape.

Then a security man asked me to show him my camera. Just a simple Kodak Instamatic I always carried for souvenir photos. He looked it over and told me to take a picture. This would prove that it was really just a camera, and not a weapon in disguise. So I picked it up, raised it to my eye, pointed it, and snapped the shutter. And three burly, armed, businesslike Egyptian security men hit the ground.

Ooooooooooohhhhhh. You mean, "Take a picture, but don't point it at *you*?" These guys thought bullets were about to shatter their chests. They thought they were history, about to be the first to drop in a powerful conspiracy to kill the president.

The picture turned out great.

A few years later, President Sadat was assassinated on the reviewing stand during a military parade. Where every soldier's weapon was supposed to be empty.

When word of the shooting reached us in London, we were out the door before our seats were reserved. That's how it sometimes works: you race for the airport while somebody back at the bureau tries to book your seats. ABC Newsers were racing to Egypt from all over Europe. It was our version of an "all points bulletin": "Sadat has been shot. If you can get to Cairo, do it."

Bill Blakemore, another correspondent, beat us there. He had come in earlier. From Rome. And he had secured the first interview with Abu Ghazala, Egypt's minister of defense, who had been near Sadat on the reviewing stand when he got shot, and was now in charge of the nation's security during the high state of alert that followed. Abu Ghazala told Bill that Libya was probably behind the assassination. Egypt and Libya might have been Arab brothers, and neighbors, but neither would turn its back on the other for a second.

Bill asked if ABC could visit the tense border between the two countries. The defense minister said yes, "If you get there by dawn tomorrow. And leave by midday."

Bill couldn't. He was already in the middle of another assignment. So, along with a producer and crew, I went in his place.

Now, picture a map. A big map of North Africa. There is only one place along the entire length of the border that matters. It is where the highway from Egypt's second city, Alexandria, meets the highway from Libya's second city, Benghazi. Well, they almost meet. Machine gun nests and dug in tanks and barbed wire barriers and other fortifications on both sides block the way.

We had no time to prepare for the trip. To be there by dawn tomorrow, we had to leave right away. You'll see on the map that it's hard to get lost. I mean, if you leave Cairo going in the right direction, toward Alexandria, you basically drive due north about a hundred miles across the desert and take the first left. If you miss it, you're in Alexandria. If you don't, you're on the road to the border.

By the time we took the turn, it was dark. Just a straight strip of black asphalt with desert all around. The wind blows down from the Mediterranean just a few miles north, and sand blows into drifts on the highway. Makes for a fun overnight drive.

There are only three villages en route. One is Al Alamein, site of the decisive World War II tank battle where England's Montgomery beat Germany's Rommel. There are only two things in abundance there nowadays: graves and flies. There are thousands of each.

Al Alamein was our first gas stop. About 250 miles from Cairo. I went into the rustic gas station office to pay, but it was so dark, I couldn't make out the numbers on my money. There was a single light bulb burning inside, but it was completely covered by flies. Might as well not have had it on at all. I had to go out and use our headlights.

Generally, Al Alamein is a lifeless, miserable looking place. It made me think about the thousands who died there. On both sides. What it actually made me think was, "I'd rather die here than live here."

It also made me think, "I still might." You see, there's not much traffic on the road, because it's really just a dead end once you reach the border. But what traffic there is, is heavy. Heavy trucks carrying tanks. Heavy trucks carrying troops. Heavy trucks carrying equipment. The only traffic on the road to the border was military traffic, and it ran all night.

Drivers have a strange habit in Egypt. It kind of sums up the reason why Egypt today is not the great nation it once was. Back at home, when we drive through a remote region at night and see the headlights of another vehicle coming toward us, we turn off our brights! Seems like the only logical thing to do, doesn't it? Saves the other driver's eyes from fatigue.

Not in Egypt, though. Driving across the desert in the dark, they don't use their brights. There's too much sand blowing across the road, reflecting the light back into the driver's eyes. That part makes sense. But when another vehicle approaches from the other direction, each driver waits until he's a hundred yards or so from the other guy, and then he *hits his brights*. Yep, he blinds the other driver, just as he is blinded himself.

Before you get as cynical as I am, listen to the explanation, provided by one of our bureau drivers: "We are all tired when we drive across the desert. There is always the danger of falling asleep at the wheel. We shine our high beams in the other driver's face as a favor. We do it to help keep him awake."

Great. Wake him up to kill him.

We made it to the border right at dawn. They knew we were coming and put on a show for us. Every man was on alert. Every gun was trained on Libya. The trouble was, they were posing. Through the binoculars and gun sights they let us use, we never saw a single Libyan. I'm not saying that Egypt wasn't really on a high state of alert. I'm just saying that maybe Libya wasn't.

We made the return trip to Cairo through the second half of that day and into the night, limping into the bureau sandy, sore, and exhausted. We showed some of our footage to *World News Tonight's* senior producer, who by then had flown in. He said, "Looks posed."

Well, duh. I said, "It was."

He said, "Let's not use it."

I said, "Good night," and went off to my hotel.

Sometimes, they paid us just to be tourists.

CHAMPAGNE FROM A STYROFOAM CUP

Tehran, Iran

PERSIA. IRAN. Now, the Islamic Republic of Iran. Many rulers, different names, all the same place. It is one of the world's oldest countries. Five thousand years of history, including a period two centuries long when the Persian Empire was the world's most powerful and most advanced civilization.

More important today, Iran is a country with almost a thousand miles of coastline along the Persian Gulf. The oil-rich Persian Gulf. That, along with its determination today to be a nuclear power, gives Iran global importance. Furthermore, it is a country that shared a border with the old Soviet Union. Since the Soviets had some key missile bases not far from that border, Iran served as an important set of eyes and ears for its friends who wanted to know what was happening on the Soviet missile testing fields.

Until 1979, Iran's best friend was the United States. The United States bought most of Iran's oil and placed two strategically important listening posts in Iran near the Caspian Sea, their huge dishes aimed directly into the USSR. It also strongly supported Iran's ruler.

At the time, that ruler was Reza Shah Pahlavi, known to his friends as simply "The Shah," which in English is humbly translated as "King of Kings." The Shah was popular among those of his nearly 60 million citizens, those very few who shared in the nation's oil wealth, and a greater number, although still a minority, who shared his vision for the Westernization of Iran.

However, most Iranians were poor Muslims and many were illiterate. They saw not a penny from the oil and liked not a morsel of Western ways.

For them, oil corrupted the economy, and Westernization corrupted the culture; in the conflict-ridden elections of 2009, they are the ones who continued to support the extremist president Mahmoud Ahmadinejad. Furthermore, back in the seventies, the Shah had a vicious secret police unit called "Savak." Since it was hard to meet an Iranian citizen who didn't have a friend, a neighbor, a relative, or a workmate who had suffered, maybe even disappeared at the hands of Savak, the Shah's dictatorial regime was doubly unpopular.

In 1979, after more than a year of mass demonstrations against the Shah and fatal confrontations between his troops and his opponents, he fled into exile. Then, in a violent brushfire revolution, fundamentalist Muslim fighters won control of all key points of power, and their long-exiled leader, Ayatollah Ruhollah Khomeini, took control of the country.

The Ayatollah's domestic policy was to govern the nation by strict Islamic law. His foreign policy was to export the Islamic revolution. He put Iran on that dual path by executing as many former supporters of the Shah as possible and eventually rubbing out all overt critics of his regime, including some who had helped him win power and establish his government. In other words, a mean regime, the Shah's, was replaced by a worse one, Khomeini's.

•   •   •   •   •

It started bad, and then got worse.

ABC desperately needed me, or at least someone who did what I did and knew what I knew, in Tehran. Somehow, the revolution was picking up speed, the Shah was hanging on by a thread, and we had just one overworked news coverage team in the nation's overheated capital.

Martial law was in force. The airport, among other centers of power, was shut down. Now don't get the wrong picture of an idle airport in your mind. This isn't anything like Chicago's O'Hare shutting down in a winter storm. There, in the pinch of an emergency, they'll clear the runways and let you land. But in Tehran, it wasn't snow that blocked the runways; it was tanks. One at each end, another every few hundred yards in between. Kind of hard to land in a place like that.

What this meant was, no flights. Nothing in, nothing out. Cement blocks would have achieved the same end.

But yo! The American people were depending on me. Or so ABC seemed to think. Likewise, Britain's population depended on Derek Taylor, correspondent for the commercial British network ITN, which was in a worse fix than ABC; ITN had no one in Tehran at all. So we flew together on a commercial jet from London to Amman, Jordan. There, we transferred to a chartered Lear jet and took off with a two-man flight crew for Tehran.

Tanks on the runway, you say? No problem if you're armed with a printed telex from the prime minister's office giving you *permission* to land in Tehran, and signed by none less than the prime minister himself, Shapour Baktiar. We assumed our telex had also been shown to the proper authorities on the ground. We assumed wrong.

We figured that out the moment the Iran Air Force began escorting us just after crossing into Iranian air space. Two F-14s appeared out of nowhere, suddenly flanking us on either side, wingtip to wingtip.

Remember, we're not just flying high, we're also flying fast. Somewhere around 500 mph. And these two guys are almost close enough to touch. But not close enough to talk. After all, they were in military jets on a military radio frequency. We were in a civilian jet on a civilian frequency. In other words, we could see the whites of their eyes and they could see ours, but we couldn't talk to each other.

It was obvious they didn't know about our precious telex, signed by the prime minister himself. And we couldn't tell them.

They spent the first few minutes just scaring us. One would stick to our wingtip while the other would peel off and do a full circle around us—we were moving at maybe 500 mph, and one of them was going around us like we were standing still—and then they'd trade roles. We didn't know if they planned to show us in, shoo us away, or shoot us down.

Then the Iranian pilot on our left side, with his arm bent and his thumb cocked backward, motioned through his canopy that we should turn around and head for home. Let me tell you, at that speed and close proximity, I wasn't thrilled to see him take his hands off the wheel. But at least we now had his attention.

I tore the telex from my briefcase and held it flush to the window. Don't forget, we were more than seven miles up in the air, traveling toward Tehran in a multi-million-dollar aircraft, and he was racing alongside in a plane so fast I felt like I was riding in a '59 Buick. Yet the best we could do was communicate with our hands.

Let me make something clear: I didn't actually expect the air force jockey to read my telex; who knew if he could read English anyway? But I figured maybe he'd assume it had to have some importance or else I wouldn't be stupid enough to be holding it up the way I was.

Wrong again. Maybe I was even stupider than anyone thought! This time he abandoned the cocked thumb approach and instead formed his hand in the shape of a gun. When he drew it back as if taking aim, Derek, the flight crew, and I all got the message. You've never seen a faster U-turn.

Now, we were heading for Baghdad to refuel for the return to Amman and were just about to cross the Iraqi border when our Iranian buddies showed up again. I mean, one moment we're up there all alone, and the next, this pair of F-14s is back on our wingtips.

This time, they let their warplanes do the talking. In the war business, a quick rocking motion back and forth means, "You'd better follow me." We did. We didn't know why, but they led us right back toward Tehran.

Within sight of the airport, our Jordanian pilot and copilot called Derek and me to the front. "You must see this," the pilot told us, "you never see again." We could see it straight ahead through the windows of the cockpit. The tanks were moving off the runway. We were on final approach (with our escorts still off each wingtip), and one by one the tanks were leaving.

Our pilot was right. To this day, I "never see again."

We landed without incident, and then cautiously taxied toward the terminal. Then we met the tanks again. Directly in our path. This time though, they formed a circle around us. Nine or ten of them surrounded us like a wagon train. All guns pointed our way. So we stopped. Never say we don't know how to take a hint.

We were watching through the windows, afraid to open our door, afraid to unlatch our seatbelts, afraid to even move. Then a fancy car pulled through the cordon and up to our plane. An impressive and impeccable military man got out with lots of scrambled eggs on the brim of his hat. Aha, an officer.

Suddenly, a knock on the door.

I've got to tell you, it's real strange to sit on a tarmac in an expensive jet plane surrounded by tanks and have someone simply knock-knock-knock on your door. The Avon lady? Welcome wagon? Or do you want to shoot us?

KNOCK-KNOCK-KNOCK. Here's this powerful guy in a fancy uniform with our lives at his mercy, and he's politely knocking on the door of our aircraft as if collecting the month's rent.

Derek asked me, "Do you think we ought to open it?"

"No," I was tempted to say, "let's just let them blow us to kingdom come." But, "Why not?" is all that came out.

The copilot turned the lever, the door rose on its hinges, and we sat frozen in our seats. The officer leaned in looking grim, peered around, broke into a broad smile, and said, "Relax. We are friends." I was never so happy to meet a friend in all my life. We told him who we were and why we were there, and then we showed him the telex telling us it was okay to come.

"You know of course we had no way of knowing about this when you were in the air," we were told. Thanks, buddy, we had figured that out.

The officer, who turned out to be a general, invited us into his office in the airport's VIP terminal, served sweet tea, held us a couple of hours until our IDs and our telex could be confirmed, and then gave us a chauffeured car to get into the city. Meanwhile, unbeknownst to us as we drank our tea, the Shah slipped into another part of the same terminal, gave tearful hugs to his closest supporters, got on a plane, and left Iran forever.

Then the tanks resumed their positions on the runway.

A sidelight: on a previous trip, I met the Shah. No doubt he wouldn't have remembered it, but I do. He already had imposed martial law, which meant he was insecure, but he wanted to show the world that he was still very much in control. So in the guise of accepting credentials from a new group of diplomats, he staged a glittery reception at his palace, the home of what he called "The Peacock Throne." We of the media were invited. Not to cover it. Just to watch.

The Great Hall was a reflection of his ego. Literally. The Shah's walls were covered in mirrored glass. His uniforms were covered in gold braid. His generals were covered in humility.

Just for grins, I went through the reception line. It gave me a whole new feeling for power, because the Shah had a handshake like a wet fish. And a stare like a catatonic. The only other man I ever met like that was Ferdinand Marcos, president of the Philippines. Not an ounce of charisma. And yet the Shah and Marcos commanded the loyalty of bright men. Thousands of them. Sometimes, loyalty to the death. Power must be what you give, not what you are.

Anyway, just a few days after the Shah gave up his power and flew forever away, the Ayatollah was permitted to return to his nation. He had lived in exile in Iraq, and then in France, and now an Air France 747 carried him and his entourage and a passel of journalists back. It turned into one helluva week.

Ayatollah Khomeini's return to the country emboldened his supporters. The Shah's laws were still in effect, and his well-paid and loyal personal army, the Imperial Guard, was still in control. But protest marchers numbered a million or more, and there were several one-sided confrontations where soldiers were shooting to kill at crowds of stone-throwing dissidents, brutal one-sided massacres by the Shah's soldiers against unarmed civilian dissidents. Iran was a deadly place. That's why, for me, it was chilling to watch the bloody aftermath of Iran's controversial presidential election in 2009. Once again, the state against the people. Same story, different players.

I saw the most dramatic massacre at University Square, which they should have called University Circle, because it was nothing but a big dirt circle enclosed by a curb at the center of the intersection of six main streets. Protesters on the square, although ordered by the army to leave, held their ground. But they were unarmed and, thus, easy picking. The army thought so too. Soldiers started picking them off.

But one soldier had had enough of such barbarity. Right before our eyes, he threw down his rifle and ran into the square to rescue a protester who was down but not dead. It became obvious to us that this soldier was defecting to the other side. The problem was, protestors taking cover in doorways and behind cars didn't see his heroism. All they saw was his uniform. A member of the Shah's army. Without his rifle. So they rushed him and started beating him.

The ABC camera crew, Tony Hirashiki and Teddy John, and I rushed from our vantage point to get closer. The crowd pressing in on the captured soldier was ten people thick in all directions. We could see fists and clubs coming down on the poor soul in the center. I roared in Tony's ear, "Let's get closer, we gotta see the soldier." Tony, this veteran Vietnam combat cameraman, gave me a "What have you been smoking?" look, but I was the boss and he didn't have time to react rationally, so in we went. It could have cost Tony his life.

We pushed and shoved and shouted "*baibachit*" as much as possible, which in the local language Farsi means "excuse me," and ended up in the heart of the chaos. Tony had his eye to the viewfinder of the camera, catching every blow being rained on the defecting soldier. Teddy flanked him close on his right side, I squeezed in on his left. Our purpose was to protect Tony's blind sides.

But while we were watching the sides, neither of us was looking up. Luckily, Tony was. He caught the flash of a hand rising, and then falling fast toward his head. A hand holding a knife. In the crush of the mob, Tony had no place to retreat. So he did the only thing he could. In a single smooth move, Tony, an awfully sweet Japanese man who stands all of about five-foot-five, took his left hand from the camera's lens, grabbed the wrist of his attacker, pulled the man's face close to his own, and planted a big juicy kiss on his cheek.

That's right, Tony kissed the man gripping the knife.

And that defused the whole chaotic crowd. One kiss is all it took. And it saved the defecting soldier's life, because as the mob's attention turned to Tony and his would-be attacker, someone had a chance to shout and be heard, "The soldier's our friend, he is joining us!"

Incidentally, Tony and Teddy were one of two camera crews I had with me. The other guys were Rupen Voskamarukian and Lenny Jensen, and they had taken up residence on a balcony overlooking the square. They videotaped the whole thing we were in the middle of: the protester being shot, the soldier helping him out and then defecting to the rebels and being beaten almost to a bloody pulp. But they shot it all through the branches of a nearby tall tree that stood between them and the square. Thankfully this was February, wintertime, and the branches were bare. But still, the branches were in every shot.

It didn't bother me. But Rupen was beside himself. He had captured a single spectacular incident that symbolized the deathly discord in Iran, yet not a single frame was "clean." No one could calm him down. I suppose I came closest when I pointed out to him that if the same incident had happened in the springtime with trees in full bud, it would have been even worse. Rupen was not amused.

Wading into an angry mob in a place like Iran isn't smart. That's what Tony had been trying to tell me when I all but pulled him closer to the soldier being beaten. But hang around a place like that long enough and you'll learn the same thing for yourself.

This time, with a different crew, Michel LeComte and Patrick Etcheverry, we were covering the funeral of a mullah, a high-level religious leader just a step removed from the Ayatollah. He had been assassinated in front of a mosque on a Tehran street by two gunmen on a passing motorcycle. We Americans did not invent "drive-by" shootings!

Anyway, the funeral attracted what I estimated to be a quarter million people. In its public show of grief, the crowd trampled every grave and knocked over half the gravestones in the "Martyrs' Cemetery," called "*Bahesht-e Zahra,*" south of Tehran.

Michel and Patrick, like Rupen and Lenny, were from Paris. With me, they spoke English. With each other, they spoke French. And with angry Iranians, they spoke French because most Iranians don't. Also because France had given asylum to Ayatollah Khomeini, even flown him home. So for the time being, France was a friend to the revolution. The United States was already the Great Satan.

Language is one key to getting along in an angry mob. Speak a language your adversaries probably don't understand, but which clearly is not the tongue of the Great Satan. A few times when militants came up to us in the crush at the cemetery to either demand our credentials or spit in our faces, Michel and Patrick staved off disaster by spouting something in French, which seemed to either please or confuse people enough that they'd back off.

Me? It was still three years before I would move from London to Paris. So beyond *"bon jour," "oui,"* and *"au revoir"* (hello, yes, and good-bye), plus *"Je suis Francais,"* which I picked up from the crew because it means "I am French" and they used that a lot, I spoke not a word. I just became as small as I could behind Michel and Patrick and kept my mouth shut.

That worked as long as I was with them. It was useless when we got separated.

I don't quite know how we got separated. God knows that in this crowd of rebels looking to vent their anger, I was trying to stay as close to the crew as a dog on a short leash. But one moment we were together, the next moment we weren't. The surge of the crowd was such that I didn't even know in which direction to look. Or which way to run to get out.

Have you ever heard anyone use the insult, "He's so dull that when he's in a crowd, the crowd stands out?" I remember that thought racing through my head: *How can I become so innocuous that nobody will notice me?* The answer was, I couldn't. Within seconds, I was surrounded by half a dozen men. They started poking at me with sticks, and one of them was kicking me in the shin. In an instant, I was French.

"Je suis Francais," I confidently exclaimed, half expecting these agitated men to drop their sticks and embrace me like a brother. After all, who in this mob of illiterate, unshaven militants could possibly speak French? Answer: the one right in front of me.

When I said in French, "I am French," he said something back in French, although I can't tell you *what* he said because I had already just about exhausted my vocabulary. I stuttered and stammered and tried to spit a few more Frenchisms into the air, but he knew one helluva lot more French than I did. He knew I was a fake. What's worse, he told his friends. The snitch!

Now, they were poking harder. And kicking higher. And shouting things in Farsi I didn't understand. But I didn't have to understand what they were shouting. All I needed to understand was, they definitely didn't sound friendly.

I thought to myself, *Let's see now: can't talk with them, can't prove I'm not a spy, can't beat them in a fight.* This insightful thought took about a thousandth of a second. So I simply outsmarted them, surprising them by shouting, in English, "I LOVE YOU!" I had no expectation that they would understand. But I said it so clearly that they stopped. Just for an instant, they stopped.

And I started. First, as if I knew the first thing about boxing, I punched the two guys directly in front of me as hard as I could, catching one in the stomach and the other on a cheek, and then I just got a quick break and ran right through them. No assurance that they wouldn't catch up, but I figured one guy can move faster than six. This one guy sure did.

Within less than a minute, they gave up the chase, and I found myself on the outskirts of the crowd. At least if I were to get surrounded again, I'd see it coming. Eventually I found our car. Michel and Patrick were already inside, since it was the only logical place to meet. We made it back to base safely. Somehow, we'd gotten no comfort from our day at the cemetery.

I've already told you that Iran was a deadly place. Having covered quite a few wars and revolutions and coups d'état, I've heard plenty of speeding bullets ring in my ears and errant rockets whistle down on me. It's scary, but like a soldier on a battlefield, you take comfort in the law of averages. That's what protects you. The law of averages, and sometimes a fast set of legs.

But every once in a while, instead of surviving at the mercy of the law of averages, you find yourself centered in someone's sights. Not someone who might accidentally kill you. Someone who definitely wants to kill you. It happened several times in deadly Iran. All in *the same week*.

One day, for instance, the reporter standing on a balcony next to me was killed by a single bullet. It wasn't stray; we were too high off the street for that. Another day, my crew and I were chased by a mob swinging machetes and hatchets; we escaped by a matter of inches. On the worst of days, a tank burst out of a driveway *firing* at us. And on the first day after power had shifted to the revolutionaries, the hotel where most Western journalists were staying was attacked by an armed mob while most of us were inside. That was the week that was.

The revolution actually began in earnest just a few days after Ayatollah Khomeini came back to Tehran. On a Friday night at an army cadet base in the eastern part of the capital, a group of cadets was watching a videotape distributed by Khomeini supporters, one where Khomeini implored his viewers to rebel. A group of officers loyal to the Shah came in and tore the forbidden tape from its machine. Shouting broke out, and then shooting. By morning, there were pitched battles all over the capital, and soon after that, all over the country. Dissident soldiers were opening their armories to the rebels. For the first time, it was an even fight.

I was on a balcony directly across the street from the main gate to the cadet base. The scene below me was incredible. Men in uniform were shooting at other men in uniform. It was hard to tell who was still fighting for the Shah, and who was against him.

On the balcony next to mine was Joe Alex Morris of the *Los Angeles Times*. He had covered many more shooting wars than I had covered, and if a balcony on the third floor of a building was good enough for him, it was good enough for me, too. But they turned out to be the most dangerous balconies in the world. They turned out to be above both sides in the battle below us, and in both sides' gun sights.

The street down there was a four-lane boulevard. The Shah's loyalists had positioned tanks and other armored vehicles down at their end of the block, while his opponents had built sturdy barricades down at theirs.

There is a good reason why you shouldn't use a tank in a city. Sure, it is designed to withstand the brunt of bullets and even some rockets and missiles, but if someone can get up on top of the tank and open the hatch and drop down a grenade, it is no more than a coffin for the crew inside.

That's one of the reasons why the Shah's Imperial Guard lost the revolution so fast once the battle broke out: just three days. Putting tanks out in the desert is one thing; putting them up against buildings in the city, buildings from which rebels can jump down onto them, is something else. Not smart. Not successful.

This is what was happening on the street in front of us. The loyalists were losing. And blaming us. That's because, for a long time, the Shah's supporters held the news media responsible for their nation's self-destruction. True, if the media hadn't finally reported on decades of corruption and torture in the Shah's name, maybe the rebellion would not have happened. But the media had been doing its job, and in a manifestation of human nature that dates back at least to the days of the Greek Empire, people were blaming the messenger.

Joe Alex Morris was a messenger. One of the most experienced. One of the best. No one down on the street below his balcony knew who he was, but besides the fighters themselves, journalists were the only other souls stupid enough to show their heads. And lest there be any doubt, we usually have pad and pencil in our hands to make the I.D. ironclad.

So someone took some shots. Simple as that. Someone saw journalists standing up on these balconies and took some shots. I didn't see who did it. I suspect Joe didn't either. And I suspect whoever took the shots didn't hang around long enough to see who he hit. One less journalist, no matter whom, was all he wanted. He got it. I hope, somehow, it has gotten him back.

It was pretty obviously time to get out of there. So after putting Joe's body to rest, Rupen and Lenny, the camera crew, and I began to make our way, first down some stairs, and then zigzagging from covered doorway to covered doorway.

A local man named Hakim, who had worked in Tehran as a driver for ABC News ever since martial law had been imposed more than a year before, was waiting with his car at a big intersection five or six blocks away. Getting there was our goal. I should have stuck to it.

But on the way, I decided to do a "standup," an on-camera piece of narrative. A standup is easy when you have some control over events in the background. It's harder when things are moving beyond your control. And hardest when the things moving are bullets.

Rupen and Lenny and I ducked into a pharmacy. That wasn't hard; all its windows had been blown out. I thought about what I'd say in the standup; Rupen got all the switches and knobs in the right place on his camera; Lenny adjusted the sound levels for my microphone, knowing full well that he'd have to find an acceptable compromise between the volume of my voice and the volume of tank fire a short block behind us.

The plan was to get everything "up to speed" before hitting the street, and then jump out through the broken windows, utter my twenty seconds or so of narrative, and jump right back into the pharmacy for refuge. If we were lucky, no one would see us long enough to take aim, and no strays would choose us as a target. But we had only one chance. If any one of us flubbed it, we wouldn't get to try again.

We almost made it. We jumped onto the street, and the moment the cameraman was steady, I started saying what I'd plotted in my mind: "The battle started late last night when the Shah's Imperial Guard entered the Farahabad military base here in eastern Tehran. Fighting broke out, civilians started getting guns, and military mutinies began en-masse. And street fighters, to protect military defectors' identities, started turning on newsmen. Whenever we openly turned our camera toward the street—"

That's when a rebel spotted us, turned his machine gun in our direction, and rapid fired.

I was the first to hit the ground, because the rebel was behind the crew but facing me, so I saw him first. While talking and trying to maintain eye contact with the camera, I had seen his abrupt movement out of the corner of my eye, and probably at the same instant he started firing, I started diving for the pavement and shouting at Rupen and Lenny to do the same.

I actually heard the whistle of a bullet as it passed my ear. The crew went down just after me. The shooter went back to the fight behind him. We disappeared into a maze of doorways. Didn't try for "take two."

It is not uncommon in crises like this one that you'll record the story of a lifetime, then have no way to get it anywhere that it can be seen. This is one thing that makes broadcast journalists good candidates for ulcers. In post-election 2009, once things got rough on the streets of Tehran, the government confined foreign journalists to their hotels, which makes it pretty hard to give a credible firsthand account about what's happening outside. Some reporters found ways around their detention, but only at substantial personal risk; as in other dictatorships, it never does us much good to wave the U.S. Constitution in the faces of authorities and claim our First Amendment rights. That's why, for a while, much of the news after the election in 2009 came out through Twitter.

Thirty years earlier, we didn't have Twitter, yet the urge to get our story out was the same. Especially on that first day of fighting. We needed to ship our video; we couldn't feed it from Tehran because the country's television network had been shut down for a long time. A member of our staff from Paris, our courier Maurice, was in Iran for our coverage simply because we needed an extra body to help haul supplies. He had his work cut out for him; he hadn't bargained for this.

Amidst heavy fighting, Maurice got through to the airport, searching for any route out of Iran. He pushed his way into the terminal, teeming with frantic people trying to escape, and spotted just one plane on the tarmac. Of all ironies in this soon-to-be Islamic Republic, it was a plane from *El Al,* the Israeli airline; its courageous crew had been given permission by the government (about to fall) to land and quickly evacuate panicked Iranian Jews. But the doors from the terminal to the tarmac where the plane was waiting were locked and guarded, so Maurice made himself invisible, found the freight department, snuck through, ran toward terrified passengers scrambling up the airliner's steps, offered money and a convincing plea to whoever would carry our tapes, and got our story on the only flight out. To Tel Aviv, of all places. ABC had a bureau there, and that's where the piece was edited and fed to ABC New York.

Our story and videotape ended up being the only material on that particularly dangerous day of the revolution that got out of Iran. As a result, through longstanding credit and syndication deals ABC had with television outlets and networks all around the world, our material was seen everywhere on the planet.

"Take one" of my standup was part of it. Which led to many misconceptions. It showed me talking in a rush with lots of gunfire all

around me, and then suddenly a close, long burst of machine gun fire,
with me grimacing and going down, and then the camera going down
after me. In other words, it looked like we had been shot.

Maybe television news producers around the world would have
questioned it if news reports hadn't already gotten out that an American
journalist that day had been killed. Pending notification of his family,
Joe Alex Morris's name hadn't yet been attached to the reports. So in
newsrooms in many countries, editors read about a dead American
journalist, saw videotape of an American journalist going down in gunfire,
and came to their conclusion.

Luckily, Peter Jennings saw it on TV before my wife did.

Peter was still based in London at the time. But he had just finished
anchoring *World News Tonight* from Tehran for a week and had left only
the day before, when no one knew the revolution would be burning like
a brushfire the very next day. It was probably the worst timing in his
enormously distinguished career. Now, Peter was in Germany, out of the
action, visiting our correspondent based there, Kati Marton, who later
became his wife.

They were watching the news on one of the two German TV networks.
The revolution in Iran, of course, was the top story. My piece was the
lead. Not my narration—remember, this was Germany—but my video.
Including the never-concluded standup.

The German anchorman told his viewers that they were seeing pictures
of an American journalist being shot to death in the heat of the fighting.
The same thing happened in Japan. And Greece. And I don't know how
many other countries.

Peter had our London bureau on the line before the story even ended.
Marge Lipton was on duty. Peter asked what happened. Marge confidently
explained that whatever had happened, she knew I was okay because I
had sent out a scribbled note with the tape, explaining why the standup
was incomplete and why we didn't try to do another. I had also gone on to
audio-record the script I had hurriedly written.

Thankfully, Marge was a personal friend of ours and thought of my
wife. Carol was home in London, knew I was in the middle of the battle
in Iran, and might have seen the videotape on the news there. Or might
be about to. So Marge called our flat. Carol was there. As she later told
me, Marge said something like, "Hi, Carol, it's Marge. I don't want you to
panic. Greg's okay, absolutely okay, and that's the thing I want to tell you
because there's been a false report you might be seeing on TV or getting

calls about, which makes it seem like he's been shot, but he hasn't." Not an easy call for Carol to take, but better than the alternative.

Incidentally, and inadvertently, Marge could have been wrong. What she didn't know was, after surviving the machine gunner who tried to mow us down, a mob armed with hatchets and machetes chased, and came within a shiny blade, of catching us. That's because, even after being shot at during the standup, and never knowing when enough is enough, we were still shooting video of the fighting as we made our way to Hakim's car.

What we didn't know was, word had gone out along the street: all cameras were to be smashed. There were loads of soldiers, still in uniform, now fighting on the side of the rebels. The fear was, if the Shah's forces were to win, our photographs and videotape of these blatant defectors could be used in courts-martial against them. It would not have been pretty.

So we were spotted. A few shouts, and eight or ten men materialized into a mob in an instant. Now, instead of darting from doorway to doorway, we cut a beeline for Hakim, still two blocks or so down the big boulevard. The mob was maybe fifty feet behind us. And catching up.

Rupen was running under the weight of his camera. Lenny was running under the weight of his videotape recorder. I was running under the weight of our tripod, plus our sack of spare batteries and tape cassettes. On the other hand, our pursuers had nothing to hold but their weapons. Thankfully, no guns. Not that guns would have slowed them down. It's just that with guns instead of blades, they wouldn't have had to catch up.

Happily, Hakim saw us coming. He turned the ignition key, jammed the car into gear, and drove directly at us. All in one efficient movement that I shall never forget, right in front of us Hakim spun the car 180 degrees as if he had been trained to, and then reached around to throw open each of the three doors, and without the car ever stopping, we tossed in our gear and jumped in after it, the blades of our executioners close enough now to give us each a tan.

Hakim saved our lives. Only so we could go out and risk them again the next day.

Actually, our first stop on the second day of the revolution, Maharabad Prison on Tehran's east side, wasn't very dangerous. Everyone inside was already dead.

We went there with a group of rebels bent on breaking in and uncovering the sadism of the Shah's regime. They broke in all right. With a battering ram. It seemed like an appropriate instrument under the circumstance. No matter what your politics, this place made Iraq's Abu Ghraib look like a kindergarten.

Several rooms inside had small, round pools, kind of like Jacuzzis, but not nearly as nice. In one room, the pool was about six feet deep, and above it, suspended with a pulley, was a rope. Prisoners routinely had been hanged by their feet and lowered into the pool, eventually to the point of drowning.

In another room, the small pool was surrounded by barbed wire and had temperature controls on the wall above it. The water could be heated to the point of boiling. With prisoners inside.

A third room had shackles bolted into the wall. And electric prods on the floor beneath them. God only knows how they muffled the victims' screams. Anytime anyone used to tell me what a shame it was that the Shah had been run out of Iran, I told them about Maharabad.

When we were through there, we had just one more fight to witness.

In any war, any revolution, any coup d'état, there are a few key places the winner must secure: the airport, the broadcast center, military armories and headquarters, the legislature, the office of the leader of the land.

The rebels were four for five. It had been bloody, but they now had everything but the prime minister's palace. It is on a corner in one of Tehran's classy, old neighborhoods. Shade trees and huge homes behind high walls. The prime minister's wall was white stucco, a heavy black wrought iron gate guarding the main entrance. I had been inside only a week earlier, interviewing the Shah's compromise prime minister, Shapour Baktiar. Now, we didn't know if he was inside anymore or not. Let alone alive or dead.

If he was alive and still in control, the revolution was a failure. If he wasn't, it was a success.

The fighting for the palace was just winding down when we made it to a safe spot, a nice, thick tree to shield us from gunfire, just half a block away. We held to its protection for maybe five minutes, and then decided it was safe enough to go right up to the gate.

From the outside, it was. From the inside, it wasn't. Just as we were nearly close enough to grab it, a tank pulled out from behind the high stucco wall and burst through the gate, its machine gunner firing wildly in all directions. It didn't take a genius to figure out what to do. We ran. If we'd been lucky, we'd have run down a different street than the tank. We weren't.

The machine gun on a tank is dangerous to be sure, but when used to clear a path, it's only a scattershot approach. The 102-millimeter cannon up on the turret is a different story. Just about the time we were used to the sound of the machine gun and the tank treads bearing down on us, there was a deafening boom. A cannon shot. Right past us.

Rupen saw an opening, an open gate, in the privacy wall to our left. He shouted, "In there!" All three of us dove in together. You know the phrase, "Look before you leap?" Take it from me, it's good advice. What we dove into was a rebel pillbox. Firing out at the tank. We dove low. They shot high. That's all that saved us.

The tank, incidentally, was the last line of protection for the palace. Once it broke free, the rebels broke in. Baktiar was gone. The place was theirs.

Whew, what a weekend. No sleep, but I couldn't have slept anyway.

The next day, there was still news to cover, mainly skirmishes in the rebels' cleanup operation. They had won. In the period of seventy-two hours, they had defeated the Shah's army, taken over the whole country, and installed the Ayatollah as its leader.

The day after that, the fight was out of us. I mean, the whole press corps. Everyone was physically and emotionally spent. In a sort of silent conspiracy, almost all of us took the day off.

Of course, in the immediate wake of a bloody revolution, especially when many of the winners are Muslim fanatics, a day off doesn't mean a walk in the park. Tehran was still a very dangerous place. Suddenly, with the seizure of so many military armories, every male old enough to use deodorant had a gun. Suddenly, with the spirit of strict Islamic law infusing the population, every foreigner risked arrest or attack.

So we stayed in the hotel. After all, life there wasn't so bad. Just before the country was effectively sealed off by martial law, in a stroke of lucky timing for which I'll always be grateful, the hotel had imported tons of Scotch beef, Swiss chocolate, and salmon from the North Sea. But our day off is memorable for more than the food.

It was midday, and I for one was napping. Until my slumber was interrupted by gunshots. No, not a dozen stories down on the street. Gunshots up at our windows. Glass was flying, and so were we. The hotel where most Western media were holed up was under attack. The only thing to keep the attackers from storming in was another group of heavily armed fighters stationed there to keep us in check. Already, rebels who had fought together just the day before were divided.

For many contingencies, we always have plans. But this was a new one.

ABC occupied the largest suite in the hotel, which for years had been identified on the double wooden door as "The Imperial Suite." Our first instinct, with the prospect of invasion by fundamentalists who'd been born and raised to hate the Shah and his imperialist ways, was to find some tape and cover the name.

Our second instinct was to try to call the new leadership of the country. Not the Ayatollah; for all we knew, this was his idea. But a lot of secular assistants who had shared his era of exile in France had suddenly been propelled to top posts. Two of them we'd gotten to know were Abolhassen Bani Sadr and Sadeq Qotbzadeh.

Bani Sadr went on to become president of Iran, and then after a narrow escape from fundamentalists who resented his wish to repair relations with the West, made it to Paris to become the "exiled" president of Iran. His second round in exile. (He once told me he learned to speak English by reading trashy American novels while riding the Parisian subways during the first round. Evidently not so well though. He told me in French.) Once things went badly for them though, Bani Sadr's sympathetic foreign minister Qotbzadeh wasn't so lucky to go into exile. About the time Bani Sadr got out, Qotbzadeh got shot.

But when we were under attack at the hotel, Khomeini's trusted lieutenants Bani Sadr and Qotbzadeh, though they were virtually in charge of the country, weren't yet office holders. They promised to round up their own people and send them to fight off our attackers.

Pending that, our third instinct was to get the hell out of there. And we had company. Within five minutes of the first shots, many, maybe most of the reporters in the hotel had gathered in our recently deflowered "Imperial Suite." Because it was the biggest, and because ABC had more people in Iran than any other news organization, our suite had become the gathering place for negotiations, conferences, parties, and poker. It was also on the top floor and would take the bad guys more time to reach.

So now we had the security of seasoned strength in numbers, but still no plan. Just as our panic approached its crescendo, the hotel manager, a savvy American named Gary, came running in. Who better than the manager would know the secret escape routes in the bowels of this huge hotel?

"I have a plan," he said to the unparalleled relief of us all.

Accustomed to the topsy-turvy style of news conferences, we all asked "What?" at once.

"If they come in the front, we go out the back. If they come in the back, we go out the—"

Gary never got to finish. He was drowned in boo's. But despite everyone's fear and confusion, he cleared our heads and got us to think clearly.

Luckily, we didn't really have to. The group of rebels bent on breaking in was run off by the other group of rebels sent to stop them. The revolution against us had failed. Now, we were free once again to cover the creation of the Islamic Republic of Iran. Oh joy oh joy oh joy.

The reverence in the country at that time for Ayatollah Khomeini was unparalleled.

Once, when I was a teenager spending a few weeks in a small town in Mexico, a cardinal of the Catholic Church came through town. A colleague of the pope. Peasants who had never even set eyes on their mayor were getting to see a cardinal of their church. As his motorcade crawled down the main street, they threw themselves at his car, and most were beaten back by his guards. But it didn't seem to matter. They had touched something close to him, and he was close to God. Their lives were fulfilled. But compared to how the Iranians idolized Khomeini, the Mexicans had all but ignored the cardinal.

The Ayatollah's aides—the president destined to be exiled, the foreign minister destined to be executed—had promised me an interview with Khomeini. So I went with a crew and a translator—Behray Taidi, an out of work English-speaking Iranian TV cameraman whom we had hired to work with us—to the elementary school in Tehran that had been Khomeini's headquarters since he returned in triumph.

The schoolyard, surrounded by a chain link fence, was packed with people. Khomeini's entourage had announced that he would hold a public audience. What that meant was, he'd stand at a window and weakly wave his hand at the masses.

We pushed our way in. The pictures would be great.

Bad decision. Once we were in, we couldn't get back out. And with more people pushing in, neither could anyone else. It wasn't like squeezing ten pounds into a five-pound bag. It was like squeezing a hundred pounds into the bag.

By the time we were near the Ayatollah, we couldn't move. Not under our own power anyway. The crush was so tight that we, like everyone else, got picked up and carried by the human tide. If your arm was down at your side, you couldn't lift it. If it was up in the air, you couldn't bring it down.

Behray had a Rolex wristwatch. It came off. There was nothing he could do. To try to reach for it on the ground would have doomed him to death by crushing. Several people did die that day in the schoolyard.

Ironically, we have the Ayatollah himself to thank for our lives. Standing at the corner window, weakly waving his hand at his subjects who were pinned in too tight to wave back, he saw us in the crush and signaled to his aides. They nudged Khomeini away from the window and reached out for us, pulling us one by one across the windowsill and into the room. Ayatollah Khomeini. What a guy.

It was just a couple of days later that the new leaders of Iran gave us permission to bring in a chartered jet to ship out the corpse of Joe Alex Morris. There were still tanks blocking the runways, manned now by new masters, but they promised to open one runway briefly to let our plane land, load, and take off again. Sometimes an American television network can pull strings that even a big city newspaper cannot.

Naturally, ABC didn't want to send the plane in empty. Knowing that the three ABC camera crews already in Tehran were exhausted beyond repair, ABC had put a fresh crew from London on board. If the authorities let them in, great. If not, at least they tried. With the coffin filling the space on the outbound flight though, there was no space for any crew to leave. By virtue of a *fait accompli*, all four now in the country got to stay. And that's what provided the line that has stayed in my mind as the definitive description of journalists.

Mervin Yates was the cameraman who flew in. By the time he and his soundman got out of the airport and into the hotel with their gear, it was nighttime. The twelve or so of us with ABC were sitting around the newly renamed "Islamic Suite" (no kidding; "Imperial" was *so* 1978). We were drinking champagne from the stocked cellars of the hotel and eating caviar, which was always in stock because part of the Caspian Sea is in Iranian territory.

But there were no clean glasses or plates to drink or eat from. We'd had to improvise. Didn't anyone tell you? There was a revolution going on!

No one would have mistaken us for being high class. Especially not Mervin. He walked into the suite, took a survey of the staff, and said, "I finally know how to define journalists. They eat caviar from ashtrays and drink champagne from Styrofoam cups." Mervin was right. Still is.

Thanks to Mervin's arrival, another crew could leave when the opportunity presented itself. Tony and Teddy. After them, I'd been there the longest. I could leave too.

And maybe elephants could fly.

The streets were still dangerous. The revolution was still insecure. The airport was still shut down. It was two weeks before another aircraft got permission to land.

It was a Pan Am 707 with an all-volunteer U.S. crew. It had been sitting across the Persian Gulf in Kuwait, awaiting approval to fly into Tehran and pick up something like a hundred General Electric employees who'd failed to get out of Iran before the revolution and had been hiding in their basements for weeks. It would land the next morning and would have some available seats.

Pan Am sent a telex offering them to non-Iranian employees of our hotel, the Intercon, which Pan Am owned. Gary, the manager who would himself be on board, took count and realized there'd still be fourteen seats left over. He offered them to the press corps. In a drawing among those who wanted to fill them, ABC got three. Tony, Teddy, and I would leave. If the plane did.

We got off the ground the next day, but our departure was even worse than Friday rush hour at La Guardia. No, there was no other traffic at the airport. The problem was getting to the airport. And then through it.

We had decided to go out in a motorcade. All the GE employees would rendezvous at the hotel, where we would join them. What a dumb idea. With the streets still empty—gasoline, among other things, was in short supply—we were not just an obvious target, but an easy one. We came under fire several times, and one evacuee was hit midway to the airport. A couple of his colleagues bravely pulled out of the motorcade to get him to a hospital.

Then at the airport, officials read through our passports, one by one, as if they were chapters from the Koran. If anyone had an Israeli stamp, for instance, they were pulled out of line. (Like many journalists who have to travel between countries at war, I always carried two passports, a special privilege accorded by the U.S. government. All I had to do was make sure I didn't have Israeli visas stamped in the same passport as Arab visas, or South African visas stamped in the same passport as black African visas, and so forth. It was a juggling act, but it worked. Nowadays it's a little easier; enter Israel and just make sure you ask the immigration officer not to put a visa permanently in your passport. He'll give you a temporary visa that you can toss when you leave.)

After that, they inspected our luggage. I don't mean they felt through the toiletries, and then passed us through. They inspected our luggage as if Ayatollah Khomeini's gold fillings were hidden inside.

By the way, mine wasn't especially hard to look through. We had been told the night before to bring only what we could carry. Having purchased a couple of Persian rugs at fire sale prices from rug merchants who said they were going out of business (and were still holding their going-out-of-business sales a year later when I was in and out of Iran many times covering the fifty-two American diplomats held hostage), I chose to carry those hard-won rugs and leave behind my personal belongings, mainly clothing and a typewriter that easily could be replaced.

Then, after luggage inspection, personal inspection. Each of us was closely frisked several times. *Very* closely. This was the scariest part because the inspectors seemed so scared themselves. They were *never* without their newly acquired machine guns or rifles slung over their shoulders. God only knows what they feared from us, but what I feared from them was a gun going off while I was being frisked.

Then, after four or five hours, they let us board the plane. Then, on board, they made us go through the whole routine again. Passports. Luggage. Personal frisks. Tony and Teddy and I were toward the back. Early on, someone up front was removed. We didn't know why, but after that, neither we nor anyone else felt secure each time the focus was back on us.

You think maybe I'm overstating Iran's paranoia? Then listen to this: when we finally got on the Pan American jet, the whole crew—flight attendants and pilots, including Pan Am's chief pilot who had volunteered for this mission—were spread-eagled on the floor. They'd been kept there since the moment the airplane landed.

But when we got on, they got up, and some eight hours after getting to the airport, we all got off the ground. That brought a rousing cheer. Most passengers had been living underground for weeks, wondering whether they'd ever be saved. The rest of us had been above ground, which was even worse.

Then the pilot made an announcement: "Folks, you may be pleased to know we are right now passing out of Iranian airspace and into Turkey." The place went wild. And when our wheels touched down in Frankfurt, West Germany, the screams for joy were louder than the winning crowd at the Super Bowl. We dispassionate journalists were probably screaming louder than anyone.

So I was *almost* home. Trouble was, there was one more wall in the way.

When we'd pulled away from the hotel in Tehran early that morning, a lifetime ago it then seemed, half a dozen colleagues who were staying behind asked me to carry their work to the outside. I became the pigeon. Typically, we'd all ship our film and video cassettes and so forth in mesh bags with the name of the company in bold print on the outside. So I made sure I was the first one off the plane so that I could hold up those bags and the couriers from *Time* magazine and CBS News and the BBC and a few others sent to retrieve their companies' cargo would see me.

That's where I learned the lesson: if you're coming from a major news story that the whole world has been watching, don't *ever* be the first one off the plane. What you run into is a wall of reporters and microphones and flashbulbs and TV cameras and questions yelled in a dozen voices all at once. I've been part of that wall countless times, but for the first time, I was seeing it from the outside. It's ugly.

All I wanted to do was get to a phone and call Carol and tell her I was out, I was safe, I would see her tomorrow.

Guess what! I walked right through the wall. Through the cameras and questions and microphones. Not a word left my lips. Whoever was behind me probably didn't know you could do that. Poor guy. But I knew. And I did.

I got home to Carol the next morning. With a tin of caviar in my pocket. We ate it off a plate.

Now, the postscript. Art Buchwald, the very funny political columnist, told me before he died, "Don't write a book without some sex." So here it is. A postscript of the most permanent kind.

I came home from Iran pretty shaken. It had been a hairy experience. I came closer than comfortable to death. Joe Alex Morris hadn't been so lucky. Carol was shaken too. A single phone call made the difference between her hearing that I was dead, and her hearing that I was erroneously reported dead.

So, almost nine months to the day after my homecoming, our first son Jason was born. Do the math.

If you can hear me in heaven, Art, how's that?

HOW WOULD I LIKE TO *WHAT?*

Kampala, Uganda, and across the border in Kenya

UGANDA, IN EAST-CENTRAL AFRICA, *is one of the most beautiful countries on the continent. It has snowy mountains and tropical forests. A sixth of its territory is covered by water, mainly Lake Victoria, the second largest freshwater lake on earth. It has enormous game parks and some of the most exotic creatures in the world.*

Although it suffers to this day from wars that spill across its borders and also from one of the world's worst AIDS epidemics, Uganda's most infamous period of misery was an era of eight years under one of the world's most gruesome tyrants, Idi Amin Dada. In 1971, as a major general in the Ugandan Army, Amin overthrew the nation's first leader after independence from Great Britain, Milton Obote, and set up a military government.

One of his first orders of business was to expel an estimated fifty thousand Asians who had been living in Uganda and running most of its commercial businesses. He confiscated their money and used it to reward soldiers who were loyal to him. With the army behind him, he began his reign of terror.

Citizens who openly disagreed with Amin's policies began to turn up dead or disappear. Citizens from rival tribes were dragged from their homes and tortured and killed. Eventually, anyone who appeared to pose a threat of any kind to Amin's power was pursued and eliminated.

Tourists stopped visiting Uganda's game parks. Exporters stopped trading with Uganda's businesses. The nation's population was terrorized, its reputation ruined, its economy destroyed.

The country next door, Tanzania, had its own problems with Amin's unstable administration, and eventually in 1979 provoked a border dispute to set in motion his overthrow.

Since then, there has been no leader as evil as Amin, but fighting between rival political and tribal factions, and the forceful overthrow of governments, have continued. The Ugandan people have never regained the prosperity they enjoyed before Idi Amin came to power.

●　　　●　　　●　　　●　　　●

Before the Internet became ubiquitous, everyone in the news business overseas carried a shortwave radio. But not everyone carried enough batteries. So sometimes, in faraway places, we'd stand together like an offensive line in a football huddle, ears cupped, bodies bent, necks twisted, focusing our every sense on someone else's small black box. What this meant was, one of us had managed to hone in on a shortwave signal and tune in the BBC. It was the highlight of the hour, sometimes of the whole day. News From Outside. No, we could care less about goings-on everywhere else. We just wanted to know what the world knew about what was going on where we were. On our plain of wind. Or jungle of mosquitoes. Or desert of dust. Wherever we were.

Funny thing is, we already knew what was going on. That was our job. That's what we were doing there. But how was it playing in Peoria (or Plymouth, as the case might have been with the BBC)? Was anyone on the outside paying attention to what we were seeing on the inside? That's what we wanted to know. If "The Beeb" were to bury the story—or worse still, altogether ignore it—maybe that meant it was time to cut our losses and head for home.

That was the case in April 1979.

There was a war going on, but there were no reporters covering it. None could. It was in Uganda, which had suffered for eight years as Idi Amin's plaything. The world knew of his atrocities, but left it to his next-door neighbor, Tanzania, to try to put him away and put the atrocities to an end.

My assignment: get into Uganda. Show the world what Idi Amin did to his people. Hey, thanks guys! Which interstate highway should we take? Or shall we jump on the next shuttle?

Just getting in was one of the biggest challenges. And that's what got me, along with about a dozen other journalists—including Ron and Carlo, an ABC camera crew from Rome—to a primitive Kenyan village on Uganda's eastern border, near the shores of Lake Victoria.

It seemed like the right place to be. A partly paved two-lane highway passed nearby, and a stucco customs post sat right on the frontier. It was dusty, it was desolate, it was far from the action. But for a place that normally sees only a handful of people a day, it was busy. We could question refugees fleeing the war as they came across the line. "Is this the road to the capital Kampala? Is it in the hands of the good guys or the bad guys? *How can you tell* the good guys from the bad guys? Will the good guys know that we are good guys too?"

The very first refugee I stopped was a Scandinavian diplomat. His advice needed no interpretation. "Don't go in. Amin's men are robbing and butchering everyone they meet." Whether this was the road to Kampala or not, this guy convinced me that it was the wrong road for us. But remember, the wrong road sometimes means the right road. So we waited longer, kind of like a sickly patient seeking a second opinion.

"Excuse me," I began with the second group of men to cross, "do you speak English?" One man did. He was wearing a dark blue business suit, white shirt, and tie. Cheaply made and dusty from two days' walking. It had been a quick getaway.

"I have been told that this is a dangerous road to take," I said.

"Who told you?" he asked me.

"Another man who came across a couple of hours ago," I replied.

"What did he look like?" asked the man in the blue suit.

"He was a caucasian—" I started, referring to the man's color, but got no further for the bear hug in which he squeezed me. It turns out the man in the blue suit was a caucasian too, but a real Caucasian with a capital "C," from the Caucasus, the mountains between the Black and Caspian seas. He and his escaping party of Soviet diplomats had split up, and he and his best buddy, a fellow traveler and fellow Caucasian, got separated. He thought I could put him on the road to finding his friend.

I explained I had only meant caucasian with a small "c." In other words, a white man. Too bad for him. But the conversation was a lucky break for me; one guy says, "Don't go down that road," another says, "I lost my friend along that road." I was two for two.

Incidentally, in the additional long hours we spent at the border post, no other Caucasians with a capital "C," like this guy's friend, ever came along.

Now, I was depressed. Here we were, trying to find a reasonably safe path to war, but the shortest route wouldn't work. That kind of thing is bad enough when it's the biggest story of the year. But it's even worse when there's no word of the war on the BBC, which means you're looking to risk your life for a story the world already has forgotten.

You can't cry on your colleagues' shoulders; they have their own tears to worry about. So, time to call home. And this leads to lesson number one in basic communication back in those days from the field: there hardly was any. Remember, it's 1979. If someone said "cell phone," you'd think of a telephone in a jail.

We made our way to a Kenyan village called Busia, and the best thing about it, in fact the *only* thing about it, was that it had a phone. Busia was one general store on a dirt road, a few dozen straw huts set back in the jungle, and a lodge of sorts. The lodge was a wooden building that, out in the bush like that, almost seems like a national landmark. We found rooms there: two single beds, four men to the room, the beds so soft that the guys who won the coin toss *chose* to sleep on the floor.

Lesson two: there are phones, and there are phones. In Busia, the phone was at the store, and when you cranked a rotating handle long enough, the operator came on the line.

"I would like to place a collect call please to New York in the United States." I gave the number of the assignment desk at ABC News, hoping that after telling the office we were still alive, I could get the call forwarded to my home in London where I might give the same good news to my wife.

I already knew what to expect, and I wasn't wrong. "Please stay by the telephone," the operator told me. "As soon as I reach your party, I will ring you back." In those days, in that part of the world, that might take six minutes or six hours.

Naturally it was the latter. So naturally, I did not stand patiently by the telephone. I put a $5 bill in the hand of the proprietor and told him to come for me when the call came through.

It did, and he did. At nearly two in the morning.

The line to New York wasn't bad. Not good, but not bad. I took care of my business with ABC, and then asked the company's switchboard operator to forward the call to London. But that was asking a bit much of the system. The only reason I knew she had succeeded was because a couple of minutes of clicks finally ended, and there was some kind of faint sound coming through the earpiece.

"HELLO!" I shouted.

"Hello!" I barely—and I mean *barely*—heard back.

"CAROL?" I shouted, the volume too low to tell whether I did in fact have my wife on the line.

"Yeah, hi!" she boomed back, reaching me at the decibel level of a creeping cat. I remind you, our voices were traveling from Busia to somewhere else in Africa, and then across the Atlantic to North America, and then across it again to Europe. And every word took a roundtrip. In short, it was next to impossible to converse, but evidently Carol had something important to tell me and thought it was worth the try. I heard the question, "How would you like to see my father?" come down the failing line.

How would I like to see her father? I was on the edge of Uganda, he was a contractor in Kansas City, and the question made no sense at all. So I came up with the shortest, loudest possible reply under the circumstances: "WHAT?"

She tried again: "How would you like to see my—" Click. The last click of the call. The line was dead. And so was any chance of another call. We were heading to a new potential entry point at daybreak. I would just have to wait awhile to find out why my wife believed the paths of my father-in-law and me would soon cross.

Daybreak. A new path to Kampala. Across the water. If the eastern part of the country was overrun by the bad guys, maybe we could sail across Lake Victoria and land near Kampala, which rumor had it was in the hands of the good guys.

The camera crew and I linked up with four journalists from Europe: two Swedish newspaper reporters and two guys from a German magazine. We were not competitors. We had strength in numbers. We decided to work together. The plan was to hire, maybe buy, an outboard fishing boat. Wait for nightfall, make our way across the lake, row to shore, cover the war, scoop every other newsman in the region.

Sitting on a bluff a hundred feet above the lake, and eagerly eyeing the Ugandan shore just barely visible way off in the distance, we discussed the plan.

We refined the plan.

We evaluated the plan.

And in a moment of sanity, we three from ABC News voted against the plan. We just didn't feel confident that we'd land in safe territory. There was no earthly reason to. We didn't know which parts were safe and which weren't.

So the Europeans went by themselves. They bought an outboard fishing boat. They waited for nightfall, made their way across the lake, rowed to shore, found themselves on the wrong side of the war after all, and surrendered at the first village they came to. I found out what happened because I finally got into Uganda the other way. With the Tanzanian Army. Why didn't we think of that in the first place? If you want to be with the good guys, go in with them.

So we got ourselves to Dar Es Salaam, Tanzania's steamy equatorial capital, and flew into Uganda with other journalists on a Tanzanian troop transport, landing under fire at Entebbe Airport, site of the infamous anti-Israeli hijacking several years earlier.

We saw a lot of craters in the tarmac and broken glass on the ground, but never got to see the terminal. Contrary to previous reports (including the BBC's!), neither the airport twenty miles west of Kampala, nor the capital itself was secure.

That was the day our adrenaline rushed as fast as the bullets. The Tanzanians had to fight their way down the two-lane road, mile by mile. They were in charge, but there was resistance.

At one point, a car came careening into our column, and Tanzanian troops opened fire. It turns out the car carried four young Libyans, sent by Colonel Gaddafi to help fellow Muslim Idi Amin's army. Evidently they had gotten cut off from their main force. At the end, all four Libyans lay in their camouflage uniforms on the broiling asphalt, blown apart in a war that wasn't even theirs. I remember wondering, *Did they even have the chance to realize they were dying utterly alone?*

So the march down the highway was bloody. But it was also exciting. Kind of like moving with Patton's conquering army. At every milepost, citizens came out of the bush. They were cheering us, hugging us, trying to tell us their stories. For the better part of a decade, they had been hiding.

"Under Amin," one man told me in a characterization of his life that I shall never forget, "everyone with nice clothes disappeared. Everyone with books disappeared. Everyone with eyeglasses disappeared. Everyone Amin thought was smart or savvy enough to be a threat to his power was picked up, and we never saw them again. If we were lucky," he concluded, "we could run away and live in the bush."

Then we reached Kampala, and the man's story made sense. Decaying bodies in every roadside ditch. A couple of dozen fresh ones in a pile right behind Parliament. We found them from the smell.

And ultimately, the worst place of all, the not-so-misleadingly named "State Research Bureau." That was Amin's euphemism for concentration camp.

It was our second day there, the capital was still violently contested, and along with a couple of British journalists, we went on a Tanzanian search and destroy mission. No one knew whether Idi Amin had gotten out of Kampala or not. The troops' job was to search for him and destroy his support if they found it.

We fought our way (well, the Tanzanians fought, we just tried to stay alive behind them) to Idi's ante-bellum style house. Clean, freshly painted, the grass mowed, the garden manicured. With its white clapboard facade, green shutters, and tall columns in front, the place looked like it was modeled after Mount Vernon. But Amin was gone. Just barely. There were all those signs you see in the movies that signify a quick departure.

We went through the house. Through the file cabinets. There were hundreds of photos of a grinning Amin, standing proudly with his arms around prisoners as thin as toothpicks.

The Tanzanians looted: clothing, food, furniture. I looted too: Idi Amin's holster, sitting on his bedside table, now hangs in a picture frame on my office wall. (My wife has never been thrilled with it. Holsters aren't quite her idea of *House Beautiful*.)

Then, when Amin's house had been thoroughly examined, someone's attention turned to a low-profile building nearby. Then all our attention turned to this building that looked like a schoolhouse. Gentle roof, stucco walls, chain link fence. But it was on the same grounds as Amin's home, and he was no teacher. No indeed, he was a torturer.

With a sense of urgency—and I don't know why—Ron, the cameraman, Carlo, the sound technician, and I went running toward the building, and when we rounded a corner, we almost tripped over the corpses. They hadn't been dead but maybe an hour. Amin or his men had had one last ecstasy of execution. At least these victims died in fresh air.

We followed the Tanzanian soldiers down into the building. Down the stairs into the dungeons. Battering their way through the iron doors to find more stairs. And more dungeons. A skeleton still hanging from a noose. Other skeletons chained to the walls. Beside one, a pair of eyeglasses. After our march down the road from Entebbe and all the stories people rushed to tell us about what little it took for Idi Amin to brand them as enemies, I understood.

Ironically, my worst horror struck when peace finally began to surround the city. The crew and I were standing in the rubble of the main shopping street. Every window was broken, every store cleaned out.

Ron and Carlo were shooting film and I was behind them when a black man walked up to me. "You a journalist?" he asked me.

"Yes," I said.

"I have been looking for journalists," he told me. "I have a story to tell." It ended up striking close to home.

He was from a village in eastern Uganda. A week or so earlier, four white men had come walking up with their hands in the air. "We are journalists," they had said in accented English. "We are not armed, we are not spies. We are lost, we want to give ourselves up."

"Our village chief went looking for the authorities," the man went on, "and came back with troops loyal to Amin. They put the four men on trial as spies right there in the center of the village, and in the space of one hour convicted them, sentenced them to death, and shot them right there in front of everybody."

It had taken this man several days to even get out of the village. Amin's soldiers had left the European journalists where they fell, to decompose in the African sun, and for three days this man and his fellow villagers were forced to see the corpses, but not allowed to touch them. Finally the soldiers left, the villagers wrapped the bodies in banana leaves and buried them, and the man set out to get word out of the murders.

I had little doubt as the story went on that the victims were the Germans and Swedes who had crossed Lake Victoria in the boat, the plan from which we had decided to withdraw. But I asked the black man who was telling the story to describe them. He said nothing. He just reached into his pocket, pulling out drivers' licenses and press cards. He had removed them from the bodies before they were buried, because he knew someone would want to know. He was right.

I had no need yet to reach ABC headquarters in New York; our stories of the war were worthless until we could physically get film and facts out of the country. But now I had to tell somebody what I had just learned. So that night, despite my need for at least a sleepless rest, I left the long-abandoned high-rise hotel where we bunked with the Tanzanian troops to get out word of the journalists' deaths.

Let me tell you, the decision to leave was a major step in and of itself. This hotel, you see, had been sealed shut for three years. I mean, at some point three years earlier, management just decided (or was forced to decide) to lock the doors and walk away. That would be okay if they made the beds first. Or let in some fresh air. Or flushed the toilets.

But no, they did none of that. When our army escort broke through the front door the day after we reached Kampala, we found a hotel in time warp. It was as if someone had sounded an alarm three years earlier, and everyone had rushed outside and then found the doors locked behind them. Beds were still rumpled from the last guests. Unflushed toilets were full of three-year-old excrement. The only saving grace was, it was dry; the water in the toilet bowl had long since evaporated. But needless to say, the air was foul.

Actually though, the hotel wasn't absolutely empty. What had revolted us had attracted others. The place was overrun with roaches and rats. As some might put it, the roaches were "a trip." But the wrong kind; there were so many, you could trip over them. Even when just standing in the room that I shared with another reporter, they would crawl all over my shoes and up my leg. When I was lying down on the long-unchanged bed, they crawled across my tummy like it wasn't there.

At first, I was terrified. Then I came to terms with my terror and was merely horrified. Then horror turned to anger, and I struck back. Whenever I felt cockroaches crawling across me, I hammered at them with the soles of my shoes. Sure, sometimes I hit my own chest so hard I knocked half the wind out of me and felt like I'd cracked a rib. But if I could cut the roach population even by one, it was worth the pain. However, the system wasn't foolproof, and I learned a lesson: never cover a war with *waffle-soled shoes.* Half the roaches survived in the cracks!

There was something else challenging about the hotel. Naturally, in a city at war, there was no electricity. Translation: no working elevators. This means we walked up and down the fire well stairs. In total darkness. Every time we'd come and go. In the case of this hotel, where the Tanzanians took the first eighteen floors and gave the press corps the top two, it was a wearying walk. Let me tell you, if you left something essential in your room and didn't think about it until you got down to the lobby, you just learned to live without it that day.

So, the night I learned of my colleagues' murders, I gingerly descended the dark fire well and left the hotel and dashed through the gunfights on city streets to Kampala's main post office, where I had heard Uganda's one working telephone could be found.

Me, and a thousand others. Armed Tanzanian soldiers wanting to phone relatives they had left at home. Ugandan survivors wanting to phone relatives who had escaped. Journalists wanting to file copy. And me, wanting to get word to four families whose fathers, or brothers, or sons, were dead. All of us were crowded into a series of decrepit hallways and stairwells. But I was too tired to wait behind a thousand people. My couple of hours of sleep each night since we'd gotten into the country had been fitful: lots of shooting outside the hotel and all those cockroaches inside.

So I was determined to bribe someone to get to the front of the line, and it was saltine crackers that got me through. Soggy, stale, old-fashioned saltine crackers. I had picked up a pack in Dar Es Salaam for emergencies. The food we had to eat was lousy, but that wasn't an emergency.

By "lousy," I mean what the Tanzanian Army gave us: each day, a lousy cup of rice, laced with pebbles. Not what I'd have fixed at home, but if it was good enough for a Tanzanian soldier, it was good enough for me. Especially when there was nothing else to be had. Each day, one cup of rice and a warm bottle of Coke.

There is little in life less pleasant, by the way, than beginning your day in an already equatorial climate with a swig of warm, sweet, sticky Coca-Cola. But thank goodness we had it. Kampala's reservoir, believed poisoned by Amin's troops, had been shut down. There was no running water in the city. So a daily bottle of cola, courtesy of the Tanzanian Army, was our only fluid.

Anyway, there I was at the post office with those sumptuous saltine rations still crushed in my belt pack. And a thousand would-be callers lined up ahead of me. I pushed to the front. The operator sat on a stool without a back, facing a switchboard that looked like it came straight from the lab of Alexander Graham Bell.

He was going nuts. Everyone was shouting at him to place their call first. He looked angry. And hungry. I told him so. He said, "I have been on duty for two days now and have not had a single bite of food to eat." Music to my ears: the crackers were his. The phone was mine. The call was made. The bad news was sent. The duty was done.

There was of course still a second call I *wanted* to make. What in the world had my wife meant the week before when she asked me that strange question over the phone, "How would you like to see my father?"

However, at the main post office in Kampala, the only place in all of Uganda with a working phone, but with a thousand chaotic voices and quite a few guns behind me, I didn't even try again to get through to London.

Just a few days later though, armed with some pretty revealing stories and film about the despotic era of Idi Amin, we did finally get out of Uganda, and making that call was priority number one. I made it from Nairobi, where if you get cut off, you just call again. But no matter; I got Carol on the first try. I didn't take a half-minute to ask, "What did you mean when you asked me on that terrible connection, 'How would you like to see my father?'"

"Noooooooooo," she laughed, "I asked you, 'How would you like to *be* a father?'"

That's how I first found out I'd be a dad. That homecoming from Iran just months earlier had been short, but sure.

There's one thing that puts all the danger and frustration and confusion into context. We got out of Uganda with spectacular footage and horrendous tales to tell, only to find out that what we suspected at the beginning was true: nobody really cared.

Just the day before, the nuclear reactor at Pennsylvania's Three Mile Island had broken. Fears of a nuclear leak, right in the heart of America. Uganda was too many miles and cultures away. Only by pleading, we got one story about Uganda on *World News Tonight*. A minute-fifteen.

"WELCOME TO MY COUNTRY," BUT NOT FOR LONG!

Kabul, Afghanistan

AS THE WORLD LEARNED when the United States went after the Taliban following the terrorist attacks of September 11, 2001, Afghanistan is a rugged, mountainous, landlocked, undeveloped, and isolated nation, nestled in southwestern Asia between China, Pakistan, Iran, and the third-world nations of the former Soviet Union. As a measure of the country's remoteness and backwardness, not to mention its terrain, it doesn't have a workable inch of railroad track.

As the world also learned, the technology of television has advanced these days to the point where you can set up a portable satellite dish in the middle of nowhere and broadcast pictures and sound to wherever you like. It wasn't always so. But back to Afghanistan.

Afghanistan often has been in the sights of conquering armies. In centuries past, it was a vital link between trade routes. More recently, it was a convenient neighbor to Iran, which was rich with oil, and which put this beleaguered country in the sights of the superpower to its north, the Soviet Union.

At the very end of 1979, in the week between Christmas and New Year's, Soviet troops invaded. Moscow claimed they had been "invited" to enter the country to restore stability to its government.

What the Soviets did not anticipate was strong opposition. As Communists, they were atheists, while almost all Afghans are Muslims. They opposed the government installed by the Soviets in the capital, Kabul, believing its policies were antithetical to their religion.

In a loose confederation of guerrilla forces, and with financial and

97

logistical help from the United States and other Western and Muslim governments, citizens from the countryside banded together to force the Soviets to pull out of the country.

Eventually, after tens of thousands of casualties, Soviet forces did withdraw. But by that time, millions of Afghans had fled the country, and countless more had died from bombing raids and direct battles. And worst of all, the fighting between the resistance and the Afghan government continued, which ultimately led to the triumph of the Taliban over the Afghan people. The rest, as they say, is history.

•   •   •   •   •

Afghanistan? Today, everyone knows where it is, but at the end of 1979, I could hardly find it on the map, let alone spell it. But the Soviets seemed to find it all right. If they could get in, why not us?

Of course, they marched in from next door. At the time, I was a bit farther away. In Belfast, Northern Ireland. Waiting for someone there to die.

Two people, actually. The death toll from "The Troubles" in Northern Ireland had reached 1,998. We were keeping track of the victims the same way sports reporters keep track of home runs and stolen bases. "Barry Bonds is just two home runs from the record," some sports announcer might belch over the radio. "Northern Ireland has just reached the milestone mark of two thousand deaths," I would soon belch over the TV. It's no fun waiting for the morgue to get busy. You feel dirty, not to mention bored. You must constantly resist the temptation to *hope something happens soon,* just to put an end to the wait.

In fact, it wasn't really much fun in Belfast back in those days even when nobody was being blown away. This city at the flank of the British monarchy was the most depressing place I'd ever been. In some ways, because of the physical environment, it still is.

The bricks from which most structures are built are a dreary dark red. During "The Troubles," they matched the city's mood. You couldn't move far without passing a "no man's land," a line of brick buildings once occupied, but now boarded up and abandoned because they sat on the different dividing lines between warring Catholic and Protestant neighborhoods.

Depressing? This was Europe, yet the police had to drive around in armored cages on four wheels, and British soldiers walked their foot patrols in combat readiness, the way you've seen American soldiers do it in Iraq: a point man, two sharpshooters, and a fourth soldier walking backward, rifle aimed warily to the rear. But it was Belfast, not Baghdad.

Even the weather is depressing, war or no war. Dismal, drizzly, dark, and dreary. Like the bricks.

And the people. You could have a roaring good time at the pub, but you could never escape the hate. Not every Catholic hates every Protestant; not every Protestant hates every Catholic. But plenty on both sides were born and raised to hate. And to terrorize. And to kill. Some still are.

Get the message? I didn't want to be there. And given where I had come from to wait for two more people to die in Northern Ireland only made it worse, because I came to Belfast from the Bahamas, a treasured Christmas week vacation in the sun with my long-unseen wife and brand-new baby son, a vacation cut short by my contract with ABC. To paraphrase the key clause, "When we call, you jump." They called the Bahamas; I jumped to Northern Ireland.

So when my pager went off early on the third day of the deathwatch, I jumped eagerly to a phone to call ABC in New York. Maybe someone there saw the insensitivity of the deathwatch and wanted to call it off. Maybe they concluded it was too costly to have us wait around for corpses that might not materialize for weeks. Maybe I could actually rejoin my family in the Bahamas.

And maybe I was dreaming. The editor on duty explained that four days earlier, the Soviets had invaded Afghanistan. "Thanks," I said sarcastically. "They don't print any newspapers here in Europe."

"We want you to go," he continued, skillfully ignoring the kind of insult from a reporter in the field to which the men and women at Mother Headquarters grow immune.

"Great," I told him, "I'll just catch the next nonstop from Belfast to Kabul." But he was in no mood for jokes. Nope, he was in a hurry. "We found an Afghan DC-10 in Amsterdam that was caught out by the invasion and it's getting ready to fly home. They're selling tickets."

ABC was not abandoning the Belfast deathwatch. The producer and camera crew who were with me would stay. Poor souls! At least I would get to Amsterdam, maybe beyond. A new adventure, maybe a new country. The only problem was, there was no commercial flight out of Belfast for hours.

"That's all right," I was told. "We're sending a charter from London to pick you up." What about a producer and camera crew? Or was I supposed to take Polaroids and send them out by mule train? "Jacques is chartering up from Paris. Jim and Bob have a separate charter from London. They're going straight to Amsterdam just in case your plane doesn't make it."

Just in case mine "doesn't make it"? Oh well, what's the difference between dying in a chartered jet and dying in a distant war!

Mine made it from London to Belfast all right and then, with me on board, it made it to Amsterdam. So did the second jet with Jacques, the producer, from Paris. And the third one with Jim and Bob, the camera crew, from London. All that commotion, all that fuel, all that *money*, just to get the four of us to another airport!

And thank goodness we rushed! The Afghan flight was operating as if on a normal schedule, meaning about six hours later than planned. That was okay by me, though. Remember, I began this trip in the Bahamas. Neon shorts and flowered shirts. I had added a necktie and warm jacket in Belfast. I would need a lot more for winter in Afghanistan. Happily, there is nothing you can't buy at the Amsterdam airport. I bought it all.

And then we took off. The whole passenger manifest was ABC News, NBC News, Britain's ITN News, *Newsweek* magazine, the *London Daily Telegraph*, and four Afghan citizens who found out about the flight and decided to go home and choose up sides in the revolution.

It's a long trip. Too long to make in one hop. We had to stop in Tehran in the middle of the night for fuel. Tehran, where just a couple of weeks earlier, right before going to the Bahamas, I had been reporting on our diplomats held hostage in the American embassy. Tehran! Where I had been chased, and spit on, and beaten. Tehran! Where the power and might of the United States was cut to pieces.

And we were just stopping for gas. I never had to get off the plane and set foot on Iranian soil. It almost made the long flight worth it!

But I couldn't just kick back and read a good book, or close my eyes to rest. I was on my way to Afghanistan where, don't forget, I still wasn't even sure how to spell the name of the country and surely didn't know anything at all about how it ended up in the mess it was in.

And neither did John Hart. He was NBC's London-based correspondent on the plane and he had had to rush to make it just as I had. But he had an advantage over me. A file from his office. His file of clippings about Afghanistan. Something I hadn't carried to my vacation in the Bahamas!

John hadn't looked a whole lot at the file yet himself; he was saving that for our arrival. So when I told him I knew not a word about the country, he generously handed over what he had, closed his eyes, and fell asleep. This is typical in such situations. Not the sleep, but the help. In friendlier settings, we are fierce competitors and won't give each other much more than the time of day. But we all know that in a place like Afghanistan, it's going to be us against the world. So without giving away any scoops, we support each other. As John supported me.

His mistake. The first thing they did when we landed was rifle through our suitcases and briefcases and equipment cases and remove every printed word. "Propaganda," they told us, "not permitted." I ended up briefing John from his own file.

The second thing they did was take us all to the ministry of culture and information, which was advertised on a big sign outside as the "Ministry of Cultra and Information." I couldn't spell "Afghanistan"; they couldn't spell "Culture."

Inside, we met with the minister of *cultra* and information who said to us in rather good English, "Welcome to my country." Of course, that quickly changed.

Then he gave us the ground rules: "There are only two things you cannot mention in your dispatches: the Soviets and anything bad about the revolution." Aside from that, the sky was the limit! The only things we couldn't mention were the only things we had come to see.

Furthermore, we were supposed to submit all reports to a censor. I should have known that a government official who still referred to our work as "dispatches" would not subscribe to modern notions about freedom of the press.

Then, the chase.

It was obvious from the outset that we were going to be closely monitored. The first sign? The Intercontinental, the modern hotel to which we were assigned. It had been absolutely empty until we arrived; when we walked in, hotel staff were warming their hands over coals burning on the marble floor of the lobby! (Reporters who got to Kabul in 2001 to cover the war after September 11 found the Intercon in basically the same condition as we did: cold, dark, and empty.) When I checked into my room, a worker was fixing my floor lamp. New wiring. I didn't think much about the lamp repair until dinner that night, when a colleague mentioned his own floor lamp getting fixed the same way. Turns out that *most* of the journalists' floor lamps had suddenly needed new wires.

All that ever tells us is, when together in the privacy of the room, talk a lot, because somebody's listening. Talk about all kinds of things you want them to hear. To mislead them. To confuse them. To upset them. We never really know if it works, but we sure get a kick out of trying. Actually, we got a kick out of fooling our government monitors every step of the way.

You see, CBS's Dan Rather, now my colleague at HDNet Television, got around Afghanistan a year or so later, famously unshaven and wrapped up in a dirty, old blanket like locals, but he wasn't the only one who knew how to hoodwink the authorities. He wasn't even the first. Because of his deserved celebrity, "Gunga Dan" got a lot of attention and a cool nickname when he did it. But we dressed that way almost from the beginning, mainly because of another rule thrown in front of us by the minister of *cultra* and information: Don't Leave Town.

Great! Track the Soviets, watch the war, cover the country, just don't leave town. But some rules were made to be broken. So we tried to bribe our way out of town on day one.

First, of course, we needed money. Local money. We could have gone to the bank and gotten whatever miserable rate of exchange the Afghan government would pay us for our Western currency. Or we could go to the black market. What that meant was, we could find people willing to pay us more for our Western money than the bank would, people who might find a way to leave the country and could use it in places where their Afghan bills, known as "*afghanis*," would be worthless.

It ought to be easy. Why? Because once the Soviets invaded, Afghans with any resources at all wanted to get out of the country, and they knew that on the outside, Afghan money would do them no good at all.

Think about it. If you sold shoes in Cleveland, and a guy in a tunic walked in wanting to pay for your product with some gritty old bills printed with a picture of the Afghan king (they still used money from the days of the monarchy), would you accept them? Of course not. Afghan refugees needed hard currency, just as journalists fresh in for the fighting needed Afghan currency. A perfect fit.

But unlike most black markets where you deal directly with the seller, in Kabul you deal with a middleman. Right out in the open. How do you find one? Taxi drivers are always a good start. Get in and ask about changing money. Either they'll take you to a guy who does it, or they'll do it themselves. In this case, the driver took us to a cobblestone plaza surrounded by pillars that no longer had a roof to hold up. There were lots of guys hunkered down, balanced on the balls of their feet, warming their hands over half a dozen small fires.

This was the black marketplace. It's known locally as "*Shahzada*," the currency exchange. I walked in with Jim, the cameraman. The money traders made us feel like we had money pinned to the outside of our pants. All these men, in various mixtures of Asian dress, rushed up to us. Some spoke in tongues we didn't understand, but several spoke in English. Short, sharp phrases in English. Phrases like, "Change money?", "You got dollars?", "I make you best deal." We chose one arbitrarily. The one holding a calculator. These were modern times.

He led us to a fire in the corner. The others retreated to other fires, leaving us alone.

"You like tea?" He began the negotiation the typical way in this part of the world. Not with small talk. With no talk.

It was good tea. Full of sugar. We three hunkered together in a squatting position over the fire, sipping tea, saying little, letting our karmas cross. After five minutes, maybe more, the black marketeer spoke up.

"My deal, best in Kabul."

I was thrilled. Not that his deal was the best in Kabul. I was thrilled because the balls of my feet were about to give out, and my knees felt like they were about to break, and the sooner we did our business, the sooner I could stand up again.

"How good is your deal?" I asked.

"This depends on currency." Translation: some hard currencies are better than others.

"We have dollars."

This brought a warm smile to his face, warmer than the sugary tea and the small fire had combined to create.

"How much?"

"Six thousand."

Uh oh. The smile disappeared. A frown replaced it.

"Six thousand, too much."

Terrific. Here we were at the heart of the black market in Afghanistan, maybe the heart in all the Himalayas, and we had too *much* money to trade.

Jim took over. "How much can you handle, dear boy?" Jim was British to the last inch.

"Two thousand dollars. No more."

Jim and I looked at each other, looked around the plaza at the other black marketeers, looked back at each other, and exchanged what novelists call "meaningful glances." The meaning in our glances was this: these guys work together, there haven't been foreigners in town for months, and there is a limit to their resources.

"Okay," Jim continued, "two thousand dollars. What will you give us?"

"Our rate is four *afghanis* to the dollar."

Another meaningful glance between Jim and me. We had not come unprepared. We had checked and learned that the official bank rate was *five afghanis* to the dollar. That would mean the bank rate was *better* than the black market rate of *four*. So maybe we heard wrong.

"Dear boy, did we hear you wrong?" Good. That convinced me that our glances had meant the same thing! "You are offering to give us four *afghanis* for every dollar. The bank will give us five."

"Four and a half. Final offer." Our Afghan seemed to know the lingo, but since he was still offering us a lousier rate than we could get legally, he didn't seem to know much about doing business.

"Since we can get a rate of five *afghanis* to the dollar at the bank, dear boy, you'll have to do better if you want our business."

"I cannot," the black marketeer replied.

"Why not?" I asked.

"Times are tough."

We got up and went to the bank. He got up and went to join his friends at another fire. Times were tough all around.

(And they became tougher, immeasurably tougher, after the Taliban took over. At its worst, the exchange rate soared to 35,000 *afghanis* to the dollar. *35,000!* Change $100 for local currency, and you needed a suitcase to carry it!)

But at least we now had what we needed to get out of town. Or so we thought.

You believe money always talks? Try hopping in a Kabul cab in Western clothes in the middle of a Soviet invasion and holding a fiver in front of the driver's nose to take you where you say you want to go. No soap.

But then, try the same thing after changing your Western clothes for a blanket. Wanna go to Moscow? Madrid? Miami? No problem, chief! It turns out that the obstacle to getting a ride out of town wasn't the indissoluble integrity of the cabbies. It was their fear of being caught. Make yourselves look (sort of) like locals, and money talks just fine.

Actually, there were two good reasons not to wear Western clothes in Kabul. One was to get around unnoticed. The other was just to get around *alive*. You see, we sensed from our first days there that Americans were not unpopular. Our government had spoken out forcefully on the world stage against the Soviet invasion, which common citizens seemed to appreciate. You'd think that when strolling the streets of Kabul, our clothes would identify us as the good guys.

The trouble was, the only other folks in town wearing Western style clothes were the Soviets. Diplomats, advisers, secret police, even off-duty servicemen smart enough not to walk around in uniform. They were the bad guys. And Afghans had no way to tell them from us!

Our second or third day in town, for instance, we were in the downtown bazaar. Hundreds of stalls, common canvas walls, merchants hawking shiny brass and rotting fruit while warming their grizzled hands over small fires.

Suddenly, some shouting. They speak two main languages in Afghanistan, Dari and Pashtu, but when you don't recognize either one, it doesn't really matter which one it is. So we neither knew nor cared.

Then, some throwing. Of tomatoes. And stones. *At us.* We would have run, but there was no place to go. The stall mall meandered in every direction. Insults and brickbats came from all around. We didn't have to understand the words to sense what they meant.

Then somebody shouted something at us in English. Something threatening, but in English. One of us shouted back, and that's what saved us because before another stone could fly, our crisis was defused by the guy who'd shouted in English.

It turns out, our attackers thought we were Soviets. The English speaker had used the only international tongue he knew, figuring we might understand it too, to tell us how much he hated us. But when we shouted back, he heard our accent for the pure English that it was. He recognized it from the movies. He had seen his share. Hollywood had literally come to our rescue.

And that pretty much formed our fashion for the rest of our stay: no more Western clothes in Afghanistan. So, blankets would disguise us, but who would drive us? For that matter, with security men very openly watching the front of the hotel, how would we even get out of the place to find a ride?

Easy. Through the back door. Security didn't seem to think of that. Maybe that's why Afghanistan never survived on its own.

We used the lessons we learned, that money does talk and blankets do disguise, during one particular trip to the countryside. It began at a meeting with the Saudi ambassador to Afghanistan, who disliked the atheist Russians and had become a pretty good source of information. He told me that his maid, an Afghan woman, had just returned from a weeklong vacation in the northern part of the country, close to what then was the Soviet border. When she returned to Kabul, she told him that her bus had been pulled to the side of the road and sat still for hours while hundreds of tanks rolled past, heading into the heart of Afghanistan.

Hundreds of tanks! Not exactly expert testimony, but not useless in a country otherwise sealed off from the world. After all, the whole question in the earliest days of the Soviet invasion was, *How big is it?*—how many soldiers, how many tanks, how many aircraft; were Soviet forces fanning out all over the country, or just mobilizing to support their new puppet government in the capital, Kabul? We couldn't just show up at Soviet military headquarters and ask; they would just as soon have shot us as answered our questions.

So the maid's little nugget about the tanks was a nifty piece of information. I had to take into account the fact that the woman was not a military expert and, like many citizens with no military background, might not know a tank (plenty of firepower, small crew) from an armored personnel carrier (protection for a company of troops, but limited firepower). So the ambassador let me talk with her. To overcome the language barrier, I drew a few pictures on a pad of paper, and could at least conclude that the machines she saw ran on treads, not tires. I also had to consider that as a maid in Afghanistan, perhaps she never had gone to school and didn't know how to count. But it was a starting point, and as it turned out, fairly accurate.

In fact, it compelled the crew and me to sneak out of Kabul and see for ourselves. And that's where fashion and personal appearance played a role. Resplendent in our moth-bitten blankets and unshaven cheeks, the four of us from ABC found the back door of the hotel still unwatched and, once outside, found a willing taxi driver, one who recognized Western currency when he saw it, and pointed the way north.

It is a fairly straight, fairly flat road, and you can see the brown barren mountains further north from a long way off. Looking at it another way, of course, *we* could be seen from a long way off. But to our surprise, we came to no barriers, even though this was the road down which the majority of Soviet ground forces were entering the country. In fact, there was a constant column of Soviet armored personnel carriers heading into the country, which meant tens of thousands of troops at the very least.

For good measure, we spent several hours lying on our bellies in the tall grass around the Bagram air base, not fifty miles north of the capital, counting Soviet airplanes and helicopter gunships landing and taking off. Jacques and I made observations, Jim and Bob made videotape of the military movements. Just one cassette, but that's more than enough to tell the tale. (Bagram became the main staging point for American forces during the war against terrorism that began in 2001; it still is.)

We were amazed every step of the way: no barriers to get where we were going, no one spotting us once we got there. But it was a different story on the way back. The first roadblock. Manned by Afghan soldiers.

It was kind of like a good-news-bad-news joke. The good news was, our driver could communicate with them. The bad news was, he could tell them what we had been doing and we wouldn't even know he was telling them. To this day, I don't know whether he told them or not. All I know is, the soldiers saw the TV camera on Jim's lap; it was too big to hide and looked bad in a blanket.

They demanded the videotape. I thought the jig was up. But Jacques knew better. He carried on a sign-language debate of sorts about their right to open our equipment. They insisted. He resisted. Finally, all of us now at gunpoint, Jacques ordered Jim to open the tape recorder and surrender the tape inside. Guns talk too.

The soldiers examined the cassette. Clearly they never had seen one before. So Jacques helped them. He lifted the bracket that protects the magnetic tape and began pulling the video tape out. *Pulling it out.*

I thought he was crazy, forsaking our last chance to salvage the story. The soldiers thought he was compliant, overcome by their authority. But he was neither. Back when we were approaching the roadblock, Jacques had quickly and quietly told Jim to put a fresh, unexposed cassette in the tape recorder and stick the one with the Bagram pictures in an unlabeled box.

It sure fooled me. More important, it fooled the Afghans. We got away clean.

Then came the second roadblock. Damn, it wasn't manned by Afghans. We could tell from the uniforms. The Afghans wore wool that would itch on a rhino. These guys wore something sewn in the twentieth century. They were Soviet grunts. An unknown commodity. We were afraid to communicate with hard currency and unable to communicate in their tongue.

Now picture this: the soldiers speaking Russian, the journalists speaking English, the taxi driver speaking a language none of us understood. That's when the hands go to work. And the tone and volume of the voice. Words aren't everything.

The message was, they wanted the videotape. That much we could tell just from the *sounds* of their sentences. We had hidden it under the top of the floor mat at the foot of the front passenger seat. That is where I had been sitting.

The soldiers started their search. We started our shell game. They'd lift out a floor mat, we'd turn it around and use it to replace another. They'd tear out a seat, we'd shift the position of our equipment so they couldn't be sure which end was supposed to be up.

For several minutes, it went on this way, the Soviets prying into every corner of the car except the one where the cassette was stashed. They never knew what they missed.

But our driver did. He had watched us hide the cassette as he rolled to a stop, and now, it wasn't hard to tell that he was grappling with his conscience. Should he side with the Soviets, turn up the floor mat, and give up the fortune we had assured him he would make for taking us? Or, should he keep his silence, keep the secret, and hope we could keep our shell game going long enough to keep him alive?

He was shaking like a leaf. Maybe it was the weight of the money I was furtively stuffing in his pockets. The louder the soldiers shouted, the faster I stuffed.

He made five hundred bucks that afternoon. Not bad in a country where the average annual income is less. So we made it back to Kabul with our cassette. And the soldiers had a diversion for their day. Everybody won.

Until later. It must have been about ten at night. We were watching our hard-won tape in Bob's room. That's where the equipment was kept.

A knock on the door. Really hard, like these guys had seen it done in Western movies.

There were two classic thugs, one speaking slow and heavily accented English: "We know you broke the rules today and left the city. We know you drove north. We know you took pictures you weren't supposed to take."

Of course we knew all these things too, so we weren't real impressed. Not yet.

"Show us whatever you were working on when we came." That got our attention.

"We were just reviewing President Kamal's news conference," I told him, hoping he'd think the event from the day before was still foremost on our minds. Kamal was the Soviet puppet-du-jour.

"Good, show us!"

No time this time to switch cassettes. No time to hide anything. These guys were standing there like statues. The evidence against us was already in the tape recorder, ready to roll. But what did Winston Churchill say when confronted by the superior force of the enemy? "We shall fight them in the trenches, blah blah blah ..." We had come this far and weren't about to lose it all now. I told the Afghans (or maybe Soviets; I didn't know) we'd have to re-cable our machines.

"Do it!"

So I talked very very very fast to Jim and Bob, with too much gobbledygook (I hoped) for our English speaker to follow. Amid the gobbledygook, I told the crew to wire up and fire up a second tape machine so that as we showed our forbidden tape to our guests, we could simultaneously make a copy to keep and they'd never know.

Sure enough, after watching our scenes of Soviet fighters and choppers going in and out of the Bagram air force base, and of a few tank columns rolling down the road, they angrily reprimanded us and demanded the tape. Contritely, we handed it over. Contritely, until they left the room. I basked in my colleagues' whispered praise for my brilliant scheme to make a copy of the tape on short notice.

Then Jim outdid me. When he gave these guys the cassette they so cleverly had confiscated, he didn't even give them the original, which had the clearest pictures. They got what was called "the second generation" copy, which didn't. We kept the original and smuggled it out. I don't know if the viewers back home knew the difference, but we sure did! You could say, shooting and salvaging the Bagram tape was the smartest thing we ever did. Among other things, it got us kicked out of the country!

After all, anytime we keep a secret, we don't keep it forever. We only keep it from the people who would take it from us. We save it for the people who tune in to watch us. Which means eventually our chicanery comes back to haunt us.

A few days after we smuggled the "confiscated" Bagram tape to our people outside (by removing the tape from the cassette, coiling it tight around a pencil, and convincing a Westerner who was fleeing the country to carry it with him and call an ABC number when he reached his destination), we had another visit. "You spied. You told us lies. Within three days, you must leave Afghanistan."

As far as I was concerned, the only greater punishment was to stay longer!

But true to our duty, we found a catch-22. The same way we needed an "entry visa" to enter Afghanistan, which they'd given us at the airport, we needed an "exit visa" to leave. Needless to say, as *personae non gratae*, we got it without a problem. And for how long was our exit visa valid? Five days. In other words, on the day before our deadline to get out, we obtained our exit visas, which entitled us to another five days in the country.

That gave ABC enough time to replace us, which was our real goal.

The correspondent who flew in to take my place had never operated anyplace quite as rustic as Afghanistan. In fact, he was fairly new with the network. As I would leave on the plane that brought him in, I was at the airport to greet him. He had just flown thousands of miles for what feels like thousands of hours, yet he stepped off the plane in a dark blue pinstriped suit, *starched* white shirt, and perfectly knotted tie. What's worse, as a recent anchorman at a local TV station, he had applied pancake make-up, just in case he had to do an immediate "standup" and ship it out with me. Should I tell him *blankets* are de rigueur in Afghanistan and suits look silly?

I had to. Otherwise, ABC might have wanted to send me back! So before my replacement had set both feet on the tarmac, I told him, "Take off the tie, lose the coat, smudge your shirt, mess your hair, and for God's sake, get rid of the pancake make-up. They play hockey here with the heads of their enemies." I'd seen it.

A postscript to the trip: the crew and I got out on that once-every-two-days-flight across the Pakistani border to India. Couldn't head right home, though; ABC in New York wanted us to stay on to cover the forthcoming Indian visit of Kurt Waldheim, then the secretary general of the U.N., and ask him some questions about the Soviets in Afghanistan. But he wouldn't hit town for a couple of days. So while waiting for Waldheim, we went for lunch one day at the recreational complex for U.S. embassy staffers and dependents. Then we went bowling. Trying for a spare, I threw out a disk in my back.

After nearly a month in Afghanistan during the start of a long, bloody conflict between the Soviet military machine and the determined Muslim Mujahaddin, I hurt myself in an air-conditioned private bowling alley in New Delhi. I went home hunched over and had to stay in bed for a month. After being with my new son, Jason, for all of seventeen days in the first three months of his life, I finally got to know him. It was the best thing that ever happened to me.

Several years later, ABC wanted me to go back to Afghanistan. This time though, there'd be no Afghan DC-10. Virtually all American journalists were *personae non gratae* in Afghanistan. The only way in was with the Mujahaddin. I would travel in on foot.

Or not at all.

"Not at all" was my choice. Not because a five-day walk from Pakistan with a bunch of armed illiterates under occasional Soviet helicopter attack and with a single meal each day of lamb bone stew eaten from a common pot was unappealing.

No, because Carol now was pregnant with our second child, and I wanted to live to see him. Or her.

What's more, plenty of journalists had snuck into Afghanistan with Mujahaddin mule trains. But I knew the one guy who got caught. His name was Jacques Abouchar. He was a correspondent for French TV. He and a camera crew had been marching with the Mujahaddin into Afghanistan when they got ambushed. Some ran, some hid under rocks. Most got away.

Jacques didn't. He was captured, taken to Kabul, put on trial as a spy, sentenced to death, and thrown into the fortress prison just outside Kabul called *Pol-e-Charkhi*. That is where he waited to be shot. I had been in *Pol-e-Charkhi*. Back when I first got into Afghanistan in '79, the authorities had announced that hundreds of political prisoners would be released. We went to watch.

The prison is built of big stones. Most buildings, most villages in Afghanistan look like they could blow away in a strong storm, but *Pol-e-Charkhi* is there to stay. Big stones, turrets, and a solid iron gate.

Family members were outside by the thousands, praying that their loved ones would come through the gate. Many got what they prayed for. Others didn't, and with no one stopping them, they went inside to search further.

We did too. The hallways were dark and dank. Cells where the doors had been thrown open were empty. Other cells weren't. The release of prisoners had been selective. If someone was still locked up, his fate was sealed.

Once he was put there, that's how Jacques Abouchar felt. Every night, as he later told me the story, a cellmate, a neighbor, or some unseen victim down the hall would be dragged from his cell. Not escorted. *Dragged*. Minutes later, gunshots outside. The prisoner would never be seen again.

The only thing that saved Jacques from the same fate was his French government. Although often criticized for playing both ends against the middle in international affairs, such an approach can have its upside. In Jacques Abouchar's case, the French still had sufficiently cordial relations with the Soviets, who controlled Afghanistan, to negotiate for his release.

Would the United States government have had the same leverage, or for that matter the same will, if I got caught and thrown into Jacques's cell? I thought not. So I did not return to Afghanistan. But I did live to see Alexander be born. The other best thing that ever happened to me.

The right choice.

IS IT QADHAFI? OR QADDAFI? KADDAFI? GADHAFI? DOESN'T MATTER, IT'S FOR TELEVISION.

Tripoli, Libya

NOBODY REALLY UNDERSTANDS LIBYA. *Not Western journalists, not other Arabs, not even many Libyans themselves. Actually, it is not the Libyan nation itself that we don't understand; it is Libya's leader, Muammar Qadhafi.*

Until the 1960s, Libya was an unremarkable country, one of Italy's colonial properties, ruled by a proxy king, and home to two giant American air bases. Almost a thousand miles north to south and another thousand east to west, larger than Alaska, the country is mostly sand, the upper rim of Africa's Sahara Desert. Almost all the population, estimated today at more than 6 million, lives in the northernmost strip along the Mediterranean Sea.

Libya was unremarkable until oil was discovered under the desert sand. But like a lot of Middle East states with oil, until it flexed its muscle, the profits weren't kept in the colony; the Libyan people didn't get any sense of ownership. Qadhafi, a colonel in the Libyan Army, led a successful revolution against colonial domination and then became head of the government that followed.

To his credit, Qadhafi shared much of the country's newfound wealth. Most Libyans, until then peasants and nomads, got TVs and cars. Education for Libyan children became universal. Health care was available to all. Foreign landlords were stripped of their property; every citizen overnight

112

became the owner of his home. For measures like these, Qadhafi became a popular leader on his own turf.

But to Qadhafi's discredit, he also used some of Libya's oil wealth to finance terrorists. He was blamed by different Western intelligence agencies for backing the terrorists who massacred eighteen passengers (and injured another 120) in 1985 at airports in Rome and Vienna, and for supporting the ones who planted a bomb and blew up Pan Am 103 in 1988 over Lockerbie, Scotland. For acts like these, Qadhafi was widely denounced by Western leaders, his diplomats were kicked out of Western countries, and Libya became a consistent if infrequent object of journalists' curiosity.

In recent years, Col. Qadhafi seems to have mellowed. He has cooperated with investigations into the Pan Am murders, he has helped develop better relations with Western diplomats (President Bush's secretary of state, Condoleezza Rice, visited Tripoli in 2008), he has muted his anti-Western rhetoric, and maybe most important, although it's hard even with satellites to know if terrorists still have training camps in his territory, he has not (at least openly) supported the forces considered America's most dangerous enemies.

Why? Only he knows. But the most popular Western theory is that ever since American warplanes killed Qadhafi's little girl (among about forty others) during a retaliatory attack on Libya in the years when President Reagan was calling Qadhafi "the mad dog of the Middle East" and blaming him for terrorist attacks on Western targets, he has calculated that the costs of terrorism were greater than the rewards.

●　　●　　●　　●　　●

What strikes you more than anything else when you get to Libya is the use of the color green. Everything, I mean *everything* that counts for anything at all, is green.

The flag for instance. It is all green. No symbols, no stars, no stripes, just a rectangular piece of fabric dyed green.

The main public square and site of "popular" rallies in the capital city, Tripoli, is not just called "Green Square," it is actually painted green, every square inch of asphalt, painted and repainted green three or four times a year.

Col. Qadhafi's political dogma, his philosophy in print; that's green too. In fact it is even called *The Green Book* and is rife with chapters you can't put down, such as "Popular Congresses and People's Committees," "How

Does Society Readjust its Direction in Case of Deviation from its Law?," and "The Economic Basis of the Third Universal Theory." *The Green Book* serves as Libya's Magna Carta. Or as Qadhafi puts it in his introduction, "the final solution to the problem of the instrument of governing." "Final solution"? Where have we heard *that* before?

Anyway, the evolution of the revolution in *The Green Book* is, government is abolished. All power is in the hands of the people. "Democracy," declared Col. Qadhafi at the time he abolished traditional government, "is the supervision of the people by the people." So the nation is administered by "people's committees," which we might call government ministries. The "committees' representatives" are the guys we would call ministers. Sure sounds like government to me. Col. Qadhafi, incidentally, is simply "The Leader." First among equals. Or at least that's how they explain it.

And, there's the fruit punch. Yes, the tropical fruit punch is green in Libya. This is a non-alcoholic country after all (officially, anyway), but you can still go stand around a bar. The difference is, you don't have to tell the bartender what you want; punch is all he's got. Green punch.

Life in Libya is built around the color green. Three things explain it.

First, green, seen as the color of life, has always been the color of Islam, and Libya is a Muslim country. However, no one else, not even the fervently religious Saudis, carries the application of the color quite so far.

Second, in a country where 90 percent of the land is monotonously covered by brown sand, the use of any other color at all, for sanity's sake, makes sense.

And third, green fills the empty spaces. Libya has a lot of them.

But it wasn't always like that. When Qadhafi took over in Libya, the cities of Tripoli and Benghazi were vibrant ports with bustling bazaars where brass pots and woven rugs and handicrafts of every kind were produced.

Then came Qadhafi's brand of socialism in which, according to *The Green Book*, "the producers are partners in production." Practically speaking, that meant Libyans could not produce things without including all of society as a partner. Which meant they could not work for themselves. Which meant all small businesses had to shut down.

By the time of my first trip to Tripoli a good ten years after Qadhafi took power, the great downtown bazaar already was abandoned. Crumbling paint, cracked paving stones, dusty stalls in disrepair. By then, only two trades had yet to be collectivized: bakers and barbers. I don't know why barbers made the cut (hahahaha) but I think I have the bakers figured out:

their most popular pastry was this thin sort of phyllo roll with a—yeah, you guessed it—a *green* glaze.

Everything else fell under a single roof. Virtually all consumer goods, from carrots to cameras to cars to caviar, were sold in these huge "hypermarkets" that Qadhafi had built to replace the bazaars. And virtually all consumer services, except haircuts of course, were there too. These were huge, impersonal places with bare walls and tile floors and enough air-conditioning to cool the Pentagon. They were uninviting. But there was no longer anyplace else to go.

Having eliminated the need for private production, everything inside was imported. Libya was rich with oil. Libyans could afford it. Let other cultures exploit their workers. Libya wouldn't. Of course, when oil prices dropped through the floor—as they do from time to time—so did the imports. No more caviar, no more cars. For that matter, with private producers out of business, no more pots, no more rugs.

This is not to say the country was broke. It is simply to say its leader, Muammar Qadhafi, stopped sharing. What money he had left, he spent on "foreign matters," as he once described it to me. Translation: terrorism. That was what got us rushing down from London on one particular occasion.

It was the year 1985, and terrorists had just pulled off a joint attack on passengers waiting in lines at the airport ticket counters of Western airlines in Rome and Vienna. Whether Western intelligence had any irrefutable information to prove Libya's connection, I don't know; the whole fiasco with intelligence about Iraq in the run-up to the war there enhanced my skeptical and somewhat educated view that a lot of American intelligence is based on what we learn from the locals we employ on the ground, who tell us what they *want* us to hear, which is not always the same as what we *need* to hear. And sometimes, intelligence doesn't even have a foundation as strong as that; sometimes, it isn't based on much more than a hunch. But right or wrong (and probably right), Qadhafi was implicated as sponsor, if not perpetrator, of the murders in Europe.

However, although these terrorist attacks and the appearance of a Libyan connection were the headline story of the week, the headlines originated elsewhere, not in Libya. Very few news organizations actually sent people to Libya.

Two reasons: first, the world had been down that road before. It wasn't the first time Qadhafi was fingered as a major suspect, and it wouldn't be the first time a major paper or magazine or network would spend a ton of money to get people to Libya, only to see the same anti-imperialist-dog rallies they'd seen a dozen times before and to hear the same venomous denials of responsibility they'd heard a hundred times before.

Second, Libya was a darned hard place to get into. Of the half dozen or so times I went there, I had a visa, to secure my entry in advance, only once. The rest of the time, since commercial airlines won't carry you to Libya without a visa, we had to charter our own plane and beg with the Tripoli tower for clearance to land, and then prostrate ourselves before Libyan authorities for permission to formally enter the country.

The one time it didn"t work, our London-based charter already had dropped us and quickly turned around and left, and we waited more than thirty hours at the airport before there were available seats on a departing commercial flight in which we could make our exit.

This time though, after the attacks in Vienna and Rome, we made it in. And felt, as they say, all dressed up with no place to go. If Qadhafi says journalists can come into his country, they can come. But if Qadhafi says they are to have no news to cover, they will have no news. And that's how this trip seemed to be shaping up. In response to our requests to interview Qadhafi and to shoot stories around the city, we were told we couldn't. We had to just wait in our hotel until they called us. And so it was, until the fifth day. Sunday.

I got a call in my room, long before dawn. We were being invited by our government escorts, our "minders," to go on tour. I knew from previous trips that when invited to go on tour, as likely as not you'll actually end up going on a real tour, seeing some of the country's authentic Roman ruins. Libya has some of the best. But on those previous trips, I had already seen every last one of Libya's ruins. I had trod every well-worn path, inspected every ancient amphitheater, rubbed every storied stone. Usually under an unbearably hot sun.

In other words, I was overdosed. Ruined out. Furthermore, Roman ruins weren't why we were there. I would skip the tour.

On the other hand, I was getting no closer to the reason why we had come, which was to have a talk with Qadhafi. Get him to level with us like he had never leveled with anybody before. Get him to say things he didn't want to say. Get him to admit it all! Sure, those were goals, not expectations, but that's how you have to approach just about anything you cover, otherwise you won't cover anything at all.

Furthermore, on a Sunday morning in a city without movies or restaurants or shops, and after reading all the novels I had brought and having nothing to drink but green punch, I had no choice. I would take the tour, just to change the routine. I didn't insist that Patrick and Robert, my crew from Paris, join me. But I called and gave them the option. They were bored too. They would come. So would Joe, the editor. Joe is a camera nut. He had never been in Libya before. Roman ruins sounded just fine. Joe had a lot to learn.

So they picked us up, still before dawn, and off we went in a small bus provided by the Libyan government, with just a handful of local journalists in a few other seats, and that kind of made me curious, because if I already had had my fill of the Roman ruins, what about them? But for all I knew, they loved history and archeology, and it was too early to think any more deeply than that. So I didn't.

All I could figure out was, it looked like we'd spend Sunday in the Libyan countryside. It could have been worse, I suppose. It could have been Syria. The Libyans, you see, are sweet as sugar. Syrians aren't. A Libyan will give you the gown off his back if you need it. I hope I never do. This is true across North Africa. Warmth and generosity are hallmarks of the culture. If only you could put politics aside. Which you can't.

So there we were, weaving our way across the countryside, wondering whether more ruins loomed on our horizon, when we pulled to a sudden stop. I was on the left side of the bus, half asleep, staring out my window. At empty fields. Patrick was on the right side. Staring at something else.

"*Mon dieu*, look at that!" he said.

I was almost too bored to turn my head. But the sound of everyone else grabbing their gear and clamoring to get off the bus got my attention.

It was a long field of grain, about a quarter mile from the road to the far end, maybe more. A phalanx of five tractors was downfield, moving away from us in the formation of a wedge. Had they been motorcycles, it would have looked like a presidential escort. Close enough. Flanking the lead tractor, the one at the head of the wedge, were half a dozen men on foot, running to keep pace. Once I squinted my sun-dosed eyes a bit, I could see that the long objects in their hands weren't hoes. They were machine guns. They were protecting the Libyan leader. Qadhafi. Or do you spell it Qaddafi? Or Kaddafi? Gadhafi? Or is it Qathafi, the way the transliterators spell it in *The Green Book*? No matter. I worked in television. We don't have to spell his name right; we just have to say it right. It was him.

I was one of the last off the bus, but first to the tractor. I could credit high school track, but it's more a case of having nothing to carry for a quarter-mile run through the mud.

"*Salam Alechum*," I tried when I reached him, hoping he'd comprehend my try at "hello" in Arabic.

"Hello," he came back in accented English. So much for the language barrier.

"What are you doing?" I asked Qadhafi, shouting above the roar of the tractor. A Massey Ferguson incidentally. Made in Canada.

"I am tilling the soil for my people."

"Do you do this often?"

"Yes, many times every year. Libya is land. Land is life." Just another humdrum talk with a farmer.

Well, we chatted on for another minute or two, both to let Qadhafi get comfortable in English and to let Patrick and Robert catch up, catch their breath, connect their equipment, and start shooting. Once they were "at speed" as we say in the biz, I decided to hit the colonel with the hard stuff.

Trouble was, the tractor was still running, and Robert, with the mike, could hardly hear him, and asked me to ask Qadhafi to turn off the tractor.

"Of course," he said, all humor and light, and started fumbling around for the key. And around. And around. But he couldn't find it. Here was the leader of the Libyan people, who tills their soil "many times every year," and he couldn't even figure out how to turn off the tractor. Maybe he usually works on foot.

Eventually, one of Qadhafi's machine gunners sensed his boss's embarrassment and reached over, placed Qadhafi's fingers on the steering column, and literally finessed them around the key until the engine was off.

Oh, there was also another piece of evidence that this was more of a photo op than a harvested crop. Qadhafi's suit. Bib overalls? Wouldn't hear of it. The leader was dressed in what I can only characterize as a Pierre Cardin après-ski jumpsuit. To be fair, Qadhafi was partial to jumpsuits. All the better to conceal the bulletproof vest that he reportedly never removed. But a reflective, metallic jumpsuit with collar and pleats in the middle of a field of grain? What is the Arabic phrase for "Gimme a break!"?

Nonetheless, once the tractor was off, we could talk. First subject: the multiple murders in Vienna and Rome. I asked Qadhafi what he thought of them. He said it was sad to see innocent people die, but that innocents had died at the hands of the Zionists (Israel) and the Imperialists (the United States) for many years.

"You have said one man's terrorist is another man's freedom fighter. How did you or Libya help the 'freedom fighters' in Vienna and Rome?"

"As I told you, we support the freedom fighters everywhere, particularly our brothers, Palestinians. And we are not responsible for their attacks."

"Did they come from here, do you know?"

"No. You know, first of all, Palestinians are everywhere, even in America. They may come from America. There are thousands of Palestinians, refugees, in America. They may come from America. That means Americans are responsible for these attacks."

"But did they come from here, is the question. These men, in Rome and Vienna?"

"Do you have any evidence?"

"I'm asking you."

"I ask you also."

The Libyan journalists around me were shocked. You just don't talk back that way to Moammar Qadhafi. But he didn't blink an eye. And eventually, persistence paid off, not necessarily with an honest answer, but with an answer: "If they are here, they can be my responsibility, but they are not here because they haven't. If they need, I will give them, I am not afraid, because they are freedom fighters."

This was a case where between what the interviewee said and what he didn't say, the audience could reach its own conclusions. The interview proceeded for five or ten minutes more in English. Qadhafi meant to come across as the salt of the earth, even if he didn't have the right wardrobe for the role.

To be sure, the interview did shed light on Qadhafi's thinking, if not his actions. We did pieces for *This Week with David Brinkley*, both editions of the *ABC Weekend Report*, and Monday morning's *Good Morning America*. My talk with Lawrence of Arabia in an après-ski suit was the lead story everywhere.

What that meant was, aircraft chartered by Europe-based journalists were racing to Libya by the gross. Qadhafi was talking! In a language we could understand! Answering everybody. Threatening nobody. *Newsweek* even flew in a photographer, not to take a picture, but to buy one: a photo of the colonel on his tractor for the magazine's cover due out just a day later. Joe, our editor, had been the only guy on the bus with color film. He made a bundle.

Naturally, every new journalist to hit town made the same request through official channels: an interview with the Libyan leader. And naturally, they were all kept waiting and wondering if it would ever happen, just as we were.

Then, Wednesday night, the call came. Be on buses at the front of the hotel at ten o'clock. A little late to see the Roman ruins, don't you think?

We were driven through downtown Tripoli, past a pair of tanks guarding an imposing steel gate, and through the opening between reinforced concrete walls into Qadhafi's residential compound, the place the United States bombed a year or so later. When the buses stopped, we were herded into a great big conference room. TV cameramen and print photographers set up their gear, radio reporters put up their mikes, and then we all were herded back out so Libyan security could "sweep" the room.

Then, back to our seats. To wait. And wait some more. We waited almost two hours. Although we could all make a pretty educated guess, no one in authority had actually told us why we were there. No one had promised that Qadhafi would materialize. On the other hand, anyone who has covered events in the Middle East knows that's not unusual. It is not that people there are so secretive. They just aren't organized. Time? It is a wholly different concept than we're used to. Time is all there is. We must have the patience to let it pass. So we stayed. Anyway, the buses that brought us were theirs, not ours. We couldn't leave if we wanted to.

Eventually, Libya's leader strolled majestically into the room. This time, flowing robes with gilded gold borders and an Islamic cap. The kind Malcolm X used to wear. And something else was new. His face had changed. I mean, the man of the people from the farm a few days earlier was gone. A stern visage had replaced him.

"Be silent!" he snarled to open the session, although it was in Arabic, with English translation through earphones. His tone of voice quickly confirmed what my eyes already had told me. Dr. Jekyll and Mr. Hyde were alive and well in Libya.

"The Zionists accuse me as a terrorist. The Zionists who invented terrorism accuse me as a terrorist. They will regret their lies and suffer the consequence of their slander."

It was obvious that Moammar wasn't in the same jolly mood I'd seen on Sunday. But I figured he was still open for the game of give and take. Especially with me, his old buddy from the farm.

"But three days ago, Colonel Qadhafi, you told me that you support the people who Western governments call terrorists and who you call freedom fighters. Why do you deny it now?"

His face took on the look of a tiger. An angry tiger with pursed lips and thinning eyes.

"Do not be insolent. We cut off the heads of the insolent." I decided not to follow up on the question. Go figure.

The man was schizophrenic; he probably still is. That's the only explanation. Nothing had changed but the date on the calendar. I'm not a licensed psychiatrist, but I sure know it when I meet two different guys in the same skin in the same week.

That news conference got me to thinking more about Qadhafi. And asking more about him. Few in Libya talk openly, but scout around enough and you'll find the occasional brave soul who will whisper incriminating observations in your ear.

Just in time, too. The beginning of the next week, *Nightline's* Ted Koppel was granted an audience via satellite with the Libyan leader. *Nightline* asked me to do the "set-up" piece, the five or six minute story that would lead the broadcast and establish the theme of Koppel's interview. That's easy enough. Talk a bit about Qadhafi's positive points, and then make the transition to his dark side.

The trouble was, before transmitting from Libyan TV to ABC in New York, we'd have to show the piece to a censor. So let me digress for a moment here and tell you how far Libya carries censorship. It made the Soviets seem open.

A few English-language publications were legally sold at Libyan newsstands. Including *Time* magazine. Once, on a different trip, I had picked up a copy of *Time*. As I leafed through it, I came to a feature story about a nudists' park somewhere in the American South. It was accompanied by a photograph, which I can only tell you in retrospect showed a man and a woman in the park, each with an arm around the other, walking away from the camera. Naked. I can only tell you this in retrospect because I didn't see the full photo until I opened my own issue of *Time* when I got home to London.

In the issue I bought in Libya, the buttocks of both the man and the woman had been laboriously concealed by a censor with a black felt tip pen. He (or she) obviously had to go through every single copy of the magazine that came into the country and blot out the offensive portion of the picture. As if Libyan readers couldn't figure out, by the portions that weren't, what was hidden.

But that is just one kind of censorship, and at least it's practiced right up front. What we ran into for *Nightline* was another form, far more insidious. To begin with, the censor didn't just sit there during the transmission with a finger on the button. No, in Libya (as in certain other countries), the censor had to watch the whole piece beforehand and give it either a thumbs up or a thumbs down before we could feed it to the United States. Thumbs down meant no feed.

The trouble was, to make the transition in my story from Qadhafi's positive side to his negative one, I had to say a few things that I knew from experience would never make it past the Libyan censor. They would earn our piece a thumbs down. So I decided to revive a technique I originally had used a couple of years earlier while covering the American hostages in Iran.

Read carefully; you may need a flow chart to follow this.

I would make my most negative points about Qadhafi in the standup, the section in the middle of the story where viewers would see me standing somewhere in Libya, talking directly to the camera. Call that the "real" standup.

Then I would make some other points, not quite fawning but far less incriminating, in a second standup. Call that the "phony" one.

We would edit the final product just the way it was supposed to be when Americans saw it, with the "real" standup in the middle. But then we'd attach the phony standup to the end.

Then, we would get through to ABC on the telephone and feed just the audio portion of the real standup down the phone line. They would record it in New York. After that, we would wipe my voice from the part of the videotape that had the real standup and tell the censor that because I made a mistake, we had to destroy the sound in the middle and attach a corrected version (the phony standup) at the end.

Are you still following this?

If all went well, we'd have the censor's okay, and feed the piece via satellite, and the technicians in the videotape room at ABC would synchronize my voice from the phone line with my picture from the satellite. We would fool the censor.

We would, but we didn't.

Most censors probably would have fallen for it. They had fallen for it in Iran. But this guy had gone to college in America. Columbia University in New York. And while there, he had worked in television. At ABC News. In the videotape room. During the Iran hostage crisis. The bottom line is, he had seen me do this before. Hell, he had helped synchronize my picture to my voice before. He knew *exactly* what we were doing. But this time, his job was to stop it. Editor Joe and I tried to smooth-talk our way out of it and get the censor to let it pass, but since he could explain our duplicity better than we could, it was a lost cause.

In a way, we should have expected no less. The human race is hypocritical. Why should Libyan members be any different? When ABC was paying him, our man worked to deceive. When his government was paying him, he was an ideologue.

I saw more hypocrisy in Libya, in fact, than almost anywhere else.

Case in point: In 1979, I came to Tripoli with an ABC team from London to track down a guy named Ed Wilson. He is an American, a former CIA spook who had turned color and was working as an agent for Qadhafi, evidently providing explosives and overseeing the construction of terrorist weapons, among other things. The U.S. government wanted to catch him in the worst way.

This was the one time we came to town with a visa. We got there late at night. We had an appointment the next morning with Libya's minister of information, who had told us by telex that he might help us get to Wilson.

Liz, who was the ABC News producer, and I arrived at the ministry right on time. The minister saw us right on time. We started our delicate negotiation right on time. We told the minister some stories about Wilson that had run in the Western media. He told us he had no need to hear stories from the Western media because the Libyan media had covered the Wilson story absolutely thoroughly.

Then, like a tornado out of nowhere, the day went to hell. From the outer office, the information minister's male assistant rushed through the door and shouted something in Arabic. Neither Liz nor I spoke Arabic, but you can recognize panic when you hear it in any tongue. What he shouted was that the BBC was reporting that two American planes had shot down two Libyan planes over the Gulf of Sidra, which is in the Mediterranean just off the Libyan coast.

First thing the minister did was whip out a shortwave radio from beneath his desk and turn it on. It was already tuned to the BBC. So much for the "thorough" Libyan media.

Then, as if Liz and I weren't even there, he got on the phone to his sources. Libyan sources. They told him nothing. Fact was, they knew nothing.

Ultimately, we found ourselves sitting there with Libya's minister of information, all ears turned to a broadcast from Britain. And when that didn't tell us enough, the minister helped us get a priority call through to ABC's bureau in London, which told us more. But still nothing from the absolutely thorough Libyan media.

By the way, when this story broke, we were the only Western journalists in the country. The late John Cooley, then a reporter with *The Christian Science Monitor*, had just been in Libya for a few days doing a feature about the Libyan economy, but when the first reports of the downed aircraft came out, he was on a plane himself, taxiing for takeoff. Poor John. A truly "thorough" reporter and a news junkie, he had an earphone in his ear and heard the same shortwave radio report we heard. But on Libyan Arab Airlines, a hundred yards short of the runway, you don't just get up and shout, "Let me off this plane!" Poor John knew that instead of an exclusive in the print media, he would have to fly all the way to Athens, and then if he was lucky, catch a flight back. Probably a flight filled with reporters.

It was. For half a day, we had the story to ourselves. Libyan government reaction (which said that *they* had shot *us* down) and anti-American rallies. It was like we had bonded! Then, when other journalists landed, the *Libyans* asked *us* if our colleagues should be permitted to enter the country. We were charitable.

Incidentally, if all that doesn't strike you as hypocrisy, how about this? Once our loyal government servant, the minister of information, was convinced that Western reports about the aerial dogfight were accurate and that his own were not, he ordered his aide from the room, pulled a forbidden bottle of whiskey from the file drawer in his desk, and filled three shot glasses. Against the law? Even in the land of green punch, rules are made to be broken.

As for Ed Wilson? Once the dust from the dogfight settled, we got to him. Then, he almost got to me! That chapter's coming up.

THIS IS WESTERN CIVILIZATION?

Belfast, Northern Ireland

NORTHERN IRELAND IS A TOUGH PLACE. *Always has been. It is even tough to describe.*

Physically, it is situated at the far northeastern tip of the island called Ireland, which is to the west of Great Britain, its sister island in the British Isles. However, the country called Ireland, the Republic of Ireland, occupies the bulk of Ireland, but not Northern Ireland. In short, most of Ireland is Ireland, but not all of it—not Northern Ireland. Get it? And Northern Ireland is the place we're talking about here.

Although a land of rolling hills and lovely lakes full of fish, Northern Ireland has precious few exploitable natural resources and therefore always has had to depend on manufacturing and service industries for its living. It also is plagued with sometimes ceaseless rain.

In the heyday of the Industrial Revolution, Northern Ireland flourished because labor was cheaper than in England (the dominant part of Great Britain, to keep the geography course going), across the Irish Sea. That meant greater levels of prosperity for management and lower levels of poverty for workers. Lower, but because of universally cheap wages, never gone. Worse still, by the later part of the twentieth century, all but the smallest contracts available for heavy machinery, shipbuilding, and finished goods had dried up. Northern Ireland would die without subsidies from the outside.

For a long time now, "the outside" has been Great Britain, which is really a collection of the once independent nations of England, Scotland, and Wales. For centuries, England, and then its parent country Britain, ruled all of Ireland. But after decades of bloody conflicts over control of the island, it was politically split in two. Two uneven halves. In 1920, the overwhelmingly Catholic Republic of Ireland was established over most of the island, while the six northeastern counties called Ulster, many of whose citizens descended from Protestant English industrialists, became an adjunct to Great Britain called Northern Ireland.

But the bloody conflict in Northern Ireland didn't end. With Protestants in the majority by a proportion of roughly two to one, Catholics felt economically enslaved, oppressed, and ignored. Militants in the Catholic communities argued that they would never have equal rights as long as Northern Ireland was ruled by Great Britain. Eventually, terrorist groups evolved, the most prominent of which was called the Irish Republican Army, best known by its initials, the IRA. Its goal, pursued by committing terrorist acts in Northern Ireland and in England itself, was to force the British to pull out. Protestant terrorist groups, equally hateful and equally vicious, grew up in response.

The British government in London has long been in a quandary over Northern Ireland. On the one hand, it has pledged to keep its hold on the province at the behest of Protestants there who still fear they'd be violently overrun by Catholics if British soldiers leave. On the other hand, Northern Ireland has cost Great Britain dearly. It has cost lives. It has cost money. It has cost political stock. Some politicians believe it must be abandoned in the long-term interest of what's left of the British Empire. Others argue that Britain must never abandon its trust.

From time to time, there have been negotiations that have led to hopes for peace, even periods of peace. But from time to time, one of the violent splinter groups on one side or the other has dashed them. It is true to this day. Although the IRA has joined its longtime enemies in a Northern Ireland parliament that governs the province, that hasn't ended the enmity. Seen as a sellout for its ceasefire, the IRA is challenged nowadays by the "Real IRA," which is still committing acts of violence in opposition to the two sides sitting together. In March 2009, the Real IRA killed two British soldiers. The beat goes on.

•   •   •   •   •

Although it's unfair to indict an entire population for the behavior of a minority, it was hard not to think of Northern Ireland as a sad excuse for Western civilization.

The police, known as the Royal Ulster Constabulary, or RUC, had to ride around in armored military vehicles with iron mesh protecting the glass. British soldiers, who were stationed there ostensibly to maintain peace in the province, were the targets of violence more often than any other group.

For a long time, to enter the main shopping street in downtown Belfast, you had to pass through a metal detector or be personally frisked for bombs. And when terrorists from one religion managed to kill targets from another, they were hailed as heroes. Go afterward to their neighborhood pubs and, in all likelihood, you would hear them glorified in song. You still will, today.

It was a sad excuse for Western civilization.

Even the twentieth century's all-time best pitchman Tom Bodett—I mean, if he can sell Motel 6, he can sell *anything*—even Tom Bodett couldn't sell strangers on the Europa Hotel, where most journalists used to stay. Sure, it was about the best in Belfast. Clean rooms, decent food, modern phones, lively pub. But even Tom Bodett couldn't sell it because, first of all, it had been bombed so often that every guest had to get searched every time he or she came in, which tends to chill your typical tourist. And because, secondly, *who'd want to go to Belfast?* The city was downright depressing.

Consider the urban landscape. Most days, the range of weather runs from fog to rain. Most homes are built of brick, deep red brick, stained by the soot of coal. Dark skies, dark facades. Even in the best of times, the place isn't particularly cheery.

Making matters worse, for decades, terrorist groups on each side devoted their energies to laying traps for the other. The result: "no-man's" lands developed in the main cities of Belfast and Londonderry. They were depressingly ugly. Where Catholic and Protestant neighborhoods once had faced each other in peace if not in friendship, buildings along these urban borders eventually were boarded up, abandoned, all the better to define the dividing lines between the two groups.

And what you didn't see to depress you, you could feel. Hate hanged around the community like wallpaper. One night in 1981, in the course of covering a riot in Belfast, I saw this hate in its genesis.

We were on The Falls Road, the main road of Belfast's poorest Catholic section. Catholics—both those who supported the Irish Republican Army and those who did not—were incensed at the gruesome death of an imprisoned IRA terrorist named Bobby Sands. He had starved himself until he died, the first of the so-called "hunger strikers" to go. Many rioters were throwing incendiary devices—a.k.a. Molotov cocktails—at the almost entirely Protestant Royal Ulster Constabulary and the almost entirely Protestant British Army.

It was nighttime, or maybe the first hour of the morning after, and things were only getting worse. Every time a police vehicle got hit, more plastic bullets flew from the barrels of police guns, which made the rioters madder, which encouraged the ones tossing Molotov cocktails to toss some more.

Now let me point out the obvious: Molotovs are dangerous. Not just because they can be thrown rather wildly, but because when they hit and the bottle of burning gasoline breaks, it can spread. Get a splash on your skin, and the skin is history. My camera crew and I liked our skin. All of it. We wanted to keep it. Therefore, we wanted to stay out of range. But at one point several hours into the riot, we got caught well within range, with no place to run. Except the alley.

We had learned earlier that alleyways were not a sure thing for safety, because rioters were using them for ambushes. They would lay in wait for an RUC vehicle or an army unit to roar boldly up the street, and then dash out and attack from behind. We had learned about this some hours earlier when we hastily chose an alleyway as a safe haven and jumped right into the heart of a roving mob of Molotov cocktail makers. We jumped in. They jumped us. Only some quick shouting had saved us. But this time, later on in the riot, burning gasoline was a sure thing. The alleyway was only a risk. We took it.

Sure enough, a small band of Catholics was in the alley making Molotovs. But not to throw on the street. They were throwing them at each other.

It was a small band of *small* Catholics. These were little kids, maybe four years old, maybe five—six at the oldest. And where we might have played cowboys 'n Indians when we were children, they were playing Catholics 'n Protestants. For real! These little kids were swearing the same slogans they could hear on the streets. They were making miniature but authentic Molotov cocktails. The ones who played the role of Catholics were elated to "score" against the Protestant "enemy."

Hate was growing in that alleyway. But it hadn't fertilized there. It had fertilized on the day of birth, maybe earlier. Who knows? If prejudice is part of a man, can't it become part of his offspring? Especially if it is infused from the beginning? In Northern Ireland, it is hate deeply held. And for some, never released. Catholic hunger strikers were willing to die rather than let go of their hate. Protestant jailers were willing to allow it, rather than let go of theirs. These were ugly deaths.

Don't get me wrong. I have seen all sorts, and none are pretty. But some are harder to watch than others. These were the worst. Catholic terrorists held in the prison called Long Kesh, more commonly called "The Maze," demanded to be reclassified as political prisoners. The authorities refused to do it.

The prisoners began a protest by refusing to wear prison uniforms any longer, and walked around wrapped only in blankets or nothing at all. Then they refused to clean their cells, and wiped their own feces all over the walls. Then they stopped eating. Hunger strikers throughout history have survived for months on water alone, sometimes laced with a touch of sugar. That is a serious protest, but not inevitably a mortal one. But the hunger strikers in The Maze refused everything. They vowed not to consume a single morsel provided by the prison authority that they now refused to recognize. They would let neither food nor fluid pass between their lips.

Refuse food, and you get weak. Refuse fluid, too, and you also become dehydrated. First the skin goes dry and flaky, and blood vessels begin to pop through. Then the eyes dry up, and you go blind. Then the brain, which cannot function without fluid, withers. The hunger striker turns delirious. Then dies.

That's hate. The hunger strikers must have hated an awful lot to suffer through that. And those who allowed it must have hated an awful lot to watch.

Bobby Sands was the first to die. The riot followed. Then the wake.

ABC had two correspondents in Belfast covering the troubles. Mike Lee and me. We went together to the wake. Sure, we had ulterior motives. We were hoping to meet Sands's family members and convince them to appear on ABC's Sunday talk show. But we also were motivated by the natural curiosity of journalists. We wanted to see how a man looked after starving himself to death.

We waited a long time in line, which stretched well out the door of the Sands's home and down the street. Maybe five hundred people in front of us. And by the time we reached the open casket, another five hundred behind.

I remember Mrs. Sands. Standing there, weeping. Looking down at the emaciated corpse of her son, weeping. Not a good time to ask for an interview. So we viewed the body, hung around long enough to get a feeling for the emotions in the crowd of mourners, and headed back to ABC's office at the Europa.

Naturally, we weren't the only ones on ABC's staff to wonder how a dead hunger striker would look. Everyone wanted to know, and most wanted to go. Ultimately, Mike and I had gone without them because the whole group decided to respect the family's grief, as much as we could. Our concession to decency.

But when Mike and I returned to the office, a question flew at us before we had our coats off: "How did he look?" And Mike, without missing a beat, answered, "Hungry." Graveyard humor when the graveyard is busy isn't particularly appropriate. But in the midst of tension, it is never far from our lips.

Actually, the most comical thing about this ugliest of deaths wasn't Mike's punch line. It was the funeral itself. At least in retrospect.

Tens of thousands of people had crowded into Milltown Cemetery in the heart of Catholic Belfast. Probably tens of thousands more out on the streets. Catholics all, I would guess. It was a day for Protestants to go undercover. Anyone there without a rosary or a press card was a fool.

The casket was carried by six men wearing IRA berets to the open grave. Bobby Sands's family, including his mother, still weeping, stood along one edge. A lone drummer, in a ceaseless mournful roll, stood to the side.

And standing at the other side, a trio of armed gunmen, dressed and masked in black. Although the weapons were illegal, this was a tradition I saw practiced time and again at IRA funerals. A final salute, after which the gunmen would melt with their arms into a cooperative crowd, which by predetermined plan took from them and disassembled and concealed their weapons and their uniforms until the next time. TV cameras, perched on a wooden platform specially built just behind the family, overlooked it all.

The pallbearers lowered the coffin to the hole. But it wouldn't go in. Too tight a fit. So in front of thousands at the gravesite, and countless more watching live on TV all over the British Isles, they started stomping on the casket. A gentle prod here, a swift kick there. One man sat on the casket and tried to force it in with his rump. But nothing worked. They couldn't nudge Bobby Sands into his grave. One corner had been cut too small. God save the gravedigger.

They had to move the casket to the side and take up shovels. Mother weeping, drum rolling, gunmen waiting, cameras recording, pallbearers digging. Quite a scene. They carved a bigger corner, and returned to the casket. Oh no. Yet another corner was in the way. The third time, at least, they got it right. Bobby Sands's final resting place was his final indignity.

That may have been the biggest funeral in the history of Northern

Ireland. But then, the funeral just a week or two later for a milkman and his son may have been the second biggest. It was the consequence of another riot. The aftermath of another hunger striker's death. Altogether, there were ten.

This time, everyone knew what would happen when a prisoner died of starvation. People on both sides were waiting for the shoe to drop, and when it did, riots broke out all over Belfast. Not just in Catholic neighborhoods, but in Protestant areas as well.

That didn't stop the milkman. He was a Protestant who drove most of his route through a Catholic neighborhood. He always had. Knew the people well. Liked them. Trusted them. Not everyone in Northern Ireland was a terrorist.

His wife had tried to talk him into staying in. "Too bloody dangerous," she later was quoted as saying. But a milkman feels the same responsibility as a postman. Maybe more. Children can go a day without mail. But not without milk. So at four o'clock or so in the morning, the milkman set off on his rounds. And his teenage son, worried for his father's safety, got up and went along for protection. The milkman was loyal to his customers. The son was loyal to his dad. That's why they both got killed.

Apparently it was a Molotov cocktail. Maybe not meant for them. But those who saw it said it squarely hit the milk wagon, which wasn't much more than a three-wheeled golf cart with shelves. It swerved. And wrapped itself around a tree. The milkman and his son were killed instantly. The only two fatalities in the riot.

This typifies the injustice of Northern Ireland. That night, there were combatants all over Belfast—angry men, mean men, Catholic and Protestant alike. Their only purpose was to hurt somebody. They probably all got home safely. The milkman and his son never got home again.

And my camera crew and I almost didn't. When the milk wagon hit the tree, we were right around the corner, covering some fighting. We heard the loud crash and went running. Ended up being the first ones there. The second ones were another ABC team. The third ones were the police.

They didn't arrive in time to see us shouting for help for the man and the boy in the milk wagon. They didn't observe us checking the victims' pulses or for other signs of life. They didn't see us trying to chase the rioters to identify who might have been responsible. They only saw us recording the event, because by the time the police got there, the crew was videotaping, and I was making notes. The damage couldn't be undone, and it was a part of that night's story. The most horrible part.

In the chaos of the night, they didn't arrest us, but they did suspect that we had staged the event for our camera, either paying someone to throw a firebomb at the milk wagon, or throwing it ourselves. And they told their superiors. And their superiors told the authorities in London. And we were denounced the next day in Parliament. I never saw bad news travel so fast, *and I was in the news business.*

A member of the Conservative party, armed with an erroneous report he failed to check out by checking with us, stood up the next day in the House of Commons and read us, if you'll excuse the pun, the riot act. Worse still, he made us out to be perpetrators of the riot. The milkman and his son had been innocent victims. And we had become scapegoats, victims of circumstance ourselves. The fact is, the authorities in Northern Ireland don't like the news media. Never have. Probably never will.

For example, once a crew and I got a typical rental car at the airport and drove out to County Armagh, the heart of terrorist territory, a region known to British soldiers who had to patrol it as the "triangle of death." Plenty of cover for an ambush there, and plenty of safe houses for terrorists.

Our mistake was the make of the car we rented. A Ford Cortina. The four-door model. The very same commonplace model favored by IRA terrorists whenever they'd hijack a vehicle to use in a crime. Plus, we fit the profile. Two men in front, one in back. The very same distribution typically favored by IRA terrorists in the commission of a crime. Why not just wave a gun in the air? Same result. We weren't five minutes into the county when we were stopped.

"Who are ya?" was question number one.

"Journalists from American television" was our answer. End of friendly conversation. Our car keys were removed, our passports taken away, and an armored personnel vehicle from the Queen's Royal Army quickly took up position ten yards away to stand guard. What were they afraid we might do? Stab them with my ballpoint pen? Bind them in videotape?

They detained us for three hours. When we got back to our base, I talked to some old-timers who'd seen their share of suspected terrorists stopped on the road. If the detainees turned out to be bad guys, they were on their way to the slammer. But if they checked out okay, they were pretty quickly on their way. In thirty minutes—sixty, max.

Three hours for us.

Journalists? They must have thought we were *worse* than terrorists, because we were the ones everyone blamed for Northern Ireland's troubles, as if by dropping back into our filthy subterranean cracks, everyone still on the surface would start to live in peace. *There they go again,* I've thought time and time again, *blaming the messenger.* We've seen it everywhere from *Newsweek's* report in 2005 about a Koran flushed down the toilet at Guantanamo, which led to fatal riots in Afghanistan, to the *Washington Post's* intrepid Watergate reporting in the early seventies that brought down a president. Actually, blaming the messenger dates back to ancient Greece.

In my experience, Clark Todd was the best example of how the messenger takes the rap. Clark was a correspondent for the commercial Canadian television network, CTV. Although he covered much of Northern Ireland alongside me, eventually he died in the hills above Beirut—and again, I was nearby. The last to go over a wall after getting trapped in the middle of a battle, he took some shrapnel in the back, fell to the bottom, and slowly bled to death on the spot. As he lay dying, Clark wrote a loving good-bye to his wife and five children. On the wall. In his own blood. It was dreadful, but whenever I picture Clark dying in Beirut, I think back to what happened to him in Belfast. It was during yet another riot, the one following the third or fourth consecutive hunger striker death. I don't even remember anymore.

As we'd done in Beirut and other places, thanks to an association between CTV and ABC, Clark and I were working together, sharing a camera crew. The four of us were in the middle of a block as the rioters throwing firebombs stood their ground at one end, and the police with their rifles loaded with plastic bullets for "crowd control" started moving in from the other. We had a bit of a problem though. No alleyway. The best we could do was pin ourselves as close as possible to the building at our backs.

You may wonder, what we were scared of? Plastic bullets sound relatively harmless. No body-piercing metal, just a solid cylinder of plastic, an inch across and maybe four inches long. But harmless they are not. In the early days of Northern Ireland's troubles, the police used rubber bullets. Cylinders of the same dimensions, fired from the same weapons. No fun to be hit by a high powered, hard packed rubber cylinder, *but it wouldn't kill you.*

However, as they flew through the air, rubber bullets sometimes softened from the effects of their velocity, and veered far from their distant targets. So somebody who apparently had seen *The Graduate*—remember the line to Dustin Hoffman, "Plastics, my boy, plastics"—had a brainstorm: replace rubber with plastic. Plastic wouldn't soften. It would hit its intended target. It would control the crowd. But there was a pesky little problem: plastic bullets also *could* kill you. They were much harder than rubber. They had blown a few heads apart. I had seen it happen. A little girl caught in crossfire. A pretty little girl, from her photograph. Not a pretty sight.

So there we were, trapped in the middle of the block as the plastic bullets began to fly. Remember, they're supposed to go where the shooter wants them to go. Or pretty close.

I saw it coming. I saw the policeman fire a round toward the crowd, and then reload, and then aim again. But he glanced up and saw our contemptible TV camera just fifty yards away, and turned his body in our direction. Just a subtle turn. Subtle, but certain.

We were an easy target. More important, we were journalists. A better target. So he turned toward us, aimed again, and fired. This was Western civilization?

I shouted "Duck!" at everybody. Clark didn't quite duck in time. Nothing fatal, just a piece of his calf torn away. A piece almost as big as the cylinder itself. It took out lots of fat and a bit of bone, but thankfully, no major blood vessels.

What I'll always remember, and this is what still flies into my mind whenever I think of Clark's slow death in Beirut, are his words as he clutched his leg on that sidewalk in Belfast: "Well, we've all got one bullet with our name on it. I've had mine."

It's an important story. Important because it puts into perspective people's suspicions that journalists all have "an agenda," which we were still hearing in the first several years of the Iraq war. Yes they do. Their agenda is to cover the story. Any story. And sometimes to put their lives on the line to do it.

And sometimes to lose.

A FISTFUL OF ZLOTYS

Warsaw, Poland, and the train tracks leading in

AFTER RUSSIA, POLAND IS the largest nation in what was long known as Eastern Europe, with its northern border on the Baltic Sea. Because the Soviet Union liberated Poland from the Nazis at the end of World War II, it got to maintain control of the country long after the war was over. Poland became part of the Communist bloc. Poles found themselves living behind the iron curtain.

Having suffered under foreign domination for most of their long history, Communist rule meant more of the same: foreign domination, in the form of Soviet domination, yet again. Beginning in the mid-1950s, there were several revolutions against it. The biggest were in 1956 and 1970 when there were strikes and riots; each time, the leadership of Poland's government changed, but Communist domination did not.

Then in 1980, there were nationwide strikes once again. They started in a Baltic Sea shipyard in the city of Gdansk (which variously over the years had been known by the name Danzig when it was part of Germany). Those strikes led to negotiations with the Communist government for economic and political reforms, and to the creation of the independent democratic Solidarity Trade Union.

For a while, Solidarity actually was dictating terms to the government. Ultimately though, the government, which survived at the mercy of the Soviet leadership, imposed martial law and disbanded the trade union, but the Polish people never forgot their taste of democracy. Eventually they wrestled their way out of the Soviet Union's grasp, and in 1990, Solidarity's *leader, shipyard electrician Lech Walesa, became modern Poland's first non-Communist president.*

•   •   •   •   •

I was heading into Poland.

Martial law had just come down. And that's a pretty good way to put it, because that's pretty much what martial law does. It comes down. A big wall comes down around the country and closes around its people.

Because of the exciting years of Solidarity, ABC News had a bureau in the capital, Warsaw, and it was staffed. To the extent that it was possible to report the news, we had the people there to do it. But the wall of martial law also comes down around a country's communications. Simply put, our people could not transmit their stories. Hell, they couldn't even make a phone call.

They got our first story out—in fact, it was the first television story anyone got out—by smuggling it with a courier. Officials certainly are concerned with what leaves a country when they've sealed it off, but they are much more anxious about what gets in. This means someone with his mind set on sneaking out, or sneaking something out, may be able to because the authorities have their sights set in the other direction.

Here's how it works, not just in Poland under martial law, but in any country where the stories we've prepared would never be allowed to leave if anyone in the government could see them. It's what we did, in fact, to get around the authorities in Afghanistan. There's more than one way to skin a censor.

The first task is, we find someone to act as our courier, someone who plans to leave the country. Sometimes in the open (as we did it in Afghanistan), sometimes (as in Poland) in stealth. We remove our "objectionable" videotape from its plastic cassette and wind it tightly around a pencil until it's about the size of a thimble. Then we give it to our civilian courier, along with the address and telephone number of an ABC News bureau on the outside. Someplace safe. Someplace staffed. Someplace findable. Then, we give him or her some money. Sometimes lots of it. We are asking these couriers to take a risk, and furthermore, we are entrusting them with the product of countless hours of work and a sometimes considerable financial investment. We call each courier a "pigeon."

Trouble is, we never know if the pigeon will deliver.

That's how it started at the outset of martial law in Poland. After the first piece of videotape made its way to our people on the outside, many more did not. Each had been given to a pigeon along with a fistful of greenbacks, but the deliveries were never made. Maybe the pigeons were uncovered and relieved of their forbidden cargo. Maybe they were caught and detained. Maybe they got out and never made the call. Maybe they never tried to get out. We never get the chance to find out. Pigeons are the best system for a bad situation, but they don't always fly.

That's why ABC's Warsaw staff finally decided to send a story out with the correspondent. Getting rid of the reporter may not make sense now, but it did at the time, because while this was the second story they actually *got* out, it was the ninth or tenth story they *tried* to get out. Someone trustworthy was going to have to carry it. The company can't spare the camera crew, which records the pictures and sound; can't let go of the producer, either, because that's who keeps the operation together. Of course you can't ask the Polish members of the support staff to jeopardize everything they've ever gained in their homeland for the sake of a piece on the news. So the correspondent who had been there was the logical choice to get the story out, which meant ABC needed me to get in.

The borders were sealed, but early one morning about a week into martial law, ABC's London-based assignment desk found one small leak. A Polish train, caught out in West Berlin when they closed the country, was going home *that night*.

When I got the call, my schedule gave a new definition to the word "packing." I wasn't packing just for me, but for everyone in the Warsaw bureau, and in a small way, for other Western journalists in Warsaw.

We knew there was a shortage of food there. There hadn't been a whole lot before, and now, nothing else was getting in. We knew there was a shortage of equipment, too. Our people had only a normal inventory of fresh batteries and raw videotape when the country shut down, and they had to be near the end of their supplies. We knew there was a shortage of communication. No mail was crossing the border. All phone lines for public use were cut. I'd better take an awfully big suitcase. It turned out to be my suitcase, my briefcase, and forty-three other cases. Wooden and cardboard cases with everything we could think of to take.

A member of the staff from the London bureau went to a suburban supermarket to shop. Big bags of coffee, sugar, rice; large sacks of apples, bananas, oranges; huge cans of tuna, spaghetti, beef. I went to the specialty store near Piccadilly Circus called Fortnum and Mason's. They don't carry rice. They do carry fine French cheese, and succulent caviar, and rich dark chocolate truffles. Don't forget, our people in Poland were suffering. And I would soon suffer with them!

Someone else in the bureau collected batteries and cassettes. Enough batteries to power a locomotive. Enough cassettes to keep a camera rolling for the locomotive's whole trip. And I put out a call to other American news organizations with bureaus in London. "If there's anything important you would like me to carry in," I told each one, "get it to my office by two o'clock." Exactly *how* I was carrying things in, I didn't say. If they didn't know about the Polish train, too bad. A few sent a case or two of food, some sent supplies. And half a dozen envelopes came through the door. Personal mail, professional instructions, pornographic magazines, maybe? It didn't matter to me. I was happy to be of service.

I flew to West Berlin where I was met by Ted, a Berliner who helped ABC in those days when we came to town. Ted, and his truck. We loaded my cargo on Ted's truck and raced from the airport to the railroad station. Four strong porters with four strong carts got my trunks on the train. And none too soon. By the time the last case was thrown on board, it was ten o'clock. Poland's government may have stepped backward in time, but its train was leaving on schedule.

I had a seat on the left side, and as we crawled out of the station, I lowered my window just to say thanks to Ted. But as I passed him by, he was standing on the platform with a uniformed railway man, deep in conversation. For a moment. Then he started running. Running in the same direction as the train.

It was like a scene from a Hollywood film about two lovers trying not to be separated. The train was speeding up. Ted was racing after it. And losing. He was frantically waving his arms. And shouting something. In German: *"Konnen Sie mir bitte helfen!"*

"What?" I shouted back, the gap between us growing. I don't speak German.

"Konnen Sie mir bitte helfen! Write it down!"

"Tell me in English!" I shouted back. Did the guy think I'd learned fluent German in the half minute we'd been apart?

"Will you help me please! *Konnen Sie mir bitte helfen!* Will you help me please! You will need it! You will have to ..." But then he was gone. Or rather, I was. Ted had run as far and as fast as he could. He was out of platform. My train was out of the station.

I jotted down and memorized what he told me, although I still didn't know why I'd need it. But I soon found out.

Fifteen minutes after pulling out of the station in West Berlin, we pulled into the station in East Berlin. And stopped. I didn't realize it, and Ted only realized it too late, but I was only on a German intercity shuttle. I'd have to figure out how to change trains with my suitcase, briefcase, and forty-three other cases! The Polish train was waiting somewhere here at the station in East Germany. Eastern Europe. Behind the iron curtain. If you think you know how it would look from the movies you've seen, you do, because Hollywood got it right. Three platforms, each with a powerful procession of railroad cars on either side, the engines spouting steam like wild animals pent up and waiting to break from a cage. And the sound of power from the undercarriages.

It was night. The locomotives' moisture clouded the dirty, old glass in the station's roof forty feet above, through which sunshine should flow in the daytime. Dampness seeped through the iron arches under which the trains come and go. Only one thing missing: movement. No trains moving, no people moving either. In fact, the only people on the lonely platforms were in uniform. Dandy. I didn't speak the language and I hardly knew where I was, but I had to figure out where the Polish train was and then how to get on it. I had to change trains, *fast*. With forty-three food and equipment cases, one suitcase, and a briefcase.

But I had Ted's crash course: *"Konnen Sie mir bitte helfen."* I asked the closest man in uniform. I didn't even have to look at my notes.

No response. Like I wasn't even there.

"Konnen Sie mir bitte helfen." I asked more carefully this time, each syllable separated from the next. But he didn't just look at me quizzically. He didn't look at me at all.

Well, that's how it is in these Communist countries, I thought to myself, having suffered dreadful service in other places in Eastern Europe where workers had no financial incentive to be polite. So I ran to the next guy in uniform. I *really* needed a porter.

"Konnen Sie mir bitte helfen." Another blank stare. Like he couldn't see me or hear me. Time was ticking by. It wasn't just that I didn't have many minutes to get my stuff off one train and onto another. It was that I didn't even have a clue where the other train was.

By now, though, I had learned how to take a hint. I quickly left the second disinterested German and ran to the third, dressed just the same. I suppose my mouth was halfway open to ask for help yet again when my eyes dropped to this third man's uniformed breast. The word on the badge was in German, but it wasn't hard to figure out, *"Volkspolizei."* Known to all who loved them as the *Vopo*. The East German People's Police. Only one thing at this point was now clear: I was on my own!

There was a long luggage cart just sitting there on the platform right next to my train, one of those motorized five- or six-piece sets of flatbeds connected together and pulled by a diesel tractor. Should I load my cases onto the flatbeds and hijack the whole thing?

Yes. I am in a hurry. Never say die.

Would I like to add East Berlin to my list of jails briefly inhabited?

No. It's only for a story.

A compromise came to mind. A measure to which the *Vopo* might not react. Something safe. Sort of. I disconnected the caboose. The final flatbed. I dragged it to the door of the train that brought me in. By now, everyone else was off.

Time was short. Frantically, I pulled my burdensome cases off the train and piled them onto the flatbed. One by one. They stood high. And heavy. I picked up the handle, the long pole meant to connect this flatbed to the one ahead of it. Then I pulled. Nowhere. So I pulled again. Nowhere again. I ran around to the back and pushed. It moved a bit. I pushed again. It moved a bit again.

But I couldn't steer the flatbed from the backside. I couldn't even see down the platform from the backside. Moreover, I still didn't know where I had to go. So I gave my overloaded flatbed a great big running push, enough to keep it moving until I could dash past it, grab the handle in front, and maintain its speed before momentum was lost. This was founded on the hope that it didn't crash into a sitting train first.

The operation was a success, at least for the moment. I was at a full run. Not to cut the time in half, but to keep the flatbed from flattening me. I barreled past all three *Volkspolizei* with my huge load. I wonder if they were sorry they passed up the tip. Now joined at the hip with my overloaded flatbed, I got to the front of the platform, the place where people normally would prance out from the station. But it was past midnight. There were no people. Only the *Vopo*. And somewhere, my train.

"*Warzasa?*" I shouted at a cleaning woman pushing a mop down the aisle of a rail car. One Polish word, badly pronounced, possibly incomprehensible to a Turkish cleaning lady in East Germany. One word that was meant to ask, Is-this-the-train-to-Warsaw-and-if-it-isn't-where-is-it-and-if-it-is-how-soon-does-it-leave? "*Warzasa?*" The result was too good to be true. Just as I got the essence of *Volkspolizei* a few minutes earlier, she got the idea of "*Warzasa*" now. She pointed to the train just across the platform. And to her wristwatch. But the train looked empty. I asked again. She pointed again.

An empty train? It figures. Who wants to ride *into* a country under martial law? Anyway, I had just barely stopped the flatbed from my frantic run before it ran over me. I had neither the energy nor the courage to get it moving again. So I started removing my cases from the flatbed and placing them on the train. Maybe ten were loaded when a figure emerged from the car ahead of me. I don't precisely remember the German that he bellowed, but from the tone alone, I sure knew what it meant: all aboard.

Now I was throwing the cases. Just pulling them from the flatbed and throwing them through the door of the train. Gee, I hope the jar of caviar isn't breakable. I threw the last case through the door of a *moving* train. And jumped on right behind it. Off came the coat. And the sweater. And the shirt. An unheated train station had turned into a steam bath. But we were moving. East. To Warsaw.

My car was empty. Once I cooled off, I roamed in both directions. On the whole train, there were just two passengers besides me. Each had a single suitcase. I had definitely over packed. I returned to my private car and dragged all my cases into a four-bunk compartment. Then I pulled down an upper bunk. And went to sleep. But just briefly. We stopped at the border between East Germany and Poland. Both were Warsaw Pact countries. The border was friendly. The East German immigration agent was not.

"Passport please," he said, but "please" can be uttered in a mean enough way that you know he would just as soon take your passport forcefully.

"Where are you going?" At least he spoke English.

"Warsaw."

He was leafing through my passport's foldout pages. "And where is your visa?"

My visa? I was heading for a country hermetically sealed by martial law, and this guy wanted to see a visa?

"I was told I shall have one when I arrive in Warsaw." Sometimes the lie works. But sometimes it doesn't.

"No. You cannot continue on this train without a visa."

Great. Wouldn't it be nice to be stuck in some small town on the scenic German-Polish border? Maybe I could empty out all my cases and build a house with them.

"I am a journalist, and my colleagues in Warsaw sent me a message that my visa will be approved when I arrive."

"I approve or not approve. You cannot continue on this train if I do not approve."

Now, an aside: most countries on earth make the Chicago of the sixties and seventies look clean. I don't mean free of litter, I mean free of corruption. This was one of them. You see, at first I was told I could not continue on the train without a visa. Now, I cannot continue without the immigration agent's approval. The train's standing still, but we're getting somewhere.

"What do I need to get your approval?" I was learning to play.

"You must decide," he told me. Then he stepped out of the compartment.

I decided fast. I folded a crisp hundred-dollar bill and hid it between two pages in my passport. Surely the visa would not be so important anymore. The agent stepped back in, spun on his heels accepting the passport without a word, and stepped out again. Not a minute later, the train was moving. And I was still on it.

I waited for the immigration agent to come back in with my passport, but he didn't. I went out to search, but didn't have to search far. The agent was gone, but my passport was sitting on the floor just outside my compartment. Either he was in cahoots with the locomotive crew to shake down passengers like me. Or he was working for himself. Or he dropped the passport, the money slipped through a crack, and the agent suddenly remembered a dinner date and hastily got off the train. Who knows? Who cares? Anyway, I was finally in western Poland and bound for Warsaw. And about to be shaken down again.

This time, there were two of them. Polish customs. A man and a woman. Not a word of English between them. For my part, not a word of Polish. A fine working relationship. We had been moving for maybe an hour when they arrived at my compartment door.

Actually, I didn't observe their arrival. I was asleep. Until one of them shined a flashlight in my slumbering face. The woman spoke first. But don't wait for the dialogue; she spoke in Polish. I produced my passport. I have no idea whether that's what she told me to do, but as she looked it over she seemed satisfied. And I do mean looked it over. Right side up, and upside down. She did everything but turn it inside out. It surprised me that a Polish customs agent would not at least recognize our alphabet, even if she couldn't actually read it. Or maybe she recognized it and was looking for a secret code. I didn't care. I just wanted her and her silent partner to leave the compartment so I could go back to sleep. I might as well have wanted a sirloin steak.

The silent one stayed silent, but motioned with his hands for me to step down to the floor. I had my socks on, but the floor was still cold. Still wet from boarding. He pointed to a case, one of them that was piled up on top of the rest. Then he shrugged as if to ask, "What the hell have you got in there?"

Well, I thought, *this will be easy. I'll tear it open, let 'em peek inside, say, "Nice getting to know you," and get on with my sleep.* Foiled again. The case contained food. The very first thing to catch the eye—their eyes, my eyes—was a clear plastic bag of ground coffee. Five pounds worth. When a country is governed by martial law, even the basic necessities are hard to get. Milk, medicine, a battery for your car. In this part of Poland, a luxury like coffee simply hadn't been seen for a while. The customs man lifted the bag from the case. *Aha*, I thought, *coffee is the price of my passage.*

But before I could smile at the shakedown and imply with my hands, "Go ahead, take it, I was carrying it just for you, Merry Christmas, now leave me alone," his female partner was ripping off the top and pouring the coffee on the floor. Obviously she's a tea drinker. The ground coffee was now soaking up the moisture on the floor. Had it been sawdust, this would have been a positive development.

I was able to communicate my panic and get the woman to stop pouring when only two or three pounds of coffee were ruined. But it was clear she was stopping only temporarily. They were looking for something, although I knew not what. But I do know how to cry uncle. I opened my briefcase, removed a newspaper, and spread it on the floor so that we could continue the festivities with no more damage to the coffee. Sleep would have to go on without me.

Nothing was spared. Boxes of rice, containers of cornflakes, sacks of flour. Eventually they came to a second big bag of coffee, just like the first one. Everything got searched and scanned and sifted. In fairness, I must admit they cut open only one chocolate truffle, and then gave the others a pass. Thank goodness there's still an ounce of decency in this world.

I didn't know what they were looking for. And after awhile, I was convinced they didn't know either. Then, as we raced past sleeping, snow-covered towns in western Poland, it began to make sense. This man and women had nice uniforms and badges. Right now they were on a train to Warsaw. In my mind, that was no great prize. Having been completely destroyed by the Nazis, Warsaw was hurriedly rebuilt after World War II in the architectural style of drab and the depressing color of grey. Furthermore, life there under martial law was tough. But if you were an employee of Polish customs and you compared Warsaw to the kinds of rural villages through which your train regularly passed, villages that the central government completely ignored, Warsaw was wonderful.

Of course, compared to our way of life, "wonderful" is the last word you would use, and that was because of a number of things—from restricted freedoms to limited opportunities to the way the economy was managed. Even before martial law, consumer commodities were in short supply in Warsaw and the rest of Poland. This was thanks to the miracle of central government planning. The message from the government to industrial managers within the system was, "Always build less than the people need. That way, nothing will ever go to waste." It worked. There was never enough.

For instance, on the route I always walked from my hotel to our bureau during previous visits before martial law, there was an appliance store. I didn't know that because of anything I saw inside, because there never was anything inside. I only knew because I'd been told. Well, late one night, probably at about one or two in the morning, I was returning from the bureau to the hotel. There was a long line of people, fifty or more, patiently waiting outside the store. I looked inside; still no appliances. It turns out that they were lined up because word had leaked out that some washing machines would be delivered. Maybe. Sometime.

I walked on, went to sleep, got up, got dressed, and walked back to the bureau at about ten in the morning. Guess what? The line was still there. Later that day, the truck pulled up. Two dozen washers were sold right off the back. The losers went home empty-handed to await word of the next shipment. And the store stayed empty. That was the beauty of central planning. It provided shortfalls big and small.

There was another store on the corner just down the street from the perpetually empty appliance store. This one sold candy. Not nice, dark Swiss chocolates, which I used to bring in by the bundle every time I went to Warsaw. Just hard sugar candies, the kind dentists love your kids to suck. No matter what the weather—Warsaw's winter can be about as wet and cold as they come—two lines snaked out of the store from the opening bell until closing time. One line was for working folks. The other was for pregnant women and senior citizens. Maybe if you were a pregnant senior citizen, you didn't have to wait at all. This was the only place in the whole city to buy a handful, which was the limit, of hard sugar candies. If you wanted some, but didn't have time to wait yourself, you asked along the pregnant/senior line until you found someone who didn't want any candy personally, but was waiting to be paid to wait for you. For two hours, sometimes more. That's how "wonderful" Warsaw was.

But at least a washing machine could be found there for a lucky few, and sugary candies could be bought if someone wanted to go through the pain. And at least in Warsaw there was food for the family. So maybe the efficiency of the customs man and woman on the train made sense. If you had that uniform, and that badge, and the assurance that there probably would be something to eat when you got home, wouldn't you carry your job to the extreme to make sure nothing untoward got into the country on your shift? So that you could *keep* the job? I'm not sure how tiny contraband could possibly be, but these Polish customs officials going through my things on the train left nothing to the imagination. If they had one.

Some of the cases contained not food, but equipment. Batteries, tapes, cables, and so forth. Believe me, if they could have taken the batteries apart, they would have. They did take the tapes apart. A few of them. Then they evidently decided it was too much trouble to take them all apart, so they stopped.

Good, I thought, *my tapes are home free.* They weren't. They were confiscated.

The briefcase came last. That's where I had my money and the envelopes from other news organizations. This is when I really began to sweat. One envelope really caught their eyes. Or more accurately, their noses. I had noticed it myself when it arrived at my office in London. It was heavily perfumed. Nothing else was. It was addressed to one of my competitors stuck in Warsaw, a correspondent with NBC.

By now, these customs agents and I had established a perfectly workable system of hand signals to converse. Other than the odd word between the two of them, we went about our business in silence. The man signaled to me to open the envelope addressed to my colleague from the competition. It smelled so strong, I half expected liquid perfume to pour out. But it was only a greeting card.

I should tell you, my wife and I knew this correspondent and his wife personally. Fun people. Fun enough, I knew, that the card would be fun to read. And maybe raunchy. Which is why I didn't want to look. If she had written him something private, it should stay private. But Polish customs didn't care. Then again, not understanding a word of English, Polish customs didn't know. Both agents were holding the card, each pinching a lower corner, treating it with the same confusion as my passport. Gee, maybe it makes more sense upside-down-and-backward.

Placing respect above curiosity, I deliberately looked away, but they shoved the card under my nose. Damn good place for a perfumed card I suppose, but it also meant I got an unintended glance at the cover. X-rated.

They wouldn't take it away. First one, and then the other made it very clear that they wanted me to read the card, and then somehow tell them if it contained any secrets that compromised the Communist empire. I planted my feet in coffee grounds and refused to even look. Eventually, the bureaucrats with the badges gave up. But I did give a lot of thought to what I might have learned, and what my correspondent friend could expect when he got home. Lucky boy.

I kept wondering why these two protectors of the Polish people didn't go forward in the train and roust the other two passengers. Maybe because they didn't like leafing through cold, dirty underwear? Or maybe because they liked cold cash better. When at long last they leafed through my plentiful supply of English pounds sterling, I didn't take my eyes off them. And they didn't take their eyes off the money. The man motioned for me to follow him. We had been at this futile exercise of going through every ounce of property for more than two hours. Even a trip to the compartment next door sounded good. So I grabbed my briefcase. He grabbed an opened cardboard case. It didn't seem to matter what was inside.

The compartment next door is exactly where he took me. He shut the sliding door, drew the drapes, and then sat on one bunk. I faced him from another. He put the cardboard case on his lap; I put the briefcase on mine. He took a pencil from his pocket and started writing numbers on the cardboard. That's why he brought the case from next door. But in the poor light, with shaky script on flimsy cardboard on a vibrating train, it didn't make sense.

Then he turned it around to face me. There was an "£," the traditional sign for English pounds sterling. And a figure to the right of it. It didn't reflect the total amount I had in the briefcase, but about a fourth of it. I took his pencil from his hand, leaned over to his cardboard tablet, and drew a question mark. What was he trying to tell me?

He put his hand in his pocket and pulled out some *zlotys*. A fistful of *zlotys*, the unpronounceable Polish currency (which in fact is pronounced "*zwoties*," despite the letter "l"). Then he took back the pencil and drew a question mark of his own.

As some multi-linguist once said, it was déjà vu all over again. In other words, I had been there before. This guy simply wanted to change money with me. Like citizens of beleaguered nations the world over, all he wanted was to get rid of his almost worthless local currency and put his hands on so-called "hard" currency, bills that would buy something outside of Poland. What he was asking me was, "Will you trade about a fourth of your English pounds for *zlotys*? I will give you a lot more than the bank will."

He was a portable black market. If the official exchange rate at the bank was thirty *zlotys* to the pound, he would give me a hundred. That's more than three times the legal rate. It's also illegal. But what it meant was, if from the bank, my £1000 would get me just 30,000 *zlotys;* from him, I'd get 100,000.

And he'd get £1000. Either he could use it in another country, which as a customs agent traveling on trains was a possibility, or he could use it in the other kind of black market, the kind where you can only buy essential items even in your own country with "hard" currency, like dollars or deutschmarks or pounds sterling. Meat, car batteries, soap. Why should people with something valuable to sell let go of their precious commodities for money that no one wants?

I had only two problems with his proposal.

First, maybe he was trying to set me up. Maybe as soon as I'd agree to change money, he'd clamp my wrists in handcuffs and earn himself a fancy commendation down at headquarters. After all, this guy *was* wearing a badge. But I decided to go for it. Maybe if we made a deal, he and his female partner, who so far as I knew was still next door trying to figure out the X-rated greeting card, would disappear into the night.

But second, even if he wasn't setting me up, I had no idea what to negotiate. Sure, I'd changed money on the black market in Asia and Africa and elsewhere in Eastern Europe, but you can't get a good deal unless you know what you're dealing with. I hadn't been in Poland for half a year and didn't even remotely remember what the official exchange rate was. Could have been thirty to one; could have been three to one. So I bluffed. He made his first offer. I took the pencil and made a counteroffer. He studied the figure like it was the Polish Constitution and then shook his head from side to side and counter offered again.

Now, I was into it. Kind of like the title character in Monty Python's *Life of Brian* trying to get a better deal on a hat to hide his face, as the Roman legions galloped closer to his capture. I shook my head the way he'd shaken his, clicked my tongue the way cartoonists want you to read "tsk, tsk, tsk, tsk, tsk," and wrote a figure on the cardboard that seemed so outrageously high that he might stomp out and have me arrested for insulting a representative of the government.

But he didn't. He just sucked in his breath, a long painful suck, and grimaced, kind of like this was the most difficult thing he'd ever had to do. And then he nodded. A good thing. We had a deal. I opened my briefcase, got out £1000, and held it in my hand. He drew his *zlotys* from his pocket, counted out 20,000, and held them in his hand. We were like

Soviets and Americans in the old days, about to exchange prisoners at the Brandenburg Gate in divided Berlin. Who would make the first move? Who would take the first risk? Who would give away more than he got?

I would. I placed my packet of pounds sterling on the box. He put his handful of *zlotys* on my briefcase. Never a word uttered, never a handshake, rarely a straight look in the eye. He rose, opened the sliding door, and left. I followed, but in the fifteen-second gap I allowed in order to avoid seeing him in the hallway, he evidently signaled to his partner that they got what they came for, because when I reentered my own compartment next door, she was gone too. It cost me a night's sleep, some blank videotapes, a few pounds of coffee, and a bit of grief, but at least personally I came out ahead. I thought.

When I arrived in Warsaw, one of my first questions was about the current exchange rate. How well had I done in my silent negotiations? Not as well as I thought. Not even as well as I'd have done *at the bank.*

I had dealt with a real pro. The customs man had read me like a book. The figure to which he ultimately and painfully agreed was still well below the legal rate of exchange. Had I held my ground and insisted I wouldn't do something illegal, I would have taken my £1000 to the bank and gotten *30,000 zlotys*, not the 20,000 the customs man gave me. The man with the badge made out like a bandit. I made out like a fool.

What did I learn from the fleecing? Stay off Polish trains.

I WAS ONLY DRIVING AN AMBULANCE ON THE RUSSIAN FRONT

Tripoli, Libya, and Beirut, Lebanon

BOTH BEIRUT, LEBANON, AND TRIPOLI, LIBYA, *have long been known as cities where "anything goes." But in very different ways.*

The reputation of Beirut for many years has been, you get what you pay for, or during its dark days, what you could win in battle. There was no limit to the size of your booty if you had enough money, enough thugs, or enough guns. This was true not just during the worst days of the Lebanese civil war; it has been true since the beginning of modern times, when Beirut became the trading capital and sin city of the Middle East. Because nowadays it's trying to woo Middle Eastern tourists who get hassled trying to travel to the post-9/11 United States or Europe, Beirut in some ways still lives up to its reputation.

In Tripoli, to this day, you get what the government gives you. But there is no limit to its generosity if it believes that by helping you, it can help itself. For years, with its own considerable oil wealth, Libya had no need for other people's money. But because of its many years as an international pariah stemming from its support for terrorists, Libya constantly tried to colorize its image. When the government saw fit, it used its limited capacity for goodwill to the hilt.

What both cities had in common was the absence of consistency. In Beirut, the man who was your friend one day was your enemy the next. Loyalty there during the fifteen-year civil war was almost as cheap as life.

In Tripoli, the man who propelled you one day stood in your path the next. Loyalty there fluctuated at the mercy of the leadership.

Neither society operates by the rules that guide us in Western nations. But that is not to say that they don't have rules. They do. Even less flexible than our own. The biggest difference between them and us is, sometimes you have to follow their rules not just to get things done, but to get out of the place alive.

•   •   •   •   •

Ed Wilson was a bad man.

He may still be, but the length of his reach was long ago limited by the longer arm of the law, which had him safely set aside for a sentence of fifty-two years of hard time, effectively the rest of his life, in a cell at "Supermax," the maximum security, federal penitentiary in Florence, Colorado. Wilson was put away for gunrunning, selling tons of explosives to Libya, even for conspiring to murder two of his prosecutors. But because the feds fabricated some of the evidence against him, Wilson won parole in 2004. We may never know whether he did a whole lot of harm before he got caught. All we know is, evidently he tried.

Ed Wilson had been a spook at the Central Intelligence Agency. A trench coat kind of guy who developed a taste for fur. One day, someone in Washington looked up and saw that this government employee, on a CIA salary, owned a big ranch in Virginia, several fancy cars, and yes, fur. More than a civil servant ought to be able to afford. So Wilson left the agency, under a cloud and at the start of an investigation, and became an arms dealer. Everyone suspected in fact that that's what he had been doing even before retiring from the government. He eventually even argued that he did his deals with the complicity of his former employer, the CIA.

By definition, arms dealers make deals with shady people. Sometimes drug dealers, sometimes terrorists, sometimes mercenaries, sometimes foreign governments looking to evade weapons export laws. Maybe some arms dealers never break a law. Maybe some elephants can fly. Ed Wilson can't.

Through his association with shady clients, Wilson came into contact with a cousin of Libya's leader, Col. Qadhafi. A cousin whose job was to keep Libya, and its protégés, well armed. Eventually, Wilson's association with Libya's leadership became a partnership. He would get them what they wanted; they would pay him well. Capitalism at its finest. And when the United States government began to look more closely at Wilson's dealings and threatened to put him behind bars, Libya sweetened the contract. A villa outside Tripoli, a safe haven. After all, Wilson could conduct business from a telephone in Tripoli just about as effectively as he could from one in Washington.

ABC News wasn't the first one on the story. The *New York Times* was. In its *Sunday Magazine*, the *Times* presented chapter and verse about this former CIA spy who, allegedly with help from former colleagues, had set up a profitable terrorist-assistance factory in Libya. It appeared that he was importing not just explosives for terrorists, but explosives experts. Some former U.S. Special Forces guys who couldn't turn down the big bucks Wilson could offer. He had plenty of money from oil-rich Libya. And plenty of space in the villa.

Their most notable invention: an exploding lamp. Apparently, they designed this handy little gadget to blow up in the face of the first person to turn it on. Perfect for hotels, yachts, and other places where the targets of terrorists like to hang out and switch on lamps. The *New York Times* story was credible. But unbelievable. A onetime sworn agent of the U.S. government would do *this*? ABC sent me down along with a producer, Liz, and a camera crew, to talk to Wilson.

Fine. Our government has charged the guy with selling twenty tons of explosives to Libya and wants to nab him and put him on trial, but they can't get to him. Yet I'm supposed to find him in Tripoli and just sidle on up with camera crew in tow and start chatting. Maybe elephants *can* fly.

But an assignment is an assignment. I didn't earn frequent flyer miles with Libyan Airways, but the warm weather sounded nice. So we started with a telex. To the ministry of information. "ABC News would like to enlist your cooperation on a project that will clarify the role of the Libyan people in a matter where the United States government says it believes one of its own citizens has broken the law." That was the gist of it. You see, a message to the Libyan government has to be phrased carefully. Because first, you can't afford to offend their sensitivities. And second, you don't want to actually be identified with the U.S. government. And third, officially, there is no Libyan government.

So, in our telex, we appealed to "the Libyan people." I don't know if all 5 million Libyans, the population in those days, voted on our request, but someone speaking on their behalf responded with the promise of visas and an invitation to come on down. Already, we were closer than the U.S. government.

By that evening, we were on a plane. And by the next morning, in the office of the committee's representative for the dispersal of information, a.k.t.o.a. (also known to outsiders as) the minister of information. Unfortunately, we made little progress on our request to get to Wilson before a bigger story about Libya and the United States broke right there in our laps. It was the dustup between the two American fighters and the two Libyan jets. The ones the Americans ended up shooting down. The incident ended up preoccupying us, as well as all of the "Libyan people's committees," for several days. But when the dust finally settled, we finally got back to the information minister and, after tea and pleasantries, picked up where we had left off.

"Libya looks bad," I told the minister once the Wilson matter came up. At times, I am a master of the obvious.

"So what else is new?" he responded, or words to that effect. The man was nothing if not realistic.

"Helping us talk to Mr. Wilson cannot hurt Libya's international image," I went on, "and if he tells the truth, it can help." Bear in mind, I was under no obligation to be accurate. Remember too, the minister's version of "the truth" may have been ever so slightly different from ours.

Liz and I threw in a few other arguments to win the government's (oops, sorry, *there is no government* in Libya) cooperation and then went back to our cruise ship to await a response.

Yes, our cruise ship. It was a ferryboat actually, one that normally makes the fairly short journey across the Mediterranean from Athens to Tripoli and back. But it was tied up in Tripoli's port, and we were assigned to sleep there. Were the city's hotels genuinely overcrowded? Or were we genuinely being kept under wraps, so we couldn't go snooping on our own? Just for the fun of it, we asked everyone we encountered. Never got an answer.

But on the third night of waiting—in the *middle* of the third night of waiting—we did get a knock on the door. And a voice, in English with a thick Arab accent: "We take you, ten minutes."

"Take us where?"

"You find out. No cameras." Hollywood sure has brought the world together.

In ten minutes, we were in a van. Blindfolded. Someone smarter than us might have been scared. We were elated. The more they do to throw you off the scent in a place like Libya, the closer you are to where you want to be. And they did a lot. By my reckoning, they drove us around for more than an hour. Around and around and around. Between us, we didn't have enough fingers and toes to keep track of all the turns. When finally we pulled to a stop, they let us take off the blindfolds. We were at the entrance of a concrete apartment building, eight or ten stories tall. With other tall buildings alongside.

Having been in Tripoli before, I knew we still were. There was no place else within five hundred miles with buildings this size. Which means they spent all that time driving us around in circles to throw us off when they could have achieved the same thing in ten minutes. I guess in a country like that, at a time like that, gasoline was cheap. And paranoia, high.

We were taken into the building, into an elevator, into an apartment. A barely furnished apartment, pretty obviously chosen only for this rendezvous. And there he was. A big bear of a man. With short cropped graying hair, an apparently permanent suntan, and a painfully thin but awfully wide smile, as if to say, "Gee, fella, I can't figure out why you'd wanna see lil' ol' me." His slap on the back, which almost threw me through the window, confirmed it: his strategy was to convince us there had been a misunderstanding, he was just a good ol' boy who has done no wrong, or as some Nazis said after the Second World War, "I was only driving an ambulance on the Russian front."

We sat down to explain and then negotiate.

"The story's out there," I told Wilson, referring to the *New York Times* piece. "If it isn't accurate, this is your chance to tell your side." He already had figured that part out.

"Oh, I'm willing to talk about it," he said, "but I have to have certain guarantees. You understand, buddy."

No I didn't.

"First of all, I have to know that you won't cut up what I say to make me look bad."

I was tempted to tell him what I always say in defense of the news media whenever someone charges us with distortion: "The media cannot make you look silly, or stupid, or corrupt, without your cooperation." But I held my tongue. I was afraid if I didn't, he would.

"Second, buddy, I can't let you show my face. It's not that I have anything to hide. I just don't want to be changing planes at the airport in Atlanta—as you might imagine, I do have a few other passports under other names—and have some little old, blue haired lady shout, 'Hey, isn't that the spy who's helping Libya?'" Ed Wilson was a federal fugitive.

Liz and I explained that we could not guarantee the first request because ABC News never had and never would let the subject of a story dictate the content of a story. But we could surely guarantee the second because by lighting and shooting Wilson in silhouette, we could physically preclude the possibility of anybody seeing his face. I told him so.

"I'll have to think about it," Wilson said. "I'll let you know, buddy. Thanks for coming up." As if, when invited a few hours earlier with "We take you, ten minutes," we'd had a choice.

Back to the van, back to the blindfolds, back to the ship. This time, they drove us in a fairly straight line. I guess at four in the morning, when the temperature even at night doesn't drop much below ninety, Libyan henchmen get pretty tired too.

It didn't take my new buddy Ed but a single day to decide that a taped interview might do him some good. He's a smart cookie, so I don't know why he made the decision to cooperate, but he did. I wouldn't have.

The next night, the same routine. A summons and a blindfolded ride in the middle of the night. The difference this time: "Bring cameras." We did. It was the same apartment, but now there was a bit more furniture. "Spin control" is not an exclusive American trait.

Bob, the cameraman, worked hard to light Wilson so that he could not be identified. There is no harder lighting job than one in which the subject is in silhouette, while everything around him can be seen.

Then we did the interview. I talked with Ed Wilson for nearly an hour and twenty minutes, and to hear him tell it, *he really did* darned near drive an ambulance on the Russian front. Wilson didn't just finesse each charge made in the *New York Times* story and in subsequent research done on my behalf at ABC News in New York. He flatly denied each and every point.

They weren't explosives, no, they were chemicals for pharmaceutical drugs. They weren't explosives experts, no, they were old buddies spending time on the desert ranch. And two dozen other denials. Considering that there were three or four Libyans in the room to whom we had *not* been introduced, and that Wilson has a forbidding presence himself, I did my best to pierce holes in his story and pin him down, but couldn't exactly press him to the wall. It was his wall, you see.

We finished, I assured him I would do my best to be fair when editing the story, he said, "Call me next time you're in town, buddy," and we left. Gee, he forgot to give me his card.

Maybe Wilson didn't admit any crimes, but it was still a fascinating conversation, not to mention something even more important in television news: it was an "exclusive." So Liz and the crew and I agreed that we should not let the cassettes out of our sight for the balance of our Libyan holiday and ought to catch the first flight out of the country once daylight came. The next flight to *anywhere*. We feared that maybe Wilson would decide in the next few hours that the interview wasn't such a good idea after all. Or maybe the Libyans would. We didn't want to give any of them the chance.

Luck was with us. There was a flight to London. It was on Libyan Arab Airways, so I didn't really relax until we touched down on friendly territory, but we and our cassettes were in ABC's London bureau by mid afternoon. England's dreary, drizzly climate rarely felt better.

By that time, I had listened to my personal audio recording of the interview and selected dozens of remarkable statements this fugitive had made. On my travel typewriter, I punched out a verbatim of each one. Then I organized them into a story script and faxed it to New York. Minutes later, the executive producer of *World News Tonight* called back.

"Do it all. How long is it?"

"Four minutes, maybe four and a half."

"Don't go longer." Four minutes, let alone four and a half, was an eternity on the network news. I always used to joke that if I were assigned to cover the resurrection of Jesus Christ, they'd probably give me three minutes because it would be a major story. So this was *good*. But I needed to explain how we had shot our interview.

"Something I've got to tell you. You're not going to see the guy. He wouldn't talk to us unless we'd shoot him in silhouette."

"Great!" came word from the other side. "Makes it better. Don't go longer than four and a half." Click. Such is the substance of many talks with the boss. They leave you flattered, but uneasy. I didn't know how uneasy until later.

We got right to work. First thing was to check the sound bites on paper against the sound bites on tape. There's always the chance of a glitch in the audio that was recorded on the videotape, making it unusable.

Not to worry. The sound was just fine.

But the picture wasn't. Wilson was in the dark all right, but not dark enough. Someone videotaping the broadcast, and then putting his face on "pause," *might* make out a feature or two. Tom, the guy in charge of technical wizardry in London, proposed a relatively easy solution. We ran all four cassettes through a machine called a "time base corrector." This thing could actually remove light from a picture. And did. I would be true to my word. My buddy Ed would not be identifiable. True to my word to a guy who was on the lam for breaking federal law.

It was a relatively simple piece to cut. A little slow on the eyes, but simple. A sound bite in silhouette, and then a line or two from me, and then another sound bite, another segue, and so forth. It took up less time than I'd thought—just a few seconds more than four minutes flat—and less time to edit than I'd have guessed.

The first transmission of *World News Tonight* was at 6:30 PM New York time. That meant 11:30 at night in London. Usually, when cutting a story, you work right up to the moment the anchorman says "Good Evening" and sometimes, if your stomach is strong, beyond. I didn't need a strong stomach this time though. I was through by ten o'clock. And home by 10:30. And asleep by eleven. And awakened at two in the morning. By the telephone.

You have to understand, if you haven't heard one yourself, a British telephone sounds like a fire alarm. In fact, I truly believe a British phone was used as the model for a fire alarm. Even after it rings in the middle of the day, your internal organs have to settle back into place. After it rings in the middle of the night, you need new ones.

I was already rattled by the ring. Then came the wrath!

"You lying scum son of a bitch you snowed me and you're gonna pay for it you fucking lying son of a bitch you're gonna be sorry you ever met me you son of a bitch asshole reporter ..."

It was my buddy Ed, from Tripoli. He seemed upset.

" ... You are scum of the earth you son of a bitch you double-crossed me you're gonna be sorry ..."

Or something along those lines. Honestly, I'm not absolutely sure of the *order* of the words, and I sure wasn't sitting there writing them down. I promise you though, they were all in there. And honestly, I didn't time his tirade, but I'm sure it lasted a year or two—well, a minute or two, anyway. It only seemed longer. When Ed finally ran out of breath, I squeezed in.

"Ed, I don't know what the fuck you're talking about ..."

When in Rome, *talk* like the Romans do.

" ... but I haven't lied to you, I haven't double-crossed you, and if you'll calm down and explain to me what pissed you off, maybe I can figure out what the fuck is wrong."

Might as well talk tough. When this guy threatens, even from Tripoli, he can back it up.

"I was getting into bed," Wilson starts, "when the phone starts ringing, and it never stops. Friends in the States, telling me, 'Hey Ed, you looked great on TV.' I say, 'Whaddya mean I looked great?' and they tell me they saw me, clear as day."

Right about now I'm wondering whether Bangladesh would make a comfortable hiding place.

"Bullshit," I told Wilson, "I was in the edit room every moment while we cut the story, and *you could not be seen.*" Of course, that wasn't going to convince him of much. His friends had just called him saying, "You looked great."

"Look," I pleaded, hoping my voice wouldn't *sound* like I was pleading, "There's got to be an explanation. I'll find out what happened, I don't care who I have to bother in New York, and if you give me your number, I'll call you back as soon as I can." He gave me the number and agreed to wait.

Great. Now I really could call him directly, next time I went to Tripoli. After all, we were buddies. As for the problem at hand, I didn't have much to go on, except one theory. We had taken some light out of the picture with the time base corrector before cutting and feeding the piece to New York. Maybe the technicians in New York had put the light back in, and then some. I didn't know whether they could do something like that, but I was sure hoping they had. Otherwise ...

I reached Jeff Gralnick, the executive producer. I told him about Ed's call and asked him if he could figure out what happened. He could. And did. No, nobody put light back into the picture. But the art department put another picture, Ed's picture from a file of photographs, over Peter Jennings' shoulder when he introduced the story. Sure Ed looked great; the picture was ten years old. Jeff apologized, because he remembered my explanation that Wilson would only agree to be seen in silhouette. It was a simple screwup in communication between him and the art department.

I called and apologized to Ed. To his credit, and my survival, he accepted the apology and the explanation. He made no more threats. But this time, he didn't invite me to call him next time I came to Tripoli. I don't think I would have anyway.

As a postscript, Ed Wilson didn't spend a whole lot more time in Tripoli. The United States Justice Department lured him to a Caribbean island, supposedly neutral territory, to discuss the federal charges against him and maybe negotiate a reduction. When Wilson bit, they pulled a switcheroo, a "sting," and bundled him back to the United States where he stood trial and went to jail.

Subsequently, Ed Wilson was convicted and then had his sentence lengthened for plotting from prison to kill those two prosecutors, plus five witnesses from his trial, as well as a former cellmate who became a snitch for the FBI. My buddy, Ed. Maybe he isn't such a smart cookie after all. I'm glad we didn't get to be closer friends. But now he's running free, and I'll just have to hope that in his senior years, he doesn't run real fast.

One guy who did get to be his close friend, though, was a guy named Frank Terpil. He was a lot like Wilson, but it took him a lot longer to get caught. He lived the high life in Cuba. Until 1995.

Terpil also had been a spook with the CIA, and also had developed a taste for things a government salary can't buy. For a while, Terpil and

Wilson worked together, providing arms to whoever hired them. Then they split up, a divorce of convenience. Wilson had found his fortune in Libya. Terpil found his in Lebanon.

Weapons in Lebanon were like an American Express card. No one wanted to leave home without one. Kidnappers, bodyguards, terrorists, highway robbers, militiamen of every stripe. On my most recent trip there, in late 2008, guns still were all the fashion. But back in the eighties, they were just about the only fashion, and Frank Terpil had the background and the connections to cash in on the fad. Like Wilson, he recruited some former colleagues to come to Lebanon and help him. Sure, by selling arms to foreign agents he was breaking American law, but he was doing it in Beirut. Who could touch him?

I could. At least ABC thought so. After getting to Ed Wilson in the middle of a hostile country, ABC thought maybe I could get to Frank Terpil in the middle of another one. The *New York Times* had tried. Without success. *Newsweek* magazine had tried. Without success. CBS's *60 Minutes* had tried. Without success. Now, my turn.

Naturally, in Lebanon, you wouldn't work through the government the way you would in Libya. Realistically, at least back then, there was no government to work through. Instead, you'd go to the underworld. Beirut is just a big city full of small neighborhoods. When you're wandering around this Middle Eastern city with a Western complexion, either you find the underworld, or it finds you.

You put out word that you want to meet Terpil. You put it out to everybody and then sit back and see who reacts.

And you could sit back rather comfortably. You didn't even have to say, "Contact me at such-and-such a place," because there was only one place you could possibly be: the Commodore Hotel in West Beirut, on the Muslim side of the forbidden no-man's zone called the Green Line. Home to the press corps, and to every inventive expense account scam that hadn't already been created in the first 6 million years of human life.

The Terpil trip was kind of nice, really. On other trips to Beirut, I'd have to cover the fighting, which was about as common there as breathing. It was a daily obligation. This time, I'd have to spend a couple of days poking around dark spaces, but then I'd be a free man. Sort of. That was the other side of Beirut. You were never completely free because violence was always right around the corner. Literally.

One day, for instance, while waiting to get some sort of message about Terpil, I went to lunch with a couple of colleagues at a restaurant about a mile from the Commodore. We took one of the ABC cars and armed drivers constantly at our disposal. It was a fine French restaurant. White tablecloths, silver service, crystal goblets, crème caramel.

While we were ordering, another party breezed in. Its host was Walid Jumblatt, son of the longtime warlord of the Druze political party and, since his father's assassination, the main Druze warlord himself. Lebanon still is a nation of principalities.

Once we took notice of our infamous neighbor, we took no more notice of his party. We ate, smacked our lips, and walked back to the car. Our driver had gone for a quick bite himself and then returned and double-parked beside another chauffeured car, a Mercedes. It was Jumblatt's. His chauffeur was dozing inside. We got in our car and pulled out for the Commodore. But we never made it. About halfway back, there was a huge explosion behind us. We wheeled around and rushed back toward a rising plume of thick dark smoke.

A car bomb. Everyone in sight was running from the scene. People knew from experience that sometimes a second car bomb goes off, calculated to kill the rescuers and spectators who respond to the first one, the kind of thing that became all too familiar to us in Iraq.

We couldn't get our car any closer, so we jumped out and ran toward the chaos. The Mercedes next to which we had been double-parked just a minute or two earlier was a blackened shell. The driver, who I humanely hope was still dozing when the bomb went off, was sitting at the wheel, just as we had last seen him.

Except he was dead. And destroyed. No skin, no scalp, no organs. Just a charred skeleton, still waiting for its passengers.

The others were scattered up and down the street. Including Walid Jumblatt, dazed and bloody. Luckily for him, the remote controlled bomb was rigged to blow out in one direction, as he was entering the car from the other.

Welcome to Beirut. The Paris of the Middle East.

When we wrapped up our coverage of the assassination attempt, we found our own driver and got into his car to finish our short trip back to the hotel. We told him he'd better be nice to us. Otherwise, next time we went to lunch, we'd stay a little longer for coffee.

Back to the waiting game, which didn't last much longer. After a couple more days, while sitting at the Commodore bar, a Lebanese man came up behind me and put a folded piece of paper on the bar. Before I could unfold it, he was gone. It said, "Come to the coffee shop at the Alexander. One hour." That's it. Not another word.

Bear in mind, this wasn't like an invitation to meet someone at the

Plaza in New York. The Alexander was a hotel on the Christian side of the city, which meant the *other* side of the Green Line from where I was. It was more like getting a summons in Hanoi during the Vietnam War to meet someone at the Caravelle in Saigon. There were going to be lots of guns trained on you en route.

I got up and went looking for Shakib. He was ABC's "fixer" in Beirut, a member of the Druze community. He was not Christian, but not quite Muslim either. Most important, Shakib could deal with almost all sides in the daily conflicts within the city. His own daughter had been kidnapped as part of the tribal warfare a few months earlier, yet he still treated all sides with equanimity.

I hadn't told him why I was in Beirut. I hadn't told anybody. That was for their protection, as well as mine. But Shakib knew it was some sort of shady project. Just the fact that I'd tell him I was going to disappear for a few hours, and then suddenly would reappear to pass idle hours at the hotel bar, meant I wasn't working on a conventional story.

As I had done each time I left the hotel, I told Shakib I was going out. Not where, just out. As he had on each prior occasion, he warned me that Beirut was a dangerous place for a foreigner alone, particularly a Western foreigner, and especially a Western foreign journalist! As always, he offered me a car and armed driver. As always, I said no. Operating without an entourage was the only way I was going to succeed.

I left the hotel, walked a few crowded blocks through the busy bazaar of the streets, and got in a taxi. I had it take me to a crossing point along the Green Line. In those days, a crossing point on the Green Line in Beirut was like Checkpoint Charlie in Berlin before the Wall came down. Heavy arms protected by sandbags on each side, all aimed at the other side. With snipers on the rooftops.

In one sense, journalists in Beirut were privileged people. We had passes permitting us to be on either side of the line. But still, crossing was like a game. It would only be deadly if you lost. The militia groups all knew that each of us carried every group's pass. Christian and Druze and Muslim, Hezbollah and Amal and PLO. But God help you if you showed the wrong pass to the wrong people.

I showed the right one. The militiamen on the Muslim side let me out. Yes, you even needed permission to *leave* one group's zone as well as to enter. Then, after running in a zigzag pattern from one side to another, I showed the right one again. The militiamen on the Christian side let me in. I caught another taxi, had him take me to within two blocks of the Alexander, and got out. Had I seen too many spy movies?

The hotel was on a hill. The coffee shop was long and bright. Long means there were basically two long rows of tables and booths. Bright means one long wall was all glass. The coffee shop overlooked the hotel's outdoor parking lot.

Once inside, I didn't know what to expect. Would Frank Terpil walk up and greet me? Would a gunfight break out? Would all the customers turn around and yell "Surprise" for my birthday? No, no, and no.

It was just a coffee shop with half a dozen customers, none of whom seemed to even glance up at my arrival. I took a seat in a small booth with my back to the wall. This meant I could keep an eye on the parking lot and see who drove up. I had *not* watched all those spy movies for nothing.

While I was keeping my vigilant eyes open for anything untoward, someone sat down beside me. I mean, this guy with a brown leather briefcase just materialized out of nowhere, set the briefcase under the table, and sat down beside me. He was not an Arab. Not his skin, not his hair, not his accent. He was an American. It wasn't Terpil—I had seen Terpil's picture before coming to Beirut—but he claimed to be Terpil's "associate." No name, just an "associate."

"Why do you want to meet Frank?" This confirmed that he was not an Arab. If he were, we'd have blown the first twenty minutes on polite chatter over cups of sugary tea.

"Because there are stories written about him in the States," I answered, "and I want to ask him if they're true."

"How do I know you're who you say you are and not working for the government?" This guy cut to the quick.

"Because I brought a picture. Take it, fax it to your associates in the United States, ask them if I'm a correspondent for ABC News, or not."

Of course that wouldn't really prove anything. There have been cases over the years of overtly legitimate journalists covertly feeding information to the U.S. government. Those who did so hurt the credibility of those who did not. But my offer seemed to convince the guy that I was who I said I was.

"Tell me what you want to ask Frank. Maybe I can answer some of your questions, and if you've still got more, maybe you can talk to Frank." And that's about as far as we got. Just as quickly as my contact had appeared out of nowhere, two more guys did the same. But they didn't sit down at the table. They towered over it.

My tablemate started shaking. Not a single word from our visitors, but he seemed to know who they were and why they were there, and he was shaking, and starting to mutter, and then squeal, "No, not me, no, not me, nooo ..."

It didn't really seem like a party where I wanted to stay. But it didn't seem like I could just get up and leave, either.

It felt like they stood there for a minute or so, just staring down at this guy next to me. But there was a message in their eyes: "Come peacefully, or not. Up to you."

Not.

I don't think the shaking man at my side actually made some kind of conscious decision to hold his ground. I think he was just too scared to move. So they moved first. These two thugs reached over the table, each grabbing this guy under one arm, and pulled him across. Coffee cups and cream and sugar bowls went flying, but hey, the owner can always buy more.

My contact wasn't just squealing anymore, he was screaming. "Noo, nooo, pleeeese, noooo, nooooo, noooooo!"

Three things flew through my mind: 1) Live by the sword, die by the sword; 2) Maybe instead of journalism school, I should have gone to law school; 3) I was really glad I never learned the guy's name.

Now let me tell you what happened with our eyes: mine never met his. The abductors were bad guys, but he was too, and I didn't want any part of his problem.

And their eyes never met mine. They were about as interested in me as they were in the porcelain now shattered on the floor. Thank goodness!

The other customers, veterans of life in Beirut, never looked up. Well, maybe once, but then they quickly resumed the appearance of non-involvement that had kept them alive so far through all the years of Lebanon's civil war.

That was the last time I saw the guy who sent me a message to meet him at the Alexander. The last time I even heard about him. His abductors had to drag him, kicking uselessly, all the way to a car. My hearing's not so hot, but I could hear him screaming 'til they slammed the door on their way out. I don't suppose he screamed much longer.

That might have been the end of it. But I couldn't be sure. Some mysterious American arms dealer had just been dragged kicking and screaming from a hotel coffee shop by a couple of mysterious Arab thugs, and *I was the other guy at the table.* Worse still, *he had left the briefcase.* Normally, since I figured this guy was part of Frank Terpil's operation, I'd have been thrilled to rummage through his briefcase. But what had just happened was hardly normal. I was afraid to simply stand up, grab the briefcase, and walk out. In fact, I was afraid to so much as touch it. Come to think of it, I was afraid to even look at the darned thing.

Believe it or not, the waiter came after about five minutes and asked if I wanted more coffee. I said no. My hands were shaking too hard to hold a cup.

All I did, in fact, was sit there. For almost half an hour, I sat there. Maybe I was being watched. All I wanted was for anyone paying attention to think that I didn't have anything to do with what had just happened. I wanted to *pretend* I hadn't even been at the same table.

On the other hand, how did I know what these guys were after? How did I know whether the abduction had anything to do with the victim's business with me? How did I know whether or not they'd get back to their bosses, mention "some other guy" at the table, get chewed out for ignoring me, and come back?

After deep thought, that made a quick departure seem like the lesser of two evils. And I took the briefcase. *Hell, if they come looking for me after all, what's the difference?*

I left money on the table, picked up the briefcase, and walked out. I doubt that my gait looked nonchalant, but I sure tried. I walked into the parking lot, remembering that I faced the rigorous transition back from the Christian side of Beirut to the Muslim side. With what had just happened, and the possibility that I wasn't yet out of danger, I didn't relish it.

But I didn't have to do it. As I reached the edge of the parking lot, two men got out of a car. Two men I knew. Part of ABC's armed bodyguard force. They worked for Shakib.

"Mr. Greg, we will get you back to Commodore Hotel."

Huh? I had gotten a handwritten message no one else had seen, had walked through a crowded marketplace, taken a cab, zigzagged across a firing line, and then another cab to get here, doing everything that James Bond ever did to lose a tail, yet these guys were waiting to take me back? Double-0-7 would have been ashamed.

When I got back to the Commodore, Shakib told me that he'd dispatched these guys to keep an eye on me. Not just for my trip that day to the Alexander, but also every other time I had gone out on my own while on this assignment. I felt dumb, but grateful. I also decided to cut my losses. I gave the briefcase to Shakib. "Get rid of it" was all I had to say.

He probably found something better to do with it. I wish him well.

MINT CONDITION ... UNTIL TOMORROW

Sana'a, Yemen, and the remote south of the north.
And Italy before that.

NORTH YEMEN WAS ON the southern tip of the Arabian Peninsula. I say "was" because in 1990 it merged with its Communist neighbor, South Yemen. Now there is just one nation, Yemen, which has the Red Sea to the southwest, the Indian Ocean to the southeast, and Saudi Arabia looming powerfully to the north.

No one knows why the two countries were designated "North" and "South." North Yemen actually was due west of the other Yemen, and so it follows that South Yemen was to the east of North Yemen. To add to the confusion, the top of South Yemen extended further north than the top of North Yemen. No one knows why. Maybe no one cares. For the record, the official name of the north before the merger was, "The Yemen Arab Republic." The south was called "The People's Democratic Republic of Yemen."

Yemen has a history of subservience. Parts of it were ruled by the Queen of Sheba, by the Ottoman Turks, and by Great Britain. There was a time when it was well worth ruling. Because of its position on the water, it was right in the path of seagoing trade between Europe, Asia, and Africa. Subsequently, it was useful to navies like Britain's as a refueling stop. And, useful to the U.S. Navy, until it became a liability. It was off the coast of Yemen that the USS Cole was attacked by terrorists. Today, Yemen can be bypassed, and usually is.

Most of Yemen, (north or south), is hot and dry, averaging only about three inches of rain a year. The only mountains of any note rise from the

164

*western coast to elevations above 12,000 feet. They get a foot or more of
rain. Most of the people of the old North Yemen live in the mountains and
the fertile plains around them.*

·   ·   ·   ·   ·

I never thought I'd see a place that could make Afghanistan look modern.

A nation with no paved roads outside the capital. And less than half
a dozen doctors. (You read it right: half a dozen doctors for *everybody*.)
A place so remote, its borders were missing from many maps because
nobody really knew where they were. So backward that citizens who could
afford it travelled to Saudi Arabia to shop!

Political events never would have gotten us to North Yemen. It could
have conquered South Yemen, or been conquered by South Yemen. We
hardly would have blinked an eye.

But in 1982, it was conquered by an earthquake, and first reports were
dramatic enough to put us on a plane. Overnight, Paris to Cairo, and
then by morning light, Cairo to Sana'a, North Yemen's capital. We flew
straight down the Red Sea. I remember watching the water from my Air
France Airbus, wondering if it was an earthquake that parted it when
Moses and his frightened Jews had to flee across. When we landed at
Sana'a International, I knew little more about the earthquake that had
struck the country the day before than I knew about the Red Sea miracle
in Moses's time.

Reason number one: we heard about the quake while sitting around the
Paris bureau the afternoon before, but didn't check into it because never
in a thousand years did we expect to go. The assignment desk at ABC in
New York surprised us.

Reason number two: when we went, we went in a hurry. Air France had
a one-stop direct flight leaving in an hour and a half. No time for anyone
to head home for clothes. Barely time to even make it to the airport. So
I grabbed what I needed from my desk: portable typewriter (laptops still
weren't much more than a dream yet), toiletries, fresh underclothes,
and my Yemen clippings file. As you might imagine if you glance even
occasionally at newspapers or magazines, a file of clippings on Yemen
doesn't take up much space.

We were armed with minimal information. We knew an earthquake
had struck somewhere in North Yemen. We didn't know where. It had
killed many people. Didn't know how many. We had to find someone to
get us to the center of the destruction. Didn't know who.

And I knew one other fact, which I had read on the plane in three out of the four articles from my thin file, but since it didn't seem to matter at the moment, I never mentioned it to my colleagues. At lunchtime, the men of Yemen chew *khat*. The dictionary calls *khat* "a fresh leaf chewed for its stimulating effects." My clippings called it a local weed chewed for its narcotic-like high. The articles said you can always tell when it's time for lunch, because every man you see has a forest-green fluid dripping from his lips. *Khat*. Rhymes with "pot."

The first thing we learned upon landing was, the capital was safe. But we were not. The earthquake's epicenter was nearly two hundred kilometers, more than a hundred miles, to the south. With a mountain range in between. No paved roads. No way to reach it easily by daylight.

But gathering news is a little like shooting buckshot. Follow every pellet and maybe you'll find the right path. Jacques, the producer, headed for the foreign ministry. I headed for the U.S. embassy. Patrick and Moustafa, the camera crew, stayed at the airport to gather the gear. We set a realistic rendezvous to meet at the foreign ministry ninety minutes later, and if any of us had found a way to the earthquake zone by then, we'd take it.

My job turned out to be the most interesting. I had been in plenty of American embassies before, but never, *never* had I seen one constructed of mud, baked hard in the sun. At least the front of it was built that way. Blocks of hardened earth, same color as the ground, rising to a welcoming arch for visitors. I can't call it ancient; nothing built from mud would have lasted since ancient times.

But the capital city itself is ancient. Many buildings have the same earthen walls as our embassy. Some are coated with stucco. A few are painted. Many, in the hills, sit stacked one atop another, kind of like children's building blocks piled against a wall.

This place was such a hardship post that our diplomats had to fly out just to see a Western physician. The U.S. government usually pays a premium to strapping young doctors to work in remote places for the sake of diplomatic staff, and the premium is high enough that it's usually not hard to fill the posts. But not here. Evidently this place was so bad, they couldn't pay enough to get anybody to move to Sana'a. As a creature of comfort, when I saw the embassy's entryway, I understood.

Jacques' job turned out to be the most fruitful. At the foreign ministry, they were flattered that we had come. North Yemen mattered after all! They offered whatever help we wanted, which in our minds was simple enough: an airplane to the epicenter. Of course our minds were in a fantasy world. One with airstrips wherever you need them. Hell, one with *airplanes* wherever you need them. But this was not that world. This was North Yemen.

There were helicopters though. Army helicopters. They were all in constant motion at the moment, shuttling blankets and food and fresh water to the villages that had fallen down the day before. But we could go out to the army base and try to hitch a ride. It wasn't far.

"Welcome. You are so welcome." This was the officer in charge of the base. "We are so glad you come to Yemen. We are so glad you are our guests." We were received so royally, we almost thought they were glad the earthquake had happened because it had caused us to come.

I started. "The foreign ministry said if you have space on one of your helicopters, we could ride in it down to the area hit by the earthquake."

Whoa, Westerner, reset your watch; you're a long way from home.

"Yes, but first," the man in charge told us, "first, you must eat."

"But we're in a big hurry," Jacques told him. We thought we'd be lucky to reach the earthquake zone by tomorrow. "We would like to go right now."

"No, first you must eat!" the man in charge said again quite hospitably, and led us into an adjacent room with huge platters of lettuce and lamb and yogurt and mint leaves and tomatoes and tea, all laid out Arab style on a rug. Lunchtime, whether we liked it or not. But on the bright side, no *khat.* Maybe the clippings were wrong.

Everyone knows the phrase, "When in Rome, do as the Romans do." Well, "When in Sana'a ..." So we ate. Sumptuously. Whatever was happening down in the earthquake zone would just have to happen without us.

Then the chopper came. It was a well-used Huey, one of those great big machines that looks like a dragonfly and flies like a dragon. The landing pad was made of hard packed sand. Seems like everything in Yemen was hard packed.

I told my team that I'd go on board, meet the pilots, beg for a ride, and be out in a minute. I closed my eyes to keep the whirling sand out, ran for the side door of the chopper, climbed on, and turned left toward the front. Two drapes separated the flight deck from the cargo space. I parted them and shouted above the noise of the rotors, "*salam,*" which means "peace" in Arabic and commonly passes for "hello." This became one of those moments when a foreign correspondent thinks yet again about law school. Long hours in the library. Long stints in the courtroom. Long lists of billable clients. Long days in a plush office. Long weekends in the country. Long evenings at home.

The two men in flight suits and crash helmets simultaneously turned toward me, the pilot rotating to his right, the co-pilot to his left. Both grinned and shouted back their "*salams*," through lips as green as the primeval forest.

Khat. Rhymes with "pot." Did I want to tell my partners? Come to think of it, did I want to go with these guys myself? Well, they had made several safe trips already, hadn't they? They had made it safely to the ground yet again, hadn't they? If I hadn't read my clipping file, I wouldn't even be concerned, would I?

Anyway, their cargo was search dogs, just in from Switzerland. If we crashed, we'd be found immediately because the dogs were already with us! So we went. I know I make it sound like Jacques and Patrick and Moustafa made the same courageous decision I did, to ignore the *khat* and take our chances for the noble purpose of the people's right to know. They didn't. Because I didn't tell them. Not until we got where we were going.

The good news is, we did get there. In one piece.

The pilots circled half a dozen different villages, each of which was reduced to huge piles of rubble. They asked at which one we wanted to get off. All looked the same to us. We chose one at random. The Huey landed. We disembarked. They promised to come back by sunset.

We collected quite a story in precious little time. Collapsed huts. Frantic searches. Crushed corpses. Praying fathers. Wailing mothers. All the elements anyone ever needs for a moving TV story about a catastrophic natural disaster.

But we were a long way from a TV, let alone a way to transmit our material to TVs in America. The plan, quickly established in a phone call to New York from the airport in Paris the afternoon before, was to cover the earthquake on "Day One," ship the tapes and the track (my narration) to Cairo to be cut, and then cover "Day Two" and carry it to Cairo ourselves. All we needed now was our helicopter. By sunset.

But when sunset came, the helicopter didn't. Maybe the villages all looked the same to the pilots too. Maybe *khat* takes awhile to kick in.

So we were stuck. Four guys in short sleeves with TV gear a hundred miles from nowhere. At night in the high desert. Starting to shiver.

Sometimes it pays to stick out like a sore thumb. The citizens of the rubble had more important things to do than worry about us, but one man worried anyway. "Dangerous to stay here," he said in English, which was an awfully welcome sound just then.

"How can we get back to Sana'a?" I asked.

"Maybe I can arrange," he replied, and almost instantly disappeared. It wasn't encouraging, but at the moment, what was?

Moments later, he was back, in the passenger seat of a beat up, old pickup truck. "My friend take you to Sana'a. You pay dollars." Was he kidding? I think any of us would have paid with our firstborn if need be.

Our savior occupied the passenger seat up front, and there were already some other passengers with whom we'd have to share space back in the bed of the pickup: goats. Two of them. They were to be our companions on the ride home. It was awfully bumpy, awfully cold, awfully long, and awfully smelly, but we made it.

Sana'a has a Sheraton hotel. That's where we gratefully paid the man and got off. The Sheraton has a concierge. That's where we arranged to ship our "Day One" story and asked for somebody to meet us four hours hence in a good car with strong shocks, soft seats, and a heater—definitely a heater—to get us back to the earthquake zone for "Day Two."

Ahmed was the man. Our ticket to comfort.

"Mint condition!" he boomed as he banged on the roof of his twenty-seven-year-old Mercedes. "Best car in all Yemen," which wasn't hard, considering the condition of cars in Yemen. But the fact was, his Mercedes was a mint. The body was flawless. The paint job scratchless. The leather looked like new. We probably had the best vehicle in the country to take us more than a hundred miles down to the destruction on unpaved roads across a rugged range of mountains. And back.

We picked up a few pebbles on the way down, but otherwise, the drive was long but uneventful. We ended up at what was left of a village on top of a hill. Ahmed didn't drive us to the top. We had to climb. But it shouldn't be hard; the Yemenis were climbing it like ants. Of course, they had a purpose. They were carrying up the supplies for survivors. And carrying down the corpses for burial.

We were climbing it like old men. Easy living takes its toll. And we had hardly eaten in a day, and hardly slept in two.

And it was raining. Biblical torrents of rain. It reminded me of the Red Sea so near to the west. We had to protect our equipment, which slowed us down even more.

At the top, more scenes like the day before: collapsed huts, frantic searches, crushed corpses, praying fathers, wailing mothers. But one scene was more dramatic than everything else we had seen. Four men digging with their hands. Removing stones the size of basketballs. This had been the home of one of them.

After almost an hour, they found what they had been digging for. The father's son. A little boy who couldn't have been more than four. And would never get older. He was mangled and bloody, but the father cradled him in his arms as if he were still alive. He kissed him. He rocked him. He hugged him.

Parenthood is universal. That is a lesson I have learned many times in many places like this. We have different ethnic habits and different national approaches to education and communication and prayer, but the tragic mix of love and grief are the same the world over.

By midday, we had our story. And Ahmed had our chariot. All we had to do was squeeze in, close our eyes, and get out of the earthquake zone and back to the airport. If only it were that easy! It's hard to remember how the trouble started. The memory of how it ended is much fresher.

The problem was a flood. A flash flood. Those biblical torrents of rain were falling on a land that hadn't felt water for months.

Earlier in the day, we had seen a line of men praying. I had asked our driver what they were praying for. "Help from Allah," he told me.

"What kind of help do they expect?" I asked.

"No more shaking. No more death. No more rain."

It seems Allah didn't hear them. The rain kept falling. And the hard packed earth had absorbed all it could.

This part of North Yemen looked kind of like West Virginia without the trees. Hills and hollows, with plenty of dry valleys just itching to be river valleys. We were heading down one of those valleys on a flat stretch just above a long crack in the earth. The water was rising; we were struggling to stay above it. And we might have succeeded if we weren't such nice guys. Yes, sometimes it's true: nice guys do finish last!

A Yemeni soldier, brought in to help with the earthquake rescue, was caught in the flood. He was hanging onto a strong root in the ground. Hanging on for dear life with one arm, trying to keep his rifle dry with the other. I said to Ahmed, "Do you have a rope or something to help him?"

Ahmed, knowing how fast water rises in dry valleys, didn't even slow down. Jacques, sitting directly behind our driver, was determined that we weren't going to leave the guy to drown. He shouted "STOP" so loud, someone might have stopped all the way up in Sana'a.

So Ahmed stopped, with a look on his face that said, "*You jerks are too stupid to know any better.*" But he had a rope. We tossed it to the soldier. He caught it. Like a fish, we reeled him in. That was enough for Ahmed. The soldier was saved. The last thing he needed now was the soaked soldier on his fine leather. He wanted to leave him.

Well, he had a point. The guy was alive. Shaken and shivering, but alive. We could get on our way now before the water trapped us.

"Ahmed," Jacques said in a very tight voice, "we have just saved this man's life. The water is still coming up. It would be silly to go to all that trouble, then leave him to die again." I think Ahmed was beginning to think about aligning himself with the concierge of some hotel other than the Sheraton, someplace journalists never stay.

So now there were six of us, and we all six piled into the Mercedes. Three in front now, three in back, the soldier directly behind the driver. The ride would have gone swimmingly, but for the wet, steel barrel Ahmed felt at the nape of his neck. Our shivering soldier had rested his rifle over the back of the front seat. Ahmed let out what I'm sure, without even speaking his language, was an obscenity. At least it sure got the soldier's attention. All in one fell swoop, his cold feet stiffened, his body jerked back, his finger accidentally brushed the trigger release, and a bullet went through the roof.

Mint condition? More like crackers now. Ahmed jumped out, the soldier jumped out, and the four of us from the West learned a whole new kind of Arabic.

What no one noticed was how fast the water was rising.

Before anyone knew it, we were the ones who were stuck. Ahmed tried to get the car started but couldn't. We tried to push it uphill but couldn't. The flash flood was catching us. Talk about events coming full circle! Along came a heavy-duty, four-wheel-drive army truck, looking for the lost soldier. We took the rope that had saved him, tied it to the truck, and used it to save the car.

There was only one mishap. The truck slipped down the embankment and put an army-sized dent in the left front door. But then, it got its traction and pulled the Mercedes to safety. All that came off in the effort was the rear bumper. And the oil pan. And the sheen of fine leather.

And half the hairs on Ahmed's head. Otherwise, we made the trip without a hitch.

By the time we limped back into Sana'a, Ahmed had calmed down. Or at least had come to terms with the day. He assured us he could get the car fixed just like new.

Where? In Munich? I wouldn't have guessed you could find a new floor mat in Sana'a, let alone a new chrome bumper.

But we paid him what he asked and he seemed to walk away happy. That money would buy a lot of *khat*. But the days of his mint condition Mercedes were gone forever.

Now here's the part I wouldn't tell Ahmed, if ever I were to see him again, because he already had suffered enough.

When we got to our bureau in Cairo, even though it was now Day Three,

World News Tonight still wanted our Day Two story. *Great*, I thought, *at least it wasn't all for naught*. We went to work and built the piece to its climax: close-ups of the four men digging with their hands, the discovery of the little boy, his father cradling him, kissing him, mourning him.

That said it all. That single scene showed the American people just how badly someone else halfway around the world was suffering. We went to Cairo TV, established our links to New York, and fed the piece via satellite. When it got to those final scenes, we could almost hear the tears rolling down the cheeks of our hard-bitten colleagues in Manhattan.

When we got back to ABC's bureau though, just across the street, we heard something else. The telephone. It was the big honchos at the broadcast. "Have you got some long shots you could feed us?"

"Yes, but why?" I asked. "We didn't leave any holes; the piece we fed in was complete."

"Yeah, but those scenes at the end were too gruesome." They wanted to use the vaguely defined long shots to cover the grisly close-ups and protect the audience from reality.

It was the second time I'd ever faced this. The first was also while covering a terrible earthquake, this one in 1980 in Italy's Apennine Mountains southeast of Naples. Dozens of towns and villages had collapsed; ultimately, the death toll was in the thousands.

In that case, we went by helicopter on the first day after the quake to a town where a church reportedly had collapsed and crushed a hundred people inside for an evening mass. With so many scenes of disaster from which to choose, the media were dispersed, and we turned out to be the only ones who found this town. While recording the horrors all around us, another helicopter appeared over a hill and came in to land. It was white, and when it set down not a hundred yards from the fallen church, the man who emerged from the side door was dressed in white. It was the pope, the then-brand-new Pope John Paul II.

He walked straight into the rubble that had been a church. As a rescue crew came the other way carrying a stretcher with a body covered by a sheet, he stopped, and they stopped before him. He lifted the sheet and kissed the temple of this bloody, mangled corpse. And we had *the only camera around*, and it all happened *right in front of us*. No one, anywhere else, could have delivered the kind of uniquely emotional scene we now had on tape.

That night, needless to say, the pope's kiss was the heart of my story. It said so much about the pope, about the earthquake, about the victims, about Italy. But as we completed our feed from Italian TV headquarters in

Naples, the producer on the other end of the phone, from the tape room in New York, asked me, "Have you got something we can use to cover the scene of the pope kissing the dead guy?"

It is a struggle that continues to this day. Do we show our audience what life really looks like? Or do we protect them from the ugly reality? From both earthquakes, not to mention a few wars I've covered, the sad answer is the latter. We don't want to upset our viewers. After all, *World News Tonight* comes on at dinnertime.

Thankfully though, we didn't have to excise a single second from another piece we did, the most dramatic of the five we put on the air that week.

For coverage like this, you want to find a fresh angle each day, and that becomes a challenge. Pretty soon, the "big picture" stories are done, and your job as a journalist is to find the small stories, the personal stories that illustrate the big pain of the victims.

On Day Three after the earthquake, with a helicopter at our command, we bounced from village to village. But they *all* had casualties, they *all* were reduced to rubble. What would we do differently than what we had done the days before?

After a couple of hours of daylight, we already were in our second or third village, still empty handed, and we were going to fly on to yet another site because we had to produce *something* for *Good Morning America*, when we heard a man shouting and saw him frantically gesturing atop a huge pile of rubble. He was shouting in Italian, but one member of our team knew the language and said, "He thinks he's found someone alive."

He had indeed. We scrambled with our camera gear to the top of the pile, and after a tough decision to blow off *Good Morning America*, we spent the next six hours there. Little did I know then how right that decision was. The rescuer who had shouted that first alarm had heard a squeal—just a tiny, weak squeal, but it sounded human. It was. It was a woman who, we learned before the end of the day, had been buried about six feet down, trapped by concrete and thick wood beams, the body of her dead sister on top of her.

For those six hours, we watched and recorded as rescuers got her out. They had to work painstakingly slowly. This pile of rubble was a house of cards; move the wrong stick or stone and the whole precarious pile could collapse, burying not just the survivor but the rescuers and, incidentally, us! Over time, the squeal came more often and eventually got louder. Rescuers delicately opening a passage were getting closer and closer. But in all those hours, we never saw the woman; we only heard her. And that's where Lenny Jenson comes in.

He was our sound man. He had a long "shotgun" microphone, and for six hours, he held his arm fully extended into the ever deeper hole. For six hours, he picked up the survivor's squeals, and the dramatic sounds rescuers made as they warily snapped thin twigs and lifted small stones, wondering whether each would be the one to cause this pile to collapse upon itself.

"Somewhere down there is a woman named Lisa ..." That's how our dramatic story on *World News Tonight* began, and then it kept getting even better. *"This rescue worker cut up his face, but said, 'I touched Lisa's hand, my blood doesn't matter.'"* In the story, we didn't see Lisa until the very end, when she was pulled from the hole and rushed to an ambulance waiting alongside the rubble, but viewers would hardly even notice, because we *heard* her. We heard every squeal, and every twig broken in the path to her crypt. When the piece was finally fed in, I called and left an apology for *Good Morning America*. We never did get them a piece that morning. Was I ever glad!

Although we put stories of the earthquake on the air all week, I've always thought it was that one in particular that won me the first of my two Emmys, for best spot news coverage on a network. I got a statue; so did the cameraman. But nobody at the National Academy of Television Arts & Sciences (which awards the Emmys) recognized Lenny's incomparable achievement.

They should have. We sure did. Officially, he was a sound technician, but it was his persistence as a journalist that made the story so special.

THIS MAY NOT BE HELL, BUT WE CAN SEE IT FROM HERE

Saudi Arabia, the Kuwait border, and Amman, Jordan

BEFORE THE GULF WAR, *most Americans knew just two things about Saudi Arabia. One: it pumps more oil for export than anyone else. Two: Lawrence of Arabia loved chasing through its sands. If Saddam Hussein had not come along, those would have remained the only two images in anyone's mind about the desert kingdom.*

But then, in August 1990, that changed. Iraq did not invade Saudi Arabia; it invaded tiny but oil-rich Kuwait, on the northeastern Saudi border. That was enough to scare the United States into believing Saudi Arabia was next on Saddam Hussein's list, which was enough to scare Saudi King Fahd into accepting an American-led military coalition onto his soil. The coalition ultimately defeated Iraq in a six-week war.

Most of Saudi Arabia is desert, and most of the soil, in fact, is sand. But there is so much oil underfoot that it need not even be pumped to the surface; natural pressure does the job. All told, Saudi Arabia has some of the largest oil deposits in the world. That is why the United States was so fearful of Iraq's intentions. And why, to this day, it is so deferential to Saudi Arabia.

Before the development of the oil industry in Saudi Arabia, most citizens lived in the desert. Today, there are still tribes of desert nomads called Bedouins, who tend their goats and camels and don't seem to care much about global politics, but most of the country's population, now approaching 30 million people, today lives in the cities. The government is a monarchy, led by the direct descendents of Abd al-Aziz ibn Saud, a military rebel who consolidated the many rival tribes of the Arabian Peninsula at the beginning of the twentieth century.

175

The government also is the keeper of the holiest shrine in the world of Islam, the great mosque in the city of Mecca. That is where the founder of Islam, known to his followers as The Prophet Mohammed, was born, and where Muslims from all parts of the world today go to pray. Only Muslims, in fact, are permitted to enter the city. All laws in Saudi Arabia are the laws of Islam, passed down since the time of Mohammed, which was more than 1,400 years ago.

◆   ◆   ◆   ◆   ◆

It all started, as they say, at the Waldorf Astoria Hotel in New York City. My mother happened to be in town for a conference; I was there because I finally had my Saudi visa and tomorrow would board my long Saudia flight from New York to the Gulf. Don't let them start the war without me.

Once we discovered we were both in the same city, Mom and I arranged to go together, along with a couple of her lady friends, to dinner and a Broadway play. Then I walked them back to their hotel, the Waldorf.

But this was New York, and the walk turned out to be more exciting than the play. Not a block from the theater after the play let out, just as we were crossing the center of Times Square, three guys in jeans and sweaters went tearing right through the middle of our group. And before we could count the purses in their clutches, several more in jeans and T-shirts went tearing after them. Purse snatchers pursued by undercover police.

The crowd roared. Not with laughter, but anger. "Catch the sons of bitches!" people were shouting. "Put 'em in cuffs and throw away the key," and within half a block, they did.

This was New York where only two days before, Brian Watkins, a young man from Utah in town with his parents to attend tennis's U.S. Open, stood up in a subway to defend them from robbers, and got fatally stabbed for his trouble. It was the last straw for normally complacent New Yorkers. What we witnessed that night in Times Square was their frustration with crime out of control.

But we were not New Yorkers, so we didn't stick around to wait for the paddy wagon. No, we tore ourselves away from the drama and made our way—a bit more carefully now, my mother and her friends a lot more protective of their purses—back to the Waldorf, at a faster pace than before. Then I said good-bye. But my mother was seeing her son off to Saudi Arabia and God-only-knows-where-else, and was none too happy about it. "If the war breaks out, you get out!" was her firm advice. You can imagine how I treasured this maternal good sense on the eve of my departure. Without hesitation, I'd be sure to pass it on to my handlers at ABC.

"Don't worry"—when will I learn how meaningless this phrase is to mothers and wives?—"Don't worry," I said, "I'll be okay. I know how to take care of myself in places like that."

Then I gave her a kiss and a hug, and putting one foot on the street while the other was still on the curb, got ready to head off on my last walk for a long time in nice, cool night air. The Waldorf is on Manhattan's East Side, my hotel was toward the west.

"Where are you going?" Mom demanded.

"To my hotel" I answered.

"Gregory, take a taxi!" she insisted. A long line of eager empty taxicabs was conveniently sitting alongside the curb.

"Don't worry, I'll be okay," I responded. "Bye." The desert, the mean streets, they're all the same.

"Gregory, this is New York!" my mother shouted after me. "You cannot walk the streets at this hour of the night!"

"Mom," I said, my arsenal of calming words now empty, "I'm going to Saudi Arabia tomorrow, and maybe Kuwait or Baghdad after that. I think I can take care of myself in New York City, U.S.A."

And off I set on foot. Here I was, heading for an inevitable and bloody conflict in the Middle East, and my mother was worried about me strolling across the island of Manhattan. Of course, considering the crime rate in New York in those days, maybe she was right. Nonetheless, I made it to the hotel without incident.

And to Saudi Arabia too.

One of the best ways to describe the difference between New York and Saudi Arabia is with color. In Times Square, for instance, there is darned near every color ever created. What you don't see in the neon signs, you see in the locals' pants. In Saudi Arabia, especially when the troops are in town, there is brown. And brown. And then, brown.

For starters, the landscape is brown. For 360 degrees. Sand sits on the ground, blows through the air, muddles the horizon. You can look down at your shoes or up at the sky, and the color may be the same: brown.

The buildings are brown. Wherever I've been in the world, building materials reflect the landscape. Ancient walled cities in southern France: reddish clay. Farm communities in eastern Poland: pale green. Hillside homes on Greek islands: Mediterranean blue. Everything in Saudi Arabia: brown.

The soldiers' uniforms were brown. Different shades to be sure, and sometimes many shades in a single shirt, but still, all in the family of brown. The loose dresses worn by Saudi men in the summertime start out white to repel the sun, but spend a single day in the desert and they're brown before you're through.

The food came packaged in brown. Vacuum-sealed MREs, "Meals Ready to Eat," so named because they're ready even if you're not. They've been ready for years. Some say they taste like it. Each morsel is vacuum-sealed in a brown plastic pouch, all the pouches sealed together in a brown plastic sack. And basically, the food itself is brown too: ready-to-eat spaghetti, ready-to-eat BBQ beef, ready-to-eat ham steak.

Brown camels, brown tanks, brown guns, even brown aircrafts, painted for camouflage in the desert. Add it all together, toss in a dose of brown mood, and you have a pretty good picture of pre-war Saudi Arabia. However, color alone can't be used to describe the heat. "Red hot?" Sure it was, but red is too civilized. "White heat?" No question about it, but white is too clean.

How hot was it? Well, I can tell you that one day I stopped at a Baskin-Robbins in the city of Dhahran for an ice-cream cone, and between the overly air-conditioned store and my idling air-conditioned car, a distance of no more than *ten feet*, the whole thing melted down my arm. I mean, the whole thing. To liquid. The temperature ran 130 degrees or more during the day. Walking outside was like walking right into your kitchen's heated oven.

But that wasn't the worst of it. During the day, we were out, we were working, we were expected to sweat. Nighttime is supposed to be the time for relief. But in summertime Saudi Arabia, forget it. For the first month I was there, the temperature never dropped below one hundred even at night.

The hottest night of all was the night I spent sprawled on the floor of a speeding school bus. Just above the drive shaft. I never before thought about the drive shaft of a speeding bus getting so hot! I never before tried to find out. But this night, we were being rushed to the border with Kuwait. Word was, Iraqi occupiers were releasing Kuwaiti men who, since the August invasion, had not been allowed to leave the country.

Actually, there is more to tell about this night than just the bus ride. Hours earlier, I had just put my tired head down on my thin pillow half a dozen miles from headquarters in Dhahran. We had worked at our makeshift office well into the night finishing the editing of a story about WWII tanks that were back in action. Then a bunch of us had gone out to Dhahran's one-and-only Chinese-Japanese-Korean restaurant for a good

Chinese-Japanese-Korean meal. An hour later, you may not be hungry anymore, but you do feel schizophrenic.

The phone rang. It was Rex, our man in charge at all hours, to his understandable chagrin. After all, daytime in Saudi Arabia is nighttime in New York, and vice versa. In other words, his phone never stopped ringing.

"They've opened the border at Khafji, and we think they're letting some Kuwaitis come across," Rex began. "Trouble is, we can't go up on our own. The Saudis say we have to go with them, and we have to go right away."

It was the best story to come along in days. In fact, it was the *only* story to come along in days. Everyone wondered what was really happening in Kuwait. Nobody knew. This was our first chance to find out.

"I've called Keith in his room," Rex went on, referring to one of our hotshot, war-weary cameramen. "He says he'll be in the lobby in three minutes. You'd better be too. The Saudis say they're providing a bus and it leaves in ten minutes." Keith had been to the Chinese-Japanese-Korean restaurant with us. I knew he wouldn't have to stop and eat first.

We met in the lobby, buttons still undone and shoes still untied, and jumped in Keith's car. Brown, of course. Seven minutes to make six miles through the city. But at almost two in the morning, no problem. There's not a whole lot to do at two in the afternoon in a place like Dhahran; we knew there would be no one on the streets now! We were almost right. The only other guy out there was a cop. We didn't see him until it was too late. As Keith sped right through a red light, the cop car blended in with the walls along Dhahran's biggest boulevard. Is this the only country where even the police cars are brown?

"*Ahhmahhlahhdahhhahh,*" he said to us after shining a flashlight through our car. Or something like that. Keith doesn't speak Arabic. I don't either. Officer Ahmed didn't seem to care.

"*Mahhsahhfahhlahhahh!*" he shouted next (to the best of my recollection), wildly gesturing with his hands. Evidently the Saudis are like Americans traveling abroad: if someone doesn't understand you the first time, speak louder! "*Mahhsahhfahhlahhahh!*"

We still didn't get it. And of course, every time we tried to demonstrate that we didn't have a clue about what he was trying to tell us, he got louder.

"*Flahhmahhshahhsnahhbahhahh,*" formed on his lips. Blank looks formed in our eyes.

Then, inexplicably, he got it. I mean, in the time it takes to turn toward Mecca, it suddenly occurred to Officer Ahmed that we weren't Arabs and we didn't understand Arabic. So he jumped in his squad car, leaned out the window, and stunned us by shouting in perfectly acceptable English, "You come!" We came. Who could turn down an offer like that?

It was like a wild chase, but kind of like *he* was trying to lose *us*. We were sure he wasn't, of course, but after being stopped for speeding through a red light, we thought it was kind of strange that he was driving even faster through more red lights, and pulling us like a magnet behind him.

And naturally, we had our assignment pulling us in the other direction. What was it that Rex had said on the phone? "The Saudis say they're providing a bus and it leaves in ten minutes." We were not only losing precious time and probably blowing a good story, but as we chased the policeman deeper and deeper through uncharted territory, we were getting lost.

But then we turned into the police precinct, and everything added up. For there had been someone else out on the streets at the same time we were. A bad guy. Or at least from the looks of things, a guy about to have a real bad time. He was being pulled out of another police car as we pulled up. He was shaking. Maybe Keith and I ought to have been shaking too, but we were naive. This guy wasn't. Obviously, he had done something that carries a bloody penalty. I had just remarked to Keith a minute or so earlier, "You know, when you're caught speeding, they cut off your steering wheel." When you're caught thieving though, they cut off your hand.

The good news was, we were only in the way. Officer Ahmed, licking his chops at the licking this criminal might get, had no time for us. In fact, apparently once he heard on his police radio about the criminal about to be delivered to the station house, he really had been trying to lose us so he could get in on the *real* action. So when we just stood there, awaiting booking and fingerprints—why would they do things in Saudi Arabia any differently than they do them in Hollywood?—he turned rather angrily toward us and regaled us with the rest of his English.

"You go!" he shouted two feet from our faces, and then turned on his thin heel and marched away. Fine. "You come!" means we are in trouble; "You go!" must mean we are free. So as our would-be executioner turned on his heel, we turned on ours, jumped in the car, and sped away. Justice had been served for some; no time for everybody. Sorry for the bad guy, but hey, we had to be someplace soon. He didn't.

Keith turned left and right through the empty, dusty brown streets, and eventually we found a landmark and made our way to headquarters. Twenty minutes or so had been lost. But we had overlooked one thing about Rex's admonition to be there on time: it was Saudi time. There is a joke we Westerners tell in the Arab world. The Arabic word for "tomorrow" is "*bukra.*" The joke is, "*bukra*" means the same thing as "*mañana,*" but without the sense of urgency.

Anyway, the driver of the Saudi bus hadn't shown up yet. No one was going anywhere until he did. We had gone through our little adventure with the police for nothing, save perhaps my chance to tell about it in this book.

Eventually, the bus driver came, and we headed north to Ras al Khafji. All the way to the border. Four hours at breakneck speed. Me on the floor, above the burning drive shaft. The alternative was to crumple my body into the shape of a pretzel and try to sleep on a hard bouncing seat, like the rest of the journalists on the bus. Kind of a catch-22, really: unnaturally twisted on a seat, or unnaturally roasted on the floor. They say getting there is half the fun! Obviously "they" never rode a bus to Khafji.

We did, and while it wasn't fun, it was worthwhile. We heard the first firsthand stories from inside Kuwait. Tales of torture, reports about rape, all kinds of incriminating charges against the Iraqis. We collected what we could, and then rushed back to Dhahran to prepare our pieces. It was a Sunday, and we had four broadcasts to service, not to mention ABC Radio: *This Week with David Brinkley, World News Sunday, ABC Weekend Report,* and the next morning's edition of *Good Morning America.* Usually it seems, the harder you work, the fewer outlets you have to show it off. This was the gratifying exception.

I went on a different, less gratifying story a few days later though: a trip to "The Empty Quarter." If ever any region on this planet was aptly named, this is it. "The Empty Quarter" is down at the bottom of the country. In more ways than one. From the air, it looks like somebody turned Saudi Arabia on end and let all its sand fall to the bottom. From the ground, it looks the same. It didn't take a genius to give "The Empty Quarter" its name. It is empty. It is the very definition of the word.

Mind you, one of my Saudi escorts told me it is misnamed. "'The Empty Quarter' is not empty at all," he told me on the trip down. "It is quite full."

"Of what?" I asked.

"Of sand." Desert humor, but he was right. You fly and fly and see nothing but sand.

Sad to say, a few of our American fighter pilots died down there while training during Operation Desert Shield, the run-up to Desert Storm, the war, because they saw so much sand, they didn't notice when it was piled up in monster dunes, dead ahead of their ground-hugging jets.

We were going to "The Empty Quarter" to try to interview the Saudi defense minister, brother of the king, who was going to inspect the readiness of his southernmost warriors. We were traveling on a Saudi government Lear jet. He was on his own 747. Could have saved the kingdom some money by giving us a ride with him, but I guess when they want my advice, they'll ask for it. Operators are standing by.

But the separate plane wasn't a total loss. It put me in close proximity to our escort, Saudi Arabia's information minister. He was a pretty hip guy, good humored and Western educated, who had lived for years in both Great Britain and the United States. We talked together most of the way down. And the memorable part is what he told me when we talked about women. I said to him, "You know how we in the West look upon your treatment of women. The way we see it is, you don't let them work at many jobs, you don't let them drive, you don't let them go out on their own, you don't even let them wear what they want—they have to cover themselves in public. You treat them like second-class citizens."

And the response of this hip, Western-trained Saudi prince was telling. Whether it was genuine, I don't know, but it was telling: "We do it to protect them. We put our women on a pedestal. You don't. We treat them like princesses, to protect them from the leering thoughts of men." Case closed.

And, case confirmed in "The Empty Quarter." The airport itself gave a taste of the region. First of all, only men. Sure, the typical Saudi woman stays under wraps, but at least in the other parts of Saudi Arabia I've seen, you see the wraps.

Here, just no women, period. It was as if no woman had ever set foot in "The Empty Quarter." Which would leave the men with a lot of explaining to do. But I wasn't about to demand an explanation. Not when every last man on the tarmac had a sword in his belt. Some also had old but well polished Enfield rifles slung over their shoulders, but all of them had swords.

"Is this a ceremonial occasion?" I asked my escort.

"No," he answered, "they always carry their swords because they always are ready for battle."

This was the irony of the defense minister's visit to "The Empty Quarter." If a war was about to start, it would start way up north, at the other end of the country, eight hundred miles away. If it was to spread, I'm not sure the *news* could have reached "The Empty Quarter" for days, let alone the war itself.

Turns out, my escort had told me only a half-truth. Yes, the men always carry their swords, but this day was indeed a ceremonial occasion. It wasn't often—and believe me, I could understand why not—that a brother of the king came down. And so, in his honor, a feast. I don't mean a five-course lunch with wine, I mean a feast (and *no* wine). If the Ottoman Turks left no other legacy from their centuries of rule, they did leave this.

I'm not sure how the civic leaders in "The Empty Quarter" came up with the invitation list for the feast, but it looked simple enough: every man in "The Empty Quarter" with a sword in his belt was invited. Plus us. Four of us from ABC News and two newspaper reporters and a photographer. The press pool.

We had been literally cooling our heels in a great air-conditioned reception hall along with our thousand or so swordsmen when two great doors opened. As the swordsmen swash buckled in, we were carried along in the flood, and then found seven seats on either side of a long table. I mean, a loooooooooong table. Seventy-two seats on each side. I counted because I couldn't believe it. There were eight more tables just like it.

Each was set the same. Just your typical feast for a brother of the king. Platters the size of rowboats, overflowing with grapes. Bowls as big as toboggans, filled to the brim with yogurt. And trays the size of sheep, holding sheep. Slaughtered and sheared of course, but damn near the whole animal, roasted to a delicious, aromatic brown (oh my God I'm beginning to like it), each one resting on its backside with its luscious legs of lamb reaching for the sky.

But let me give you a couple of pieces of advice, just in case you ever attend a feast in "The Empty Quarter": first, if you want to remember how things looked, you'd better look fast. By the time we seven outsiders sat down, every other hand was already on the food. Ripping apart the lamb, limb from limb. Ladling the yogurt into rich, porous pita bread. Tearing huge helpings of grapes from their stems. There was also salad and melon and gargantuan chunks of roast beef, puddings and jellies and statuary-sized ice sculptures.

Ice sculptures? What was this, a Bar Mitzvah?

People were eating like there was no tomorrow. I guess that's because they knew that tomorrow, they wouldn't eat like this again. So my second piece of advice is, besides looking fast, you'd better eat fast. Nobody politely passes you the food. Nobody says, "Anyone want the last shank bone?" In fact, nobody talks at all.

This was the strangest part. They all race into the room, dive into the food, and leave. Not so much as a *how do you do* or a *nice to meet you*. No toasts, no speeches, no conversation. Of course, it took the seven of us awhile to catch on. We were doing things Westerners do over meals, like talk. Next thing we knew, the meal was over and the swordsmen were out of their seats and out of the door. Every tray, bowl, pitcher, and platter was empty. So were we. At least we were far from full, but no matter: the brother of the king was on his way out; so were we. I don't recall whether I put in for lunch on that day's expense account. But I sure needed the expense account a few days later.

We had asked the military public affairs officers at their so-called "Joint Information Bureau" to fly us out to a ship in the Persian Gulf. We wanted to do a story about the United Nations' shipping embargo against Iraq, and the only way to get there was with military help. It took a few days, but approval came through. "Be at the flight line at "Oh Five Forty Five" (that's how they talk), "you'll be wheels up at Oh Six Thirty." Great. It would give me time to buy some T-shirts.

T-shirts, you see, are the cultural mark that we Americans now leave behind. And take with us as well. From the Valdez oil spill I have T-shirts saying things like, "The Valdez Oil Spill, One Slick Operation," and, "I Said Put My *Drink* On The Rocks, Not My Ship." From the San Francisco earthquake: "I Was Really Shaken Up In San Francisco."

So inevitably, T-shirts showed up in Saudi Arabia, and the best place to buy them was in the huge hangar next to the flight line. But it was only 5:45 in the morning, and while the flight line was hot twenty-four hours a day, the guy with the T-shirts wasn't there. *Oh well*, I thought, *I'll get them when we come back.* I didn't know how soon that would be.

By 6:30, we were wheels up, as scheduled. And four minutes later, wheels down again. A small fire in the engine of our helicopter. Or so the cockpit indicator light showed. We landed awfully hard and awfully fast at the far end of the airfield. Maintenance crews went to work. We went to the hangar. The T-shirt man was there. I bought three. One had a simple map of Saudi Arabia with sites variously identified as "Somewhere," "Somewhere Else," "Someplace Really Secret," and "Unidentified Airbase." This was because, to protect our troops as they prepared for war, we could never sign off at the end of a story with anything more specific about our location than something like, "Greg Dobbs, ABC News, in eastern Saudi Arabia."

Another T-shirt transformed the "Hard Rock Cafe" logo into the "Hard Luck Cafe, Kuwait City, Kuwait." On the back it said, "Visit Iraq ... Before Iraq Visits You." My favorite simply summed up everything the Western press corps felt about the country: "This May Not Be Hell. But We Can See It From Here."

Well, by eight o'clock ("Oh Eight Hundred"), they told us the chopper was fixed. Albeit temporarily, we would be leaving hell behind. We climbed back on board and rose again. This time, no sudden return to base. Out over the water. An hour to the ship. My brain and my eyelids both shut down. On stories like this, catch your shut-eye where you find it.

We all awakened with a jolt when we touched the ground. That's right, not a seaborne landing pad, but the ground. I was too tired to understand. I leaned out the open evacuation doorway and thought, *Gee, this is the biggest ship I've ever seen.* There were a dozen other helicopters on the deck, but also lots and lots of airplanes. Fighters, fuelers, cargo-carrying C–130s, even a Continental Airlines 747. What kind of gargantuan ship was this anyway?

We were told to jump out and jump out fast. It turns out the indicator light that put us back on the ground a few hours earlier didn't need fixing; the engine did. It had caught fire over the sea and our crew had headed for the nearest safe land. Good thinking, boys!

As I ran from the helicopter, I looked quickly around. We were not back at the main base in Saudi Arabia. I didn't know yet where we were, but learned we weren't supposed be *there* when I stopped an officer on the tarmac and asked, "Where am I?" and his only answer was, "Uh-oh."

It was Bahrain. A friendly country to be sure, but friendlier than it wanted the world to know. Bahrain, which for many years had quietly hosted a U.S. naval supply depot, was now serving as a launching pad for the Western coalition. The Continental jumbo jet had just disgorged another five hundred Marines to the war zone. No one was supposed to know. But the engine of the journalists' helicopter was not supposed to catch fire.

So someone had better get us out of there. Fast. Not by helicopter, though; none could be spared. Therefore, by pickup truck, "borrowed" for the purpose and driven through a hole in the chain link fence around the airbase.

Bahrain is kind of a city-island. The city is the nation, the nation is the city. I had been there once before, and remembered the Bahrainis' loose attitude toward forbidden fruit. Like beer. Which is how they bought us off. They took us to the makeshift U.S. officers club across town, where we had beer and hamburgers. I've eaten in the best five-star restaurants in France, but after a couple of months of Meals Ready To Eat and the other culinary delights we found on Saudi sands, nothing ever tasted better than the beer and hamburgers in Bahrain.

But it cost me. Our boys in Bahrain were starved for mementos from "the front." They feared they would miss the war. I had my brand-new

T-shirts and gave them away. All in all, a fair trade. I could get more T-shirts. They could get more beer. And when the war started, some of them probably made it to "the front." I did not. On the day we dropped the first bombs, I was rushed to New York. ABC needed 'round-the-clock coverage at the United Nations. I was it.

At least I wouldn't be ducking missiles. Mom was glad. But after a few weeks there, I began to rethink my priorities. There were tremendous risks just riding through the streets in your typical New York taxicab. Some nut tried to mug me one day while I was out jogging—all I had on was a sweatshirt, shorts, shoes, and socks, so I never figured out what he thought he could steal. After that, I opened my eyes to the untold dangers of walking down any sidewalk in Manhattan. And therefore, in the middle of the war, I applied for transfer back to Saudi Arabia. For my personal safety. And one more story comes out of that.

At a certain point during this second Saudi stint, now that the guns were firing, ABC put out a call for a correspondent to go to Baghdad. The Iraqis' allowance of journalist visas ran hot and cold. But even if they awarded one, it was limited to a ten-day stay. Ten days, of course, was about nine days longer than anyone wanted to stay in Baghdad. It was a dangerous place, although whether more dangerous because of coalition bombs or Saddam Hussein's wrath was debatable.

Anyway, ABC's correspondent and camera crew currently in Baghdad were about to get kicked out, and although ABC had a replacement crew available, it couldn't find a correspondent who wanted to go. Frankly, I've always thought this spoke to the high intellect of my colleagues.

But I had just about had it with Saudi Arabia. Every day, I found myself picturing an old-fashioned scale, with the Saudi desert sitting on one side, and Colorado's Rocky Mountains, where I live, sitting on the other. There was no contest! So when I got the appeal from New York to do ten days in Iraq, I called my boss and struck a deal. "Okay, I'll do it, but only if you let me go home when I get out. I won't leave Saudi Arabia for Baghdad, only to return to Saudi Arabia ten days later."

Things were heating up, and ABC couldn't afford to leave Baghdad without a correspondent. So he said yes. And the next morning, I was on my way. Not directly to Baghdad; because of the war, that was impossible. But to Amman, the capital of Jordan, which shares a long border with Iraq.

ABC had a temporary bureau set up at a hotel in Amman, because Jordan was the transit point for anyone going in and out of Baghdad. We had used it that way several years earlier, too, to cover the years-long Iran-Iraq war. So when I landed mid afternoon in Amman, a car and driver met me and, thanks to arrangements made by our people in Amman, took me straight to the Iraqi embassy. They would issue my ten-day visa, which the crew already had, and we'd leave on the following afternoon's once-every-two-days flight into Baghdad. Piece of cake.

But there was something wrong. The Iraqi press officer had faxed my application to the foreign ministry in Baghdad, submitted by ABC before I even got there, and hadn't yet heard back. "No problem," he said, "they must have many people asking. Tomorrow morning, for sure. Come back tomorrow morning. No problem."

I came back "tomorrow morning," since our flight wouldn't leave until the middle of the afternoon, and the press officer still had no information. Not about me, anyway. There were other Western journalists there, and he was handing them visas like Islamic worry beads. But none for me. "No problem, I'm sure. I call Baghdad on phone, make sure you get visa. You come back one o'clock, I have visa ready. No problem." There sure were a lot of problems when this guy promised, "no problem."

I went back to the hotel, packed my bag, sent the crew on its own to the airport, and returned, suitcase in hand, to the Iraqi embassy. But I never got far enough to find out whether my visa had come through. Instead, the receptionist told me there was a message to call my office. I borrowed his phone.

"Come back to the hotel," our temporary bureau chief told me.

"But they might have my visa ready, and if I don't get it now, I won't make the flight."

"I don't care. Come back right now. I'll explain when you get here."

"Should I get the visa first?"

"No. Get out of there and come back." Click.

I was confused, not to mention disappointed, because the deal I'd struck meant that if I survived those ten days in Baghdad, this would be my ticket out of the Middle East. But reluctantly and unhappily, I went back to the car and told the driver to take me back to the hotel. As it turned out, it was a good call.

Here's why. Carl Bernstein, a reporter renowned for his Watergate coverage for the *Washington Post* back in the 1970s, had just been in Baghdad for *Time* magazine. And that week's cover story was his. It was a fair and thorough look, through Western eyes anyway, at Saddam Hussein. And it wasn't pretty. The Iraqis were incensed and made it clear that Bernstein had done what they considered a hatchet job because he was "a Zionist Jew." What's more, they decided they wouldn't let any more "Zionist Jews" into the country.

But they had no reason to believe *I* was Jewish. They had no way to know. I'd been in Iraq three times in the past, back during its war with Iran, and each time, where it asked you to list "religion" on the visa application, I had listed "Lutheran." "Lutheran" made sense because my wife is Lutheran, so I always figured I'd remember what to scream when they tried to beat the truth out of me. Consistency is everything!

Nonetheless, the Iraqis had called in the correspondent I was due to replace, and questioned him about me. I mean, *all* about me. What was my father's name? Where was he born? Did I take the Jewish holidays off? Did I wear Jewish symbols around my neck? This correspondent was based in the Far East, so our paths had rarely crossed, and he didn't know me well enough to answer these questions, but he could see what they were fishing for: a Jew.

The funny thing was, they might have caught one, but probably didn't know it. So when they finally let him go, our correspondent called ABC in New York and told of his interrogation. New York concluded that there was no danger in being rejected for the visa; the danger was, Iraq might grant me the visa, let me into the country, and then accuse me of "Zionist" tendencies and hold on to me as a high-profile example to all other journalists.

So New York called Amman, and Amman called me and kept me off that plane.

All that was left for me now was to make sure that when I did catch a plane, it would take me home to Colorado, not back to Saudi Arabia. ABC tried to renege on our deal, since I hadn't actually gone to Baghdad, but I held firm, insisting that my willingness to go to Baghdad had fulfilled my part of the deal. I won. Within a day, I was on my way home.

My first full day home, by the way, my wife and I went to a movie. We left home a few minutes early because I wanted her to take my picture with the snowcapped Continental Divide as the background, so I could send it to my buds still stuck in the desert. I got it developed and enlarged quickly, wrote "Miss you terribly" in the corner, and sent it via ABC's mail, which got it there within days.

And within a few days after that, I got another photo in the mail from Saudi Arabia. There were about twenty people in the shot, all standing out in the sand; just about everyone with ABC, plus a few officers from the military's "Joint Information Bureau." Their inscription was, "Wish you were here," and the better part was, every last one of them was flipping me the bird.

I know how they felt.

THINGS WE TAKE FOR GRANTED

Budapest, Hungary; Khartoum, Sudan; Fez, Morocco

ONE THING YOU LEARN *as a foreign correspondent is how lucky domestic correspondents are. Working in the United States, all you have to do is cover a story and get it on the air. Need a meal? You know where to go. Need a room? You know where to look. Need a doctor? You can easily find one. Need a telephone? Even back in the days when everyone depended mainly on pay phones, you'd know a phone was never far away. These days, of course, the best place to find a pay phone is in a museum, but no matter, you just carry your own.*

Overseas, it wasn't always so, and in many ways because of different cultures, it still isn't. Things we all take for granted in the United States, and I don't just mean a clean room, sometimes are special treats abroad. Like talking openly with someone on the street. Or winning permission to be in a particular place at all. Getting a meal you can eat, or a doctor who can treat you sometimes becomes a challenge, not a right.

All these things can be true for any American in a foreign land. The point of this chapter is, they are even truer for journalists than for other Americans. Why? Because others don't choose to visit places where there are so many barriers to simple survival, let alone success. Moreover, there is a big difference between visiting a place, and actually having to work there.

This chapter is a small collection of stories from a small collection of places. They are stories about having to focus much and sometimes all of your energy on simply supporting yourself long enough so that you can do the work you came to do.

•　　•　　•　　•　　•

189

BUDAPEST

The case that really stands out in my head is Hungary. That's because my head hurt so much.

It started with a typical head cold. Raw throat, stuffy nose, generally miserable congestion. But I boarded the plane anyway. From London we flew to Zurich, and then changed planes for our flight to Budapest, where we were going to do a story about the nation's economy. By midnight or so, when we landed in Hungary, I knew I was in trouble. The first descent had "blocked my ears." You know the feeling: there's pressure inside, which doesn't really hurt, but you can't hear so well anymore. The second descent brought on the pounding. Kind of like a pile driver pounding away somewhere within my head. It still didn't hurt a lot, but the sound from inside my skull seemed louder than any sound outside.

By the time we got our gear and passed through customs and found our taxis and checked into the Hilton Hotel, the pile driver was more like an ice pick. Still rhythmic, but the sensation that something dull was pounding at my brain turned into a feeling that something sharp was stabbing at it. Get the *point*?

I loaded up on aspirin. Might as well have saved my money.

I tried lying down on the bed. The stabbing pain was mainly on the right side, so I thought that by lying on that side, it would somehow relieve the pressure. It didn't. So I figured right must be wrong and turned over to my left side. Was the left side right? No, left was as wrong as right. That's when I realized there was no right side. Right or left, lying down wasn't going to cure a thing. Right?

I began to consider my options, because I had been through something similar, a medical emergency in a hotel room, once before. But it was a hotel room in Washington D.C. A tumor had popped up in the roof of my mouth literally in the middle of the night. I called our Washington bureau's overnight assignment desk, which was virtually across the street. My friend there called his friend, the oral surgeon, who called a pharmacy, which called me to say that an antibiotic prescription was ready. I took a taxi to pick it up, and by noon the next day I was back home in Chicago in surgery. That's about as easy as it can be.

It didn't take me a moment though to understand that my experience in Washington had no relevance here in Budapest. The only similarity was the hour: it was past two in the morning. So I phoned the front desk.

The clerk on duty seemed to understand the urgency of the situation.

"We have no house doctor we can call at this hour, but I will call you a taxi and send you to the hospital."

"Is there someone there at this hour to treat me?"

"Oh yes. You will be better very soon."

Good. Now we're getting somewhere.

The taxi was waiting by the time I reached the lobby. It was raining hard, but the hotel clerk walked out with me under the awning and shouted "*Korhaz*," the Hungarian word for "hospital," at the driver. All this time, the ice pick is still stabbing me somewhere inside.

We drove through a bad, blinding rainstorm getting worse. I sat in front and remember spending the whole ten-minute trip using my handkerchief to wipe the condensation from the inside of the windshield so that we could make it to the hospital alive. I mean, doesn't it seem silly to go to the hospital if you're not alive when you get there? Of course, there wasn't really much we could hit, because there was nothing else moving on the streets. Not another car the whole way. It was not only too wet for anybody in his right mind to be out, but it was too late, too. Everyone else was asleep. In Budapest, in the middle of the night in those days, there was nothing to do *but* sleep.

At the bottom of the last hill, we came to an old stone wall that seemed to surround the whole block. Looked like a fortress from the days of King Arthur. It was high, and if I remember correctly, it had turrets. I had been expecting to barrel around some corner and have a huge, red neon cross on a bright white background staring me in the face. Maybe even blinking! Something that beckoned to the sick and injured, something that said, "Come in, this is where we treat you." But no. Just a long, dark stone wall.

But yes, it was the hospital. I could tell when the driver stopped, reached across my idle body to throw open my door, and several times loudly repeated the same word the hotel clerk had used with him: "*Korhaz*." But how do you get into the *korhaz*? For that matter, *where was the korhaz*? There was a tunnel, but no light at the end of it. Surely this wasn't the entrance to the hospital!

Or on second thought, it was. The driver was pointing right at it. I knew they believed in secrecy in these Communist countries, but this was ridiculous.

I paid for my ride, stepped out of the taxi, and ran for the tunnel's entrance. I was soaked to the skin before I even reached it. That's how hard it was pouring.

At the tunnel's other end, I walked out into what looked like a hilly college campus. Maybe a dozen long, brick, three-story buildings scattered here and there, muddy paths connecting one to another, mounds of grass filling the open space between. But still nothing shining in my face with words that even remotely resembled, "Emergency Room." In fact, there were only three lights shining anywhere at all. Two were on the middle floors of a couple of buildings, the third was on the top floor of another.

With the ice pick stabbing deeper and deeper, and the rain falling harder and harder, I made my way to the first building with a light on. I still didn't know if it was part of a hospital or part of something else, but evidently there was someone alive inside, and maybe they could lead me in the right direction.

There was a door on one end. I pulled at it, but it was locked. I made the rounds of the building and found a second door at the other end. It was locked too. I bent to the ground, picked up a mound of mud and tried my best to mould it into a ball that I could throw at the lighted second floor window to attract someone's attention. My best wasn't good enough. It backfired. Now, on top of the fact that my head was exploding and my body felt like a drowned rat, my face was caked in mud. This was about when I asked myself for the umpteenth time in my career, *Why didn't I go to law school*? I just know I would have been better off!

On to building number two. This one also had a single light burning in a second-floor room. And the door was unlocked! Inside was darker than outside. Sure, when you're on some sort of campus with no lamps to light your way at the height of a rainstorm fit for the likes of Noah, it's dark outside. But it was even darker inside.

I was creeping along in the ground-floor hallway. Arms out to both sides to keep from crashing into a wall. Feeling my way and searching for a stairway to the second floor. Maybe halfway along, something struck me. No, I don't mean some bright thought entered my inquisitive mind. I mean, something struck me and then fell to the floor. Instinctively, I bent down to feel around for what it was.

A shoe. Somebody had hit me in the chest with a shoe. Then my attacker growled. He, or she, tried to make it sound like an animal's growl, but when it comes to growls, I am one smart cookie. This was clearly the growl of a human, which under the circumstances made it even *scarier* than an animal's. I nearly jumped out of my skin. If it weren't so wet and muddy, I might have. I didn't creep back to the door. I ran. And when I stood outside again, the pain beyond anything I'd ever experienced and the rain beyond measure, for some reason I turned back to look. Etched in the brick abutment to the side of the door was a long word. I had a lighter in my pocket. It didn't stay lit long in the rainstorm, but long enough to make out the letters. "*PSZICHIATRIA*." I'm no linguist, especially in a remote language like Hungarian, but I understood enough to realize I had just wandered through a psychiatric ward. That was the bad news. The good news was, maybe this was a hospital after all. Two down, one to go.

The last building with a light on, the last building offering any hope at all of a remedy for my misery, was clear across campus. All I picked up along the way was more water and more mud. Like the psychiatric ward, the door was unlocked. I walked in, felt my way until I came to the opening of a stairwell, and climbed. This was the building with the third-floor light. At the top of the stairs, I found myself looking down a rather long hall. Clear down at the other end was a huge set of swinging double doors, with light seeping through the center crack. Bonanza.

I all but skated down the hall. That room was my salvation. I pushed open the doors the way cowboys used to do it in Western saloons. "Hello," I said to six people in white coats. But just a couple of them looked up from what they were doing to see what came through the door, and not for long. They were in the middle of surgery. So what? Maybe I needed surgery too.

"Hello," again. This time it worked. This time, two of them kept their eyes on me.

"Is anyone here a doctor?" Immediately I knew it was a stupid question. I was in an operating room. These people were performing surgery. *Of course* someone here was a doctor. But no one came forward.

Naturally, I assumed that doctors anywhere in the world would speak English. Some English anyway. But either I was wrong, or they don't use doctors to do surgery in Hungary. If not, pity the poor guy on the table. So I resorted to international language. Not Esperanto. No, I borrowed from Alan Arkin's character in the classic movie, *The Russians Are Coming, The Russians Are Coming.*

"*Emerhensee.*" I tried to imitate Arkin's foreign accent as best I could. I held both hands to my head and said "*Emerhensee.*" Phonetically, it was supposed to sound like "emergency."

I might as well have said "*Jkwpvmssphcpx,*" for all it was worth. To them, it sounded like nonsense. But it got a reaction. Finally. The two biggest men in white coats put down their instruments and walked over to where I was standing. For a moment there, I thought I had found my saviors. Until they hoisted me in the air, one under each arm, and began to drag me toward the double exit doors, just beyond the operating table. The way I must have looked, soaked to the bone and covered in mud and holding both hands to my head, I could understand them wanting to get me out of the room while they were operating. But this sure didn't feel like they were checking me in for emergency treatment. They weren't. They carried me to the door, pushed it open, and kicked me out.

Getting no relief for my head was bad enough. Getting booted back into the mud was worse. But above all else, for a horrible instant I thought they were pushing me three stories down. Fast. After all, I had entered the far end of the building at the bottom level and then climbed two flights of stairs. I hadn't noticed that the ground rose along the side of the building so that at this end, it came up to the third floor. In other words, the ground was at my feet. Given that this wasn't the fatal fall I momentarily thought it was, mud never felt so good. Or bad. I was back where I had started, but worse.

I remember wondering two things:

1. How do I get back to the hotel? That seemed the wisest course; it was obvious that while I was indeed in a hospital, I was doing something dreadfully wrong.

2. Dammit, why *didn't* I go to law school? Surely, if I had, I wouldn't be lying face down in the mud right now with my head tearing apart in pain during a driving rainstorm in the middle of the night in Budapest.

Mind you, some people think that's just what lawyers deserve. But that's another story.

I found my way back to the tunnel and went back through to the street. It was still just as wet, just as dark, and just as abandoned as it had been thirty minutes earlier when I arrived.

I started on foot in the middle of the street, climbing up the hill. I had no idea where to go from there, but I knew my taxi had come down that hill, so going up made the most sense. Then, suddenly, a stroke of luck. A truck came racing up behind me. If my ears weren't pounding at this point like a hammer, I might have heard it. But he saw me and skidded to a stop just in time. The driver rolled down his window and was beginning to read me the riot act, but before he got past the preamble, I got to my knees in the river of rainwater, put my hands in a position of prayer, and said, "Hotel Hilton." I tried to make it sound like "Cho-tel HEEL-tin," as if that would make him understand it any better.

Thankfully, this guy understood it well enough. Anyway, he had never before seen anyone actually pray for a ride to the Hilton. Hell, this was a Communist country. He might never before have seen anyone actually pray. He said something incomprehensible, motioned for me to climb in, and returned me to my hotel.

The same clerk was on duty. He only had to look at me to know I hadn't seen a doctor yet. And instantly he recognized why.

"Mr. Dobbs, I'm so very sorry. I only told the taxi driver to take you to the hospital. It did not occur to me that you don't read Hungarian and don't know where to go when you get there."

You got that right, pal!

He made another call for a taxi, and five minutes later, one came. The same one as before. This time, the clerk told the driver precisely where to take me, and why.

Same rainstorm, same darkness, same route to the hospital. But instead of the tunnel, the driver went around to a gate, opened it, drove through, and pulled right up to one of the completely dark buildings I had passed on foot the first time. He got out himself, went up to the abutment by the stairs, shined a flashlight on the word etched there, and motioned for me to look. It was Hungarian, but had the root of our word, "Otolaryngology." Ear, nose, and throat.

He rang a bell. I never noticed any bells next to the doors the first time, but when he rang it, a light went on. A minute later, a doctor came down in bathrobe and slippers. *So* this *is how it works!* At the hospital in Hungary, there is no "emergency room" staffed twenty-four hours a day, because for every specialty there is a separate building, staffed twenty-four hours a day. All you've got to do is find it and then ring the bell. Why don't they tell us *things like this* in the tourist guides?

The doctor diagnosed my problem as an infection and inflammation, fixed me up, gave me some antibiotics, and sent me home to my hotel. The taxi driver had stayed behind to take me.

Eventually, this same problem recurred, several times a year, and I visited emergency rooms of one kind or another in many parts of the world. The *worst* was in New York City. The longest wait, with the scariest people (one man wearing a crown of thorns, who thought he was Jesus Christ, was pacing around the whole time and never stood still). But that's to be expected. Ultimately, I had corrective surgery. I've pretty much tried to avoid emergency rooms ever since. Not always successfully, but I've tried. Overseas, and certainly in New York!

KHARTOUM

Sometimes of course, we go looking for the kind of trouble that could put us in the hospital. Which means sometimes we're not very smart, because you'd think that being world weary travelers, we'd know better than to risk our health in a country where whatever they call their best hospital probably would be shut down in any Western nation. That pretty much describes Sudan: one of Africa's poorest countries, and its biggest. Not the most populous, not the most powerful, just the biggest. We flew in because we'd heard a report of a coup d'état.

President Numiery, a friend of the West, was increasingly unpopular at home. For starters, he had been unable to win a long civil war with secessionists in the south; this was before the rest of the world ever heard of Darfur (which is in the west of Sudan). Secondly, he had been unable to mollify Islamic fundamentalists in his own northern part of the country.

We rented a small jet and chartered in, because in the immediate wake of a third-world coup, successful or not, the authorities never let airliners full of foreigners in right away. Call it prudence, call it paranoia, but they never do.

Chartering was our first mistake. Commercial passengers had continued to come in. Paris to Khartoum for my three colleagues and me, commercially, would have been a lot cheaper. Our second mistake was our assumption that the report of a coup d'état was accurate, and we began to get a sense of that from the moment we landed.

What happens in a coup? How does someone claim control of a country? Victorious forces seize the key organs and positions of power. Like Iran during the revolution: the leader's command post, the parliament building, military headquarters, weapons armories, newspaper offices, radio and TV origination points, the airport. Take the tools of leadership, military force, and communications and transportation, and the country is pretty much yours.

But they sure didn't seem worried about holding a firm grip on the airport. By the time we landed, well past midnight, the guards were asleep. It's true. The country was supposed to be in the middle of a coup, but we got off the plane, walked into the terminal, and had to awaken the people empowered to ensure that no one entered the country without permission.

Then, we thought we'd have to play a tedious shell game, which typically works this way: on a normal trip to a remote destination, we'd carry fifteen or twenty heavy cases. After all, if something breaks down in a place like Khartoum, you'd better have a backup. There's no Radio Shack. Sometimes we'd carry things we could safely predict the authorities would want to tinker with. Maybe take apart. Maybe not even allow into the country. Although there was nothing threatening about what we carried, the authorities didn't know that. But we were tired of going through the motions of soothing their fears, so we usually played a little game that cut the process short.

It was simple: just open several cases at once. As one customs officer rummages through a relatively simple case of equipment, start pulling things out of a second case. And on, and on, and on. The point is to push a few cases through that never get opened at all. Or if it's a carry-on bag with lots of zippered compartments, keep turning it 'round and 'round and opening zipper after zipper, but never open the zipper to the compartment that contains books and papers the inspectors might want to spend hours poring over.

The shell game usually works. But we didn't even have to use it in Khartoum. Oh, they opened three or four cases and conducted a cursory inspection. One case, for example, held a couple of belt-type batteries that look like bandoleers. But as in many countries, we'd just say, "TV equipment," and they'd let it in. I hate to think it, but if I were a hijacker, I know how I'd get my weapons on board.

So basically, they just waved us through. I guess they wanted to resume their dreams. Hardly the kind of behavior you'd expect from men in uniform right after a coup.

We hired a few taxis and had them drive us and our gear around town. You don't want to let tens of thousands of dollars worth of equipment out of your sight if there's a chance of it being destroyed in battle. But there wasn't any battle. In fact, we could have left the stuff right in the middle of the main street, because nobody was out. Not soldiers, not police, not civilians. Nobody. If there had been a coup, it was the quietest in history.

When morning came, we made the diplomatic rounds. The story must have started *somewhere*. But the diplomats didn't know where either. They assured us, though, that there had not been a coup. Not even an attempted one. Not so far as they could tell, anyway. And that really brings me to the climax of our coverage in Khartoum: dinner!

After a few days, we had wrapped up our work, and pretty much convinced our bosses in New York that the whole thing was a non-starter. I say "pretty much" because they were still hanging onto what they had heard the day we came, had already spent ten thousand dollars or more chasing it down, and couldn't quite accept that it was all a blatant waste of time and money. The fact that they now had their own people in Sudan, telling them that all was peaceful, was only partly convincing. So we were told to stay a little longer. Long enough, regrettably, for at least one more dinner.

Wherever in the world we went, we'd stay in Western hotels if we could. Not that they were always cleaner than local fare (although they often were), but they usually had the services we needed: late-night room service, currency exchange, working elevators, long-distance phones. What this meant, of course, was that we usually found ourselves eating hotel food.

As a veteran of hotel food, I think there's one "hotel chefs" college somewhere in the world, and almost all hotel chefs go there. Some take "High Class 101," others specialize in "Inedible," but there is something common about the food in most hotels. (The word "common" in this context is a pun.)

So why should the Khartoum Hilton be any different? Whether Budapest or Khartoum, doesn't it make sense that all the Hiltons want to look alike, taste alike, feel alike, so that the customer always knows what to expect? Sad to say, the answer is yes. That's why, given the opportunity, we wanted to eat out.

Earlier in the day, when talking with the political officer at the U.S. embassy, I asked for a list of the capital's best restaurants. He said, "There isn't one."

I said, "Oh, I don't mean I expect that you keep a printed list handy. I just want to know which ones you recommend."

"There aren't any."

"You don't recommend a single restaurant in Khartoum?"

"Just the Hilton."

"No, I mean *outside* the Hilton."

"You don't want to eat outside the Hilton."

"The trouble is, we don't want to eat *inside* the Hilton."

"Then you shouldn't eat."

This was not my idea of progress. I didn't care whether Khartoum had a Michelin Four Star. But it must have restaurants. I just wanted a few names.

"Okay," he said, "I'll get my assistant." And in came a Sudanese man who worked for the embassy. Same question: "Where can we eat tonight?"

Same answer as his boss: "At the hotel." And this guy was born and raised there!

I went through the same motions, and finally the guy agreed to give us a list. Reluctantly. "I'll give you a few names, but do not hold me responsible. I really do not think you should go to these places." To hear him tell it, Khartoum didn't even have a Michelin No Star.

He gave me three names. He was even nice enough to write them down. I don't really think he used his own handwriting though. This guy was really scared that we were going to have a horrible experience and nail him for sending us.

Lenny, our sound tech, opted out. "I have a headache," he told us. Maybe just the prospect of eating out gave him his headache. He had heard both conversations. That left Rupen, Jacques, and me. And that was fine, because Rupen, raised in Beirut, speaks perfect Arabic.

We got in a taxi outside the hotel and handed the driver our list. Rupen told him, "Take us to the first one." The driver glanced at the list, glanced at us, shook his head, and said, "*La la la la la.*" Simply put, that is Arabic for, "No no no no no."

What's going on here? All we want to do is eat "local," and everyone's telling us we can't.

I can't tell you exactly how the conversation between Rupen and the taxi driver then went, but basically the driver agreed to take us to a restaurant only if we didn't blame him for what happened! By now, Rupen and Jacques and I were rethinking our aversion to Hilton food, but by this point, curiosity was getting the better of us. Drive on.

We got to the first place on the list and gave our driver a big bill with the promise of more to come if he'd wait for us. Then we walked in. Actually, to say that we walked in is a bit of an exaggeration since there was no "in." The whole place, except the kitchen, was outside. I'd like to tell you it had the outdoor charm of a French brasserie. But I'd be lying. It had rickety tables, a dirt floor, lots of Sudanese gentlemen in dirty gowns eating and drinking and spitting on the floor, and at least one resident rat. Maybe more than one, but that's all I saw. Rupen saw it too. That's what compelled him to come up with a plan.

"You guys stay here. I'll go check the kitchen." He came back out almost as green as the fish he described to us. So, back to the taxi. If a place can't keep a clean kitchen, it can't keep us.

At restaurant number two, which looked exactly like number one, Rupen again offered to inspect the kitchen on the group's behalf. He came out with just two words, and then stepped into the taxi. "Same fish."

We debated whether to waste our time and money visiting the last restaurant on the list. After all, why would the last be any better than the first? Would it even be as good? But we had come this far. Anyway, I knew that if someday I wrote a book about a foreign correspondent's life overseas, this would make a cute little story. We pressed on.

The third place looked like the second. And the first. The only difference was, Rupen never entered the kitchen. It was a deliberate decision. Rupen said, "Let's not look at the kitchen." We concurred. What we figured was, the kitchen at the Hilton probably doesn't look all that great either. For that matter, the kitchen at La Tour d'Argent in Paris might turn you off. All those dead ducks.

So we decided if our accommodations at the third place were acceptable, we'd skip the inspection and just see how the food looked when it reached our table.

The table at which they put us was right in the middle. What I mean is, right in the middle of a ring of Sudanese men sitting at their tables, spitting all over the dirt floor. Apparently, it's something of a custom. They like to wet their whistles in this hot, dusty country, but they don't like to swallow. What's more, it's a fairly strict Islamic country, and what they're drinking is beer. So they take a swig, swish it around in their mouths, and then spit it out. Clearly not all of it, but enough for appearances. Now I understand why they don't put down linoleum. Luckily, my polished shoes already were filthy from all the soil I'd been on. At this point, a little beer and human spit wasn't going to make a difference.

A waiter came along. He wasn't holding any menus.

"What do you have tonight?" Rupen asked in Arabic. He knew how the system worked. Jacques and I didn't.

"Fish, chicken, lamb." Also in Arabic.

"We'll have all three, and beer."

The beer came first. I wasn't especially inclined to spit it at my neighbors as they were spitting theirs at me, but I did, once or twice, just for the satisfaction.

Then the food. A huge, long platter with a whole long fish. Not green. At least not anymore. A huge, rectangular platter with a whole leg of lamb. Not subdivided. Intact. And a small, round platter with a fairly scrawny chicken. Not headless.

Each of us was given a plate. I looked around and saw that some of our neighbors were working without plates. But we were Westerners. The only ones there. We got plates. No forks though, or knives or spoons or any other utensils you might expect to need when tearing into three cooked but otherwise intact animals.

It was delicious. Messy, but delicious. The lamb was juicy. The chicken was tender. The fish? Well, as I said before, it wasn't green. Anymore.

And my shoes? Well, I could always clean them when I got home.

Incidentally, none of the three of us ever got sick. But Lenny, who ate that night at the Hilton? He felt lousy all the way back to Paris.

FEZ

You've already read about communication snafus in Salt Lake City on the day Gary Gilmore was shot, and in Eagle Pass, Texas, after the Mexican mine disasters. And we had those problems *in English!* Imagine the same thing *in gibberish.*

No matter where we go, we need communication. Sometimes that means speaking the local language. Sometimes it means getting in touch with the Mother Ship in New York. Sometimes it means getting your pictures and sound from here to there the same day, what we call "a feed." None of those describes what we faced in Fez, Morocco. It was a communication problem whose source we never did discover.

There was a major Arab summit in Fez. Bitter rivals under the same roof. Iraq's Saddam Hussein and Syria's Hafez Assad. Libya's Muammar Qadhafi and Saudi Arabia's King Fahd. Yassir Arafat from the PLO, King Hussein from Jordan, King Hassan, the Moroccan host, they were all there. All except Egypt. Egyptians still were pariahs in those days for making peace with Israel.

Naturally, with so many Arab leaders and their enormous entourages in town, there was no place at the inn for us. The media were billeted in a market town more than an hour away, and taken to watch the party only when security saw fit. We had no choice. Our cars, rented at the Casablanca airport, were prohibited from entering Fez, so we'd be herded onto buses and driven to attend the Arab equivalent of a photo op. Trouble was, for reasons of security, no one in security knew for sure where the photo op would be.

On one bus ride, for example, the security chief on our bus was absolutely positive the photo op was down a particular street. But the security chief at the barrier that kept the bus off the street thought otherwise. An argument broke out. Our security guy pulled his gun. The other security guy pulled his. Pretty soon, these two bodyguards would be shooting at each other. Apparently, this was their way of protecting the VIPs somewhere inside the security cordon we couldn't pierce anyway. Their lieutenants pulled them apart. For them, a happy ending. For us, no photo op.

The entire event was riddled with frustrations. It made a carefully choreographed, presidential trip seem like a free-for-all. Still though, the red carpet arrival ceremonies for the Arab dignitaries made being there worthwhile. Flags, bands, warriors with scimitars. It was all a case of keeping up with the al-Jones.

Any king or sheik or emir worth his salt showed up in a 747. I mean, wouldn't it be embarrassing to fly in on anything smaller? Even Syria's President Assad, whose national airline owned exactly one 747, came in it. What that did to Syrian Arab Airline's schedule, I don't know. I'm sure he didn't care.

The only delegation to come in "commercially" was Lebanon's. In fact they not only flew in on an aging 707, but they flew in from Cyprus, the Mediterranean refuge to Lebanon's west. Beirut's airport, periodically closed by shell and mortar fire for much of Lebanon's civil war, had been shut down during their departure. Like refugees, they had to leave their country on a ferryboat, and then climb aboard their aging jet in Cyprus, where all Lebanese aircraft took cover whenever their home base came under fire.

Once the summit started, the photo ops, at least those we could reach, also made being there worthwhile. They gave us a new definition of brotherhood.

You'd think that for the sake of self-image, which is a critical ingredient of power in the Arab world, they would show at least a pretense of brotherhood when we were there. You'd think so. But you'd be wrong. Here they were, the leaders of the Arab world, sitting for hours on end, knowing that their rivals were there, hearing their rivals speak, sometimes close enough to their rivals to smell them, but never exchanging a single glance, let alone a word. For many of us in the media, that was the story. The whole purpose of this summit was to bring these leaders together and show the world a unified face. That's pretty hard when so many eyes won't even look at each other.

The summit wasn't working. But thanks to a communications snafu, the part of the world that depended on American television networks never got a chance to watch.

The problem wasn't Morocco's. It was ours. ABC's. For years, ABC and CBS had ceded to NBC the responsibility for arranging satellite and other transmissions by the pool of three U.S. networks. NBC had a special division set up to "book the birds," and we let them do it. Sure, that meant that since they controlled communication between New York and the feed point, they could sometimes finesse a slight advantage over the competition when time was tight. But generally, they did the job honestly and well, so we let them.

Until Fez. ABC had decided to set up its own "satellite desk" and compete for control of satellites. Why give NBC the edge? Answer: because they knew how. We didn't!

This was the first story on which ABC had beaten NBC to the punch and "booked the bird." This didn't mean NBC or CBS would be shut out from the transmission; it just meant ABC controlled the bird, and controlled the time during which each network used it to transmit its story. As long as ABC treated everyone equally, there should not be a problem. Unfortunately, ABC did treat everyone equally. Which they came to regret. Because the transmission didn't work. Not NBC's, not CBS's, not ours.

From some feed points, you'd just pick up the phone, dial the number for the New York assignment desk, and ask what went wrong. From Fez, we didn't have that luxury.

Let me try to describe our voice communication network between Fez and New York.

Barbara, an ABC producer, was stationed by the videotape machine that was wired up to transmit everyone's stories. She had just one telephone in the room, from which she could dial other extensions in the building, but nowhere else. So Patrick, the cameraman, was stationed in an adjacent warehouse garage where there was another internal extension on which he could talk to Barbara. The first link. Beautiful. Now, Barbara and Patrick, on opposite sides of the same wall, can communicate.

We didn't let that bog us down. The beauty of the garage was, by taking just five steps, Patrick could reach around a corner and shout back and forth at me, as I held onto a telephone at a bank of telephone booths specially set up for us to use to call out. The second link.

Trouble was, these were just local phones. Now, Barbara could communicate, through Patrick and me, with anyone *in Fez*. But not beyond. So, over my local line, I relayed whatever information Barbara communicated, through Patrick, to Liz, another ABC producer. And vice versa. The third link. Now, we were reaching *clear across town*.

You see, Liz was stationed clear across town at a hotel where we had paid a king's ransom (something people understood in this monarchy) to monopolize one of the two long-distance telephone lines on the hotel switchboard for one hour each day. Liz talked with me on one phone, New York on the other. That was the fourth link. The lines were lousy. But it was the only way we had to communicate with New York.

It would have been okay if all we had to relay back and forth was information like, "Roll your tape," and "Stop your tape," and "Raise your audio," and "Lower your audio." Each simple instruction would have required ten or twenty seconds to implement, but it would have been okay.

But when the satellite transmission itself didn't work on the first night, and nobody's story got on the air, our voice communication system didn't work well enough to solve it, or even figure out what was wrong. I don't mean that any of the individual links wasn't working. I mean that, put together, with a few frustrated producers and correspondents from the other networks thrown in, the system didn't work. No complex message could possibly pass through that many people over that many miles and come out clear.

So after our satellite time ended without a single second of videotape getting through, we ended up sending a printed telex to New York, asking what went wrong and suggesting that since ABC's first effort to successfully book an overseas satellite had failed, we should ask NBC to "book the bird" for the second night and give ourselves a bit more time to learn how to do things right.

But when we all reached the feed point on the second night, all that awaited us was a telex from New York saying that, yet again, it was an ABC bird. And yet again, it didn't work.

You can imagine just how pleased we were, not to mention our colleagues. Not only had we wasted two irritating days, but so had our competitors, and they were jumping on our backs. They knew we personally weren't to blame for whatever screwups there had been, but who else could they yell at?

We sent a second telex, begging ABC to give NBC control of the third day's bird. But the next morning, a return telex told us it wasn't going to happen. That's when I abandoned the story. No, I don't mean I walked away from our coverage. I just mean I made it my first priority to actually *talk with New York*. Of course, I couldn't just pick up a phone and start dialing. For starters, it was too early. Ten o'clock in northwest Africa was four in the morning back home. No one on the ABC News overnight shift could deal with my complaint, other than to offer sympathy. Sympathy I didn't need. What I needed was a working satellite. I'd have to wait until almost four in the afternoon.

Secondly, even if the hour was right, from most phones, I couldn't call outside Fez, let alone outside Morocco. Almost all the direct-dial, long-distance telephone lines were taken. Not used, just taken by the different Arab delegations. "Held in reserve" is the way one Arab attaché put it.

That meant the post office. In Morocco, as in many countries, the government telecommunications ministry controls both the movement of mail and the flow of communication. That means, if you don't have a phone at your disposal, you go to the post office, which does. Naturally though, the post office doesn't have supply to meet demand. After all, this is a *government*. So I waited. There must have been two dozen callers ahead of me, and I had to wait for each of them to make a call, and each of them had to wait anywhere from two minutes to twenty to get the call through. And most of them were just calling someplace else *in Morocco*.

So it was with me. Just worse. I figured it would take half an hour or more to get through to New York. I wasn't disappointed. But eventually, the call was connected. This was my first chance in three days to talk directly with anyone in authority. In this case, it was our foreign editor.

"What happened?" I didn't need to make my question any more complicated than that. Everyone there in New York knew what had been happening. Those of us who were on the other end, in Morocco, were probably the only ones in the company who didn't.

"The satellite desk had the wrong coordinates for the bird." What that means is, if the satellite is at X-degrees, Y-minutes, and Z-seconds in the southern sky, you'd better get those numbers right or your transmission won't work.

"But it happened twice in a row," I complained.

"This is their first time. They're bound to make mistakes."

Mistakes? These were pretty costly mistakes. Besides the lost satellite time, all three networks had five or six people on expense account in Morocco, effectively accomplishing nothing.

"Look," I said, "let's iron out the mistakes in some practice runs. But not with us as guinea pigs. Right now, that's what we are; we're the victims. We're taking a lot of crap from CBS and NBC, and all we can say is, 'We're sorry.' I'm fed up with the whole thing. I've sent you two telexes asking to give control to NBC because they know how to do it and we don't. Why haven't you done that?"

And here is his response, which I have always remembered because it says so much about the blindness that overcomes otherwise bright people in a dog-eat-dog industry like network news in a take-no-prisoners place like New York: "We're not going to relinquish control of the satellite until we know we can make it work."

Well, there you have it. We'd rather keep screwing up than admit defeat.

So sometimes, the things we take for granted are hard to achieve because of backward conditions where we're working. And sometimes, they're because of backwardness back home.

Index

clothing
in Afghanistan, 104–105, 110
"galabaya," in Egypt, 56
Islamic cap, 120
"color bars," video standard, 31
Colorado
Rocky Mountains, 186, 188
"Supermax," federal prison, in
Florence, 150
Commodore Hotel, West Beirut, 158, 159
Communist bloc, 37, 43, 135
concentration camps, in Uganda, 91, 92
Cooley, John, 123–124
cordoning off, Wounded Knee, 4, 5
correspondents
deaths in Beirut, Lebanon, 133, 134
deaths in Iran, 73–76, 82, 85
deaths in Uganda, 90, 92–93
finding food, in Khartoum, 197–200
foreign, 189
imprisonment of, 111
interrogation, in Iraq, 188
Iraq, issuing journalist visas, 187–188
leaving Iran, 83–84
in news fast lane, ix–xi
in post-election 2009, Tehran, 75–76
public opinions, expressing, 36
responsibility on network news
teams, xi
seeking medical treatment, in
Budapest, 190–195
See also reporters
County Armagh, Northern Ireland, 132
coup d'états, 78, 196
"the cripple-makers," in Cairo, 55
CTV, Canadian television network, 133
Cuba, 37
currency exchange
in Afghanistan, 102–104
in Poland, 146–148
customs agents
in East Germany, 141–142
in Khartoum, 196–197
in Poland, 142–146

Czechoslovakia, 37

D

Dada, Idi Amin, 86–88, 91–92, 95
Danube River, 38–39
Danzig, Germany, 135
Dar Es Salaam, Tanzania, 91
Darfur, 196
Dari language, in Afghanistan, 105
Day, Elizabeth, xiii
death penalty, 18, 19, 27–28, 35
deaths
of correspondents (See
correspondents)
and injuries at Wounded Knee, 13
at Long Kesh prison "The Maze,"
Northern Ireland, 129
on New York City subway, 176
in Northern Ireland, 98, 126, 129–130
in Uganda war, with Tanzania, 91–93
dehydration symptoms, 129
Denver Federal Appeals Court, 28–29
desert, description of (Saudi Arabia), 175,
177–178, 181
Desert Storm (Gulf War), x, 181
See also Gulf War
Dhahran, Saudi Arabia, 178–179, 181
See also Saudi Arabia
dictatorships, working in, 38
dissidents, in Soviet Union, 43, 46–47
distortions, by news media, 153
Dobbs, Alexander, 110, 111
Dobbs, Carol
calls from Uganda, 89–90, 95
in Egypt, 53–57
first born son, Jason, 85, 110
getting news about husband in
Iran, 76–77
mother-in-law, 176–177, 186
second born son, Alexander, 110, 111
weekend in New York City, after
Gilmore execution, 35
Dobbs, Jason, 85, 110

doctors
in Budapest, 190–195
working in remote places, 166
dollar exchange
in Afghanistan, 102–104
in Poland, 146–148
driving, in Egypt, 62
drug overdoses
Barrett (Gilmore's girlfriend), 24–26
Gilmore, 21, 23–25
Druze party, in Lebanon, 159–160

E

Eagle Pass, Texas, mining disaster, in
northern Mexico, 32–35
earthquakes
in Italy, 172–174
in Oakland, California, xi
in Yemen, 167–170
East German People's Police "Volpo,"
139–140
East Germany, 37, 141–142
editors, responsibility on network news
teams, xi
Egypt, 50–63
about, 50–51
airbase, in Sinai Desert, 60–61
assassination of Sadat, 61–62
bargaining, in bazaar, 54–55
beggars in, 55–57
driving in, 62
Grateful Dead concert, at Giza
pyramids, 57–60
peace talks, with Israel, 52, 53
population growth in, 50, 57
sites in, 53
Egyptian Antiquities Museum of Cairo,
53, 57
Egyptian-Israeli handshake, 52
El Al, Israeli airline, 75
Emmy Awards, 174
"The Empty Corner," in Saudi Arabia,
181–183
England, 125–126

English Language Institute, Hungary,
40–42
Entebbe Airport, Uganda, 91
escorts, in Hungary, 41–43
Etcheverry, Patrick, 70–72
Europa Hotel, Belfast, 127
"evil empire," 43
Executioner's Son, The (Mailer), 19
executions
of Gilmore, 19, 28–30
by Idi Amin, and army, 91, 92–93
explosives, 150, 151, 154, 159

F

Fahd, Saudi King, 175, 201
The Falls Road, Belfast, 127
Farahabad military base, Tehran, 74
Farouk, King, 51
Federal Appeals Court, Denver, 28, 29
Federal District Court, U.S. (Salt Lake
City), 28
Fez, Morocco, 55, 200–205
'56 rebellion, Budapest, 38
firing squads, 19, 27–28
"fixers," 160
flash floods, in Yemen, 170–171
Florence, Colorado, 150
Franco, Francisco, 60
Frankfurt, West Germany, 84
freedom fighters, 118–119, 120
funeral
of hunger striker, Belfast, 130–131
of mullah (Iran), 70–72

G

Gaddafi, Colonel *See* Qadhafi, Muammar
"galabaya" clothing, in Egypt, 56
Garcia, Jerry, 57
Gary, ABC News cameraperson, in
Soviet Union, 47
Gary, American manger of hotel
(Tehran), 80, 83
Gdansk, Poland, 135

211

ABOUT THE AUTHOR

GREG DOBBS worked at ABC News for 23 years, first as a producer, then for most of his career as a correspondent, including ten years overseas. He won two national Emmy Awards in the process. When ABC asked him in 1992 to move from his home in Colorado's Rocky Mountains to New York City, it took him approximately one nanosecond to say no. That led to a second career as a radio talk show host, a newspaper opinion columnist, and the television moderator of an Emmy Award winning discussion program on Rocky Mountain PBS. In 2003, Dobbs returned to the road as a correspondent for the all high definition television network HDNet. It put him back on airplanes, reporting documentaries for the program "World Report" from around the country and around the world. A native of San Francisco, Dobbs has been married to Carol for more than thirty-five years, and both their grown sons, Jason and Alex, are better skiers for sure, and probably better writers too, than their dad.

Breinigsville, PA USA
22 August 2009
222786BV00004B/2/P